Lightly on the Land

The SCA Trail-Building and Maintenance Manual

Lightly on the Land

THE SCA TRAIL-BUILDING AND MAINTENANCE MANUAL

BY
ROBERT C. BIRKBY

ILLUSTRATED BY
PETER LUCCHETTI

WITH ADDITIONAL ILLUSTRATIONS BY
JENNY TEMPEST

Published by
The Mountaineers
1001 SW Klickitat Way, Suite 201
Seattle, Washington 98134

First edition: first printing 1996, second printing 1997

Published simultaneously in Great Britain by Cordee, 3a DeMontfort Street, Leicester, England, LE1 7HD

Manufactured in the United States of America

Edited by Linda Robinson
Cover design by Elizabeth Watson
Book design by Alice C. Merrill
Book layout by Margarite Hargrave
Typesetting by The Mountaineers Books

Cover photographs: *SCA crew building the upper reaches of the Harding Icefield Trail, Kenai Fjords National Park* (Photo: Bob Birkby). Insets: *Building a turnpike for the Greater Yellowstone Recovery Corps* (Photo: Jay A. Satz); *Pulling a stringer into place for a puncheon, Yellowstone National Park* (Photo: Carla Neasel); *Forest Service workers repairing a damaged meadow, Mount Baker–Snoqualmie National Forest* (Photo: Pam Matthews and John Schubert).
Back cover photographs: *Building new trail on the Nogales Ranger District, Arizona* (Photo: Bob Birkby).
Frontispiece: Drawing by Peter Lucchetti

Library of Congress Cataloging-in-Publication Data
Birkby, Robert.
    Lightly on the land : the SCA manual of backcountry work skills / by Robert C.
Birkby ; illustrated by Peter Lucchetti ; with additional illustrations by Jenny Tempest.
      p.   cm.
    Includes index.
    ISBN 0-89886-491-7
    1. Trails—United States—Design and construction—Handbooks, manuals, etc.
2. Trails—United States—Maintenance and repair—Handbooks, manuals, etc. I.
Title.
TE304.B57   1996
634.9'3—dc20   96–17213
                                                  CIP

♻ Printed on recycled paper

Contents

This ground, this work
burns like a fire
in the backcountry
of my heart.

Scott Paul
(1954-1993)

Foreword

LIGHTLY ON THE LAND IS A MANUAL of practical, proven work skills for anyone interested in caring for America's backcountry. Whether you are a week-end volunteer, a youth group leader, an outing club member, a crew supervisor, part of a land management agency, or simply enjoy learning about traditional and contemporary methods of backcountry work, this book is for you.

While the basic principles of backcountry work hold true everywhere, the ways in which those methods are practiced vary in different parts of America as trail crews have developed innovative solutions to the local challenges that confront them. In some regions, for example, trails climb steeply up hillsides; in others, they hug the terrain like contour lines. Crews in forested areas have become masters of timber construction because wood was available to them. Those who had rock on hand have perfected the use of stone as their primary building material.

Separated by long distances, differing visions, and sometimes fierce regional loyalties, backcountry crews seldom have opportunities to share their local wisdom with the larger community of trail workers. *Lightly on the Land* moves the understanding of backcountry work beyond home terrains and organizational boundaries by bringing together in one volume a national overview of rustic skills that can be used in any region, as well as recognizing and celebrating the regional knowledge that has been enriched by the efforts of generations of trail workers.

Although the material included here is a compilation of information and techniques found to be appropriate and useful by trained SCA crew leaders and other professionals working in the field, readers must decide for themselves what activities described in these pages can be undertaken safely. In addition to using an abundance of common sense, backcountry workers must also observe any Occupational Safety and Health Administration (OSHA) regulations and land-management agency guidelines for planning and completing projects, and avoid any activities that might endanger themselves or others.

Real work that protects and enhances the backcountry offers a meaningful way for each of us to give something back to the earth. By maintaining a section of trail or restoring an eroded meadow, people of any age can experience the satisfaction of hands-on stewardship. They can walk along a pathway they have repaired and see that they have made a difference. They can look at a campsite newly protected from overuse and erosion, and know that their efforts do matter.

This book is for those people who want to help care for the backcountry they enjoy and cherish.

One of the best things about trail work is that there is always more than one right answer to any problem. The Student Conservation Association is grateful to the following professionals committed to stewardship of our public lands who have read and commented upon *Lightly on the Land.* Their unique experience and insights have enriched this book with a wealth of diverse perspectives that the subject deserves.

Jeff Birkby	National Center for Appropriate Technology
Janet T. Bohlen	SCA
David Cole	U.S. Forest Service
Tim Ernst	American Hiking Society, Ozark Highlands Trail Association, and SCA
Russ Hanbey*	SCA
Peter Henrikson*	SCA and U.S. Forest Service
Dan Hinckley	SCA and The Center for Wooden Boats
Ruth Ittner	Volunteers for Outdoor Washington
Willie Janeway*	Adirondack Mountain Club, The Nature Conservancy, and SCA
Lester Kenway*	Maine State Parks and SCA
Bill Lester*	National Park Service
Dave McDonald	SCA and U.S. Forest Service
David Michael	U.S. Forest Service
Bob Proudman	Appalachian Mountain Club and Appalachian Trail Conference
Jeff Quinsey	SCA
Rod Replogle	U.S. Forest Service
Elizabeth Rothman*	SCA and U.S. Forest Service
Mike Shields	National Park Service
Alicia Spence*	Cascade Joinery, U.S. Forest Service, and SCA
George Tempest*	SCA
Brian Vachowski	U.S. Forest Service
Helen Welborn	SCA, Washington Trails Association, and Volunteers for Outdoor Washington
Steve Wennstrom*	SCA and Outward Bound

---

* Instructor for SCA's Henry S. Francis, Jr., Wilderness Work Skills Program

Acknowledgments

LIGHTLY ON THE LAND IS DEDICATED to all those who have mastered the art and skill of caring for the land and, in their passion for the work, have become committed to passing their knowledge along to others. All of us who practice rustic work skills can look back fondly upon a few people in our own past who got us started with conservation work, encouraged us, and taught us. They shook us out of our sleeping bags at dawn and worked us until dark, shared stories and lore with us around the campfire, and in dozens of other ways convinced us that caring for trails and for the backcountry is not only deeply satisfying, but is also a great gift to give back to the earth.

The Student Conservation Association owes a tremendous debt to countless numbers of people who, over generations of working in our programs and those of other organizations, have developed, refined, practiced, and taught the craft of backcountry conservation work. It is impossible to name them all, or to document adequately their contributions to the quality of the American trails system and the protection of the extraordinary landscape that these trails cross. Their legacy lives on in the trails they built, the campsites they maintained, the damaged terrain they nurtured back to health, and the generations of trail workers they have inspired.

But we do want to acknowledge some people in recognition of the hard labor and remarkable tenacity they applied to turn *Lightly on the Land* into a reality. The following only scratches the surface of those who have contributed significantly to our understanding of backcountry work skills, to the preparation and production of this book, or both.

The first effort to consolidate the collective backcountry skills of the Student Conservation Association resulted in *The Work Skills Manual,* privately published by SCA in 1979. Key to its success were Harry S. Francis, Jr., then SCA's Executive Director; Dan Hinckley, SCA Deputy Director of Operations; Geoffrey R. Quinsey, editor; William Turner, contributing editor; and Jack Slagle and Peggy Hoth, illustrators. Many others added their knowledge, especially Mike Shields of the National Park Service. No more than a few hundred copies were ever printed, but the thick, loose-leaf notebook served as the backcountry bible for a multitude of SCA crew leaders who carried it into the field.

In the years since, SCA backcountry work crew leaders and the instructors of SCA's Work Skills Program have been laboring, learning, and teaching in parks and forests throughout the United States. Many have also worked for land-management agencies and conservation organizations, and have been private trail contractors. Their accumulated knowledge has become national in scope, drawing together the best techniques and philosophies from every region of the country. Our ability to develop and maintain SCA's repository for this wealth of knowledge is due, in part, to the energy and leadership of past Directors of the Work Skills Program—Carroll Vogel, Missi Booth Goss, and Su Thieda.

SCA President Scott Izzo and Executive Vice President Valerie Shand gave the project the green light and provided resources for moving forward when resources were sometimes in short supply. Vice President of Programs Scott Weaver and High School Program Director Ray Auger, trail dogs themselves, helped formulate the book's outline and reviewed each manuscript draft. Chief Financial Officer Mark Bodin shepherded the creation of the business plan to make the project financially viable. Their hard work, and that of the entire SCA staff, have made this project possible.

This book would not have happened without a few talented trail builders putting down their Pulaskis and picking up their pens. The SCA has had the pleasure of working with artist Pete Lucchetti since he joined our Greater Yellowstone Recovery Corps in 1989, and we are delighted to showcase his artistry here. Thanks also to Jenny Tempest for her illustrations for the chapter on felling and bucking trees and on site restoration.

Bob Birkby is the Work Skills Program's longest-serving Chief Instructor, and perhaps the most traveled of SCA's High School Program Crew Leaders. But above all, words are his forte, and he did a remarkable job in bringing style, clarity, and wit to this effort.

And finally, we are indebted to the staff at The Mountaineers Books for their enthusiasm, professionalism, and guidance.

We cannot shake you out of your sleeping bags and work you until dark. But we do hope that *Lightly on the Land* will give you the information, and perhaps some of the inspiration, to get out in the backcountry, get your hands dirty, and do something good for the land.

Jay Addison Satz
SCA Director of Field Operations
Lightly on the Land publishing project director

CHAPTER 1

Trails

WE HAVE ALL SEEN IT—the beginning of a pathway drawing us toward an adventure. It may have been a trail in a city park or along a quiet river. It may have been the start of a short walk in the woods, or the first few feet of a route that will not reach an end for two thousand miles or more. The beginning of a trail seems both familiar and full of the unknown, for a pathway is an invitation. It is the promise of possibilities. It is an entry to another place, to another sensibility, even to another time.

Each of us makes of trails what we most want them to be. For some, a path is merely the quickest way to reach a destination. Others find escape along trails, discovering the inspiration of leaving behind the rush of urban life and coming closer to the natural world. Trails may be challenges of the first order—the lure of hiking for weeks or months along pathways that resonate with adventure, or the chance to roll a wheelchair over routes that allow freedom of movement into otherwise inaccessible terrain.

Trails are among the earliest marks left by humans on the face of the earth. Perhaps because of that, a pathway is also one of the most recognizable shapes we know, a structure so obvious and universal that we seldom stop to look beneath our feet and notice the sheer wonder of what it is.

For the most part, the trails of mankind have led to places where people had strong reason to go. Routes between villages and to sources of food and water followed valley floors, stayed near open country, and avoided rugged terrain. Travelers crossing mountains sought out the lowest passes to get from one side of a range to the other. In many cases, these trail locations were so practical that over the decades they were widened and hardened to benefit livestock, wagons, railroads, and, in more recent times, automobiles.

The construction of pathways to places where the need to go was less apparent—mountaintops in particular, and wild country in general—tended to occur after the establishment of trails and roads in more favorable locations. The design of these backcountry trails was heavily influenced by their expected uses—everything from access for fire control, mining, and the movement of livestock, to recreation—and by the shape of the terrain that they crossed. That has led to two distinct views of trail construction in America—a Northeastern approach based on a vertical orientation, and a Western and Southeastern ideal that perceives trail layout as essentially horizontal.

But how were these trails made? . . . According to one writer, "The deer were the first; then the elk followed the deer; the buffalo followed the elk; the Indian followed the buffalo; trappers then; then army officers came along and discovered a pass."

Mathilde Edith Holtz and Katharine Isabel Bemis
GLACIER NATIONAL PARK: ITS TRAILS AND TREASURES
(NEW YORK: GEORGE H. DORAN CO., 1917), PP. 73–74.

Northeastern Trails—A Vertical Vision

As in other parts of the country, many of the early pathways into the New England mountains evolved into roadways alongside rivers and through valleys. Over time, travel became sufficiently manageable and accommodations sufficiently numerous that in the latter half of the nineteenth century, tourists from the cities began coming in great numbers to visit the Catskills, White Mountains, Green Mountains, and Adirondacks. Innkeepers cut pathways up the forested flanks of nearby peaks so that their guests could scramble to the top and have a look around. The routes were steep, often ascending in a direct line from a valley to a summit. Minimal to begin with, many of these summit paths soon melted back into the mountainsides.

In addition to the crews hired by innkeepers, early New England trail construction was often conducted by college outing clubs, community boosters eager to attract tourists to their towns, and by the occasional would-be woodsman with a hatchet and a strong imagination. The quality of these efforts was dependent upon the energies and whims of the people doing the work. A standardized approach to trail work in New England remained an elusive notion until the late 1800s when regional outdoor recreation organizations began reaching a size and influence to introduce their concepts of trail construction and maintenance in the backcountry.

In the White Mountains, the earliest of the groups concerned with trail work was the Appalachian Mountain Club, formed in 1876. The Green Mountain Club, established in 1910, served a similar purpose in the Vermont Mountains, and the Adirondack Mountain Club influenced trail work in the Adirondack region beginning in 1922. The public agencies and private landowners responsible for managing extensive tracts of the New England countryside came to rely upon these and other volunteer organizations for the people and the expertise needed to establish and care for recreational trails.

The methods of trail work that these clubs brought into the twentieth century were based upon the prevailing New England tradition of cutting routes that ascended directly from the lowlands to the high country. Rocks and roots in the tread were usually left where they were found. Crews could clear pathways quickly and, at least in the initial construction, with little manipulation of the terrain. At the far extreme, some routes were so steep that trail builders installed ladders or embedded iron rungs in rock faces so that hikers could haul themselves up.

The acute angles of the trails made erosion inevitable. In some locations, the shallow topsoil washed away, leaving the granite beneath as a durable hiking surface. Other trails became ditches, or sank into mud holes. As crews began turning their attention from opening new trails to maintaining older routes, much of their effort focused on constructing stone steps up the steepest trail sections and placing wooden walkways across saturated soil.

Despite the arduous nature of many trails, the distinctive steepness of New England pathways became part of their allure. People traveling to them from the cities were often under the time constraints of weekends or annual vacations. They wanted to experience the challenge of wilderness as quickly as possible. Northeastern trails indulged that desire by allowing them, within a few steps of leaving the road, to head straight toward the heights. There were also those, as there were in other parts of the country as well, who saw the mountaintop experience as a privilege to be earned through at least a little bit of struggle. New England's trails certainly allowed them that.

The lay of the land also contributed to the direct and rugged nature of trails in the Northeast. The mountain ranges of New England confronted trail builders with a confusing jumble of humpbacked peaks unlike the more orderly ridges and linear ranges of the Southeast and West. Add to that the glacial legacy of granite outcroppings, ledges, and a scarcity of soil, and crews building routes any distance across the Northeastern mountains had little choice but to go up and down at grades that in other sections of the country would be unthinkable.

Steep routes became so ingrained in the philosophy of New England trail building that early attempts to lessen the pitch of pathways and make them inviting to a wider range of people were sometimes met with disparagement. The most interesting effort may have been the trails built under the direction of J. Rayner Edmands, who had served as president of the Appalachian Mountain Club in 1886. Edmands applied techniques he had seen in the Rocky Mountains to the construction and rebuilding of several routes in the vicinity of Mount Washington. His trails hugged the contours of the land and rose gradually up the slopes. He removed rocks, smoothed the tread, and built stone cairns to show the way. The work was done so meticulously that some of the trails are still in use today.

Even so, few Northeastern trail builders could see the practicality, on any but a very limited scale, of the ideas Edmands borrowed from the West. In 1900, the annual Appalachian Mountain Club report by the club's "councillor of improvements" noted, instead, that "In no case has the Club undertaken to make the smooth graded paths or so-called boulevards." In New England, the shape of trails would continue to be influenced by a legacy of steep routes adapted to the geographic realities of a rugged land.

(For a discussion of Edmands' trail work and a general overview of Northeastern trail development, see *Forest and Crag* by Laura and Guy Waterman [Boston: Appalachian Mountain Club, 1989].)

Western and Southeastern Trails— A Horizontal Vision

The trail construction methods that Edmands had witnessed on his journey to the Rocky Mountains were as different from the New England ideas about trail work as the backcountry of the West was from that of the East. For one thing, there was just so much more of it. In the late 1800s and early 1900s, millions of acres of virtually untouched territory were coming under the jurisdictions of new federal land-management agencies and bureaus. While the mountains of the East were relatively close to major cities, or at least within several days' journey by railroad, the majority of the West's open lands lay far from population centers. A few highly publicized destinations such as Yosemite and Yellowstone did entertain crowds of visitors, but most of the high country of the Cascades, Sierra, and Rockies simply had nothing comparable to the throngs of recreationists pouring into the Appalachians, White Mountains, and Adirondacks.

Early travelers making their way into the Western backcountry found little infrastructure to ease their journeys. Highways and railroads tended to parallel rather than penetrate the mountains, and the sheer expanse of the landscape often confronted adventurers with long, arduous treks. Except in the newly formed national parks and on some private lands, there were few inns or other tourist amenities. In addition, much travel in the West was work-related rather than recreational, done by miners, foresters, hunters, and trappers more intent on reaching a destination than enjoying the journey there.

The combination of vast expanses, extreme distances, and scarcity of population forced mountain travelers to be self-sufficient for days or weeks at a time. Many relied upon pack animals to carry their provisions and camping equipment, and they themselves were as likely to be on horseback as on foot. Since horses and mules are not fond of steep routes, trail construction in the West leaned toward the needs of livestock. To achieve a reasonable grade, the pathways were surveyed along the contours of slopes rather than directly up them. Trails were cleared of stumps, rocks, and other obstructions. Switchbacks allowed builders to zigzag routes up mountainsides and still maintain grades that would not cause pack animals to balk.

The geography of the mountain ranges of the southeastern United States made them even more inviting for trail crews to place routes along their flanks rather than up and over their summits. Graceful trails were built at minimal grades through the lengths of Shenandoah and Great Smoky Mountain National Parks, and in many of the surrounding national forests. Furthermore, unlike New England where timberline hovers at about 4,000 feet, many mountaintops in the southern Appalachians were forested rather than open. Southeastern hikers often found it more interesting to traverse long distances through the forests rather than to labor to summits that offered little visual reward.

By the time trails were being constructed in the West and Southeast primarily for recreational users, the philosophy of building them with a horizontal orientation had become the standard. An entry from the crew foreman's report of the 1915 construction accomplished on the John Muir Trail in the Sierra National Forest describes trail specifications remarkably similar to those used throughout the West to this day:

> Tread, 30 inches minimum width. Plenty of turnouts provided in dangerous places. Grade in no case except under extraordinary conditions exceeding 15 per cent. The exceptions so far as noted were extremely few.

Where grading work was done, ample clearance for packs was made in cuts, and in timber country six feet clearance between trees was obtained. Trail was placed, so far as possible, out of the way of slides, in order to decrease cost of up-keep.

Over the years, trail construction in different sections of the United States has leaned toward either a horizontal or a vertical orientation. Each has evolved into hundreds of variations to address specific needs in thousands of locations. The two approaches, and the many ways in which they can be combined, serve as the primary building blocks of contemporary trail construction and maintenance.

What is a Trail?

A trail is a narrow highway over which a pack animal can travel with safety during the usual period when the need for a highway exists.

TRAIL CONSTRUCTION ON THE NATIONAL FORESTS
(FOREST SERVICE, 1915), P. 8.

. . . a trail is a linear corridor, on land or water, with protected status and public access for recreation or transportation. Trails can be used to preserve open space, provide a natural respite in urban areas, limit soil erosion in rural areas, and buffer wetlands and wildlife habitat along waterways. Trails may be surfaced with soil, asphalt, sand and clay, clam shells, rock, gravel or wood chips. Trails may follow a river, a ridge line, a mountain game trail, an abandoned logging road, a state highway. They may link historic landmarks within a city. Trails may be maintained by a federal, state, or local agency, a local trails coalition, or a utility company.

TRAILS FOR ALL AMERICANS:
THE REPORT OF THE NATIONAL TRAILS AGENDA PROJECT
(SUMMER 1990), P. 2.

At its most basic, a trail is simply a cleared travel corridor leading from one point to another. In a way, that seems to fly in the face of environmental protection, for a trail is also a scar on the landscape. It is a sacrifice zone devoid of vegetation, a linear clearcut that can amount to a third of an acre or more per mile. And yet we accept the denuded surface of a trail as an almost natural part of the backcountry. It serves our needs extremely well and, by concentrating human use to a thin ribbon of land, it can spare the larger landscape from being trampled.

Even in areas designated as wilderness, trails are usually viewed as an acceptable construction. Quadrangle maps of the U.S. Geological Survey use green ink to indicate vegetation, blue for water, and brown for contour lines showing variations in terrain. Roads, buildings, borders, names of landmarks, and any other human creations are indicated with black. But once inside the boundary of a wilderness area, the cartographer's only need for black ink is to trace the thin, broken lines of trails.

Trails as Management Tools

Trails are among the most effective means of backcountry management available to those responsible for overseeing public and private lands. By controlling trail locations, managers can encourage visitation to certain areas and limit access to others. Every choice that land managers make about design, construction, and maintenance will affect who will be able to use a pathway and who will be discouraged from traveling on it or denied access altogether.

It has always been a daunting task for land managers to balance all the demands that are placed upon the backcountry and to make decisions about trails that are appropriate both for users and for the environment. Should a trail offer access to everyone who wants to use it, and by whatever means of transport they wish to employ? Should rugged country have rugged trails that challenge those few able to make their way along them? If horses or bicycles are not allowed on certain trails, should alternative pathways nearby be open to them? Should some trails be made passable by wheelchairs? To what extent should signs, interpretive exhibits, and blazes be used to mark trails and explain the landscapes through which they pass?

Trail decisions can also be influenced by legislation. Guidelines of the Occupational Safety and Health Administration (OSHA) may determine how trail crews can operate. The Wilderness Act of 1964 prohibits the use of mechanized travel or construction techniques on trails in designated wilderness areas. Regulations on some public lands set the standards for making certain trails accessible to persons with physical disabilities, and the Americans with Disabilities Act specifies how those trails shall be constructed and maintained.

In spite of the effectiveness of using trails to control human activity in the backcountry, there sometimes comes a point when users themselves determine matters on their own. Imagine, for example, a secluded lake located a mile from the nearest road. Hoping to minimize visitation to the fragile shoreline, the agency in charge of the area has decided not to fund the construction of a trail from the road to the water.

Fishing enthusiasts have heard, however, that the lake is full of hungry trout.

You know what will happen. Crowds armed with rods and reels will make their way to the lake despite the lack of trails, beating down vegetation and compacting the soil as they tramp through the woods. The haphazard pathways that form beneath their hip waders may be subjected to erosion, and may reach the lake at points that will endanger the area. Before long, agency personnel will probably find themselves building the trail to the lake after all. Properly designed, the trail will give people the access they want, but along a route that causes the least impact upon the environment.

User demand can also affect how existing trails are maintained. For instance, the numbers of bicyclists, motorcyclists, and equestrians who want to ride in the backcountry have grown tremendously. For reasons ranging from protecting fragile areas to reducing negative impact upon the experience of other trail users, land managers may ban livestock and wheeled vehicles from certain trails. But if riders organize themselves and petition their legislators to pressure the agency, administrators may find themselves forced to open the trails to a wider spectrum of users. Ideally, land managers will also be able to count on these new users to help maintain the trails they will be enjoying.

Trail decisions can even be driven by fear of litigation. A wilderness trail fords a stream, a hiker trying to cross in high water drowns, and his survivors sue the agency for negligence. While it is unusual for an agency to lose such a case in court, land managers may feel compelled to invest a portion of subsequent trail construction budgets to build a bridge that may be completely out of place except in the eyes of the law.

There are no easy answers to the questions that continually confront trail workers and land managers. However, if those who are in positions to oversee trails have a general understanding of trail construction, maintenance techniques, and the possibilities of site restoration, they will have the widest range of options with which to make informed decisions.

A Trail Historian's Chronological Primer

1810   Local boosters claim that a trail built to the top of Mt. Ascutney in Vermont is the first summit route constructed solely for recreational purposes.

1872   Yellowstone National Park established, the first national park.

1876   Appalachian Mountain Club formed to "explore the mountains of New England and adjacent regions both for scientific and artistic purposes, and in general to cultivate an interest in geographical studies."

1886   Division of Forestry established by Congress to oversee federally owned forest lands.

1891   Creative Act. Section 24 of the act gives the president the authority to set aside forested lands as public reservations.

1897   Organic Administration Act. Provides protective management authority and direction for the forest reserves. The act states that forest reserves are to be established only to secure favorable water flow conditions and to furnish a continuous timber supply.

1898   Sierra Club established by John Muir and others.

1905   Transfer Act. Congress transfers the forest reserves from the Department of Interior to the Department of Agriculture where Gifford Pinchot is in charge of the Division of Forestry. Shortly

	after the passage of the Transfer Act, the Division is renamed the Forest Service.
1906	The Mountaineers organized in Seattle.
1907	Forest reserves redesignated as national forests.
1910	Green Mountain Club formed in Vermont.
1911	Weeks Act. Authorizes the acquisition of private timber lands, establishing the eastern national forests.
1916	National Park Service established.
1920	New York–New Jersey Trail Conference founded to replace the earlier Palisades Interstate Park Trail Conference, which had been developing trails in Harriman Park.
1922	Adirondack Mountain Club organized.
1922	First mile of the Appalachian Trail cut, located in New York's Palisades Interstate Park.
1925	Appalachian Trail Conference formed to encourage and oversee the development of a hiking trail extending the length of the Appalachian Mountain range.
1928	The U.S. Forest Service begins to develop the Cascade Crest Trail through Washington State from the Canadian border to the Columbia River.
1930	The Long Trail completed down the length of Vermont.
1932	The Mountain League of Los Angeles County proposes a wilderness trail from Canada to Mexico along the summit divides of Washington, Oregon, and California. No significant action occurred until the 1960s.
1933	Civilian Conservation Corps established. For the next nine years, it provides backcountry work opportunities for hundreds of thousands of Americans.
1936	Parks, Parkway, and Recreation Act. The act attempts to iron out the rivalries and differing mandates of the Park Service and Forest Service in managing public lands by assigning to the Park Service the preeminent responsibility for recreation planning on all federal lands.
1937	The last mile of the Appalachian Trail built, located on Sugarloaf Mountain in Maine, thus opening the full length of the route from Maine to Georgia.
1942	Civilian Conservation Corps disbanded.
1957	Student Conservation Association founded.
1960	Multiple-Use Sustained-Yield Act. The act enhances the importance of recreation, range, wildlife, and fish on public lands to give them equal standing with timber and watershed uses.
1964	The Wilderness Act places limits on the type and amount of development allowed in areas designated as wilderness. Depending

on how each agency interprets it, the act places moderate to severe restrictions on trail types, amounts, and levels of construction, and on the tools and techniques allowed for trail work. In some areas, agency interpretation may preclude trails altogether.

1968   The National Trails System Act authorizes three types of trails:
- *National Recreational Trails,* capable of supporting a variety of outdoor recreation uses.
- *National Scenic Trails,* for recreation and for the conservation and enjoyment of the areas through which the trails pass.
- *Connecting or Side Trails,* to link the recreational and scenic trails and to provide additional points of public access.

The first trails to receive National Scenic Trail designation are the Appalachian Trail and Pacific Crest Trail. By the 1990s, other National Scenic Trails included the Continental Divide, Ice Age, North Country, Natchez Trace, Florida, Potomac, and Heritage Trails.

1969   National Environmental Policy Act (NEPA). The act requires that all work having the potential to impact natural resources be reviewed to determine the least damaging alternative, including not doing the work at all.

1970   First National Trails Symposium.

1970s   Roadless Area Review and Evaluation (RARE and RARE II) identifies all remaining roadless areas within the national forests and determines which would be administered as wilderness and which as multiple-use.

1973   The final proposed route of the Pacific Crest Trail published in the Federal Register.

1975   Eastern Wilderness Act amends the Wilderness Act by designating certain areas in fifteen eastern states for inclusion in the National Wilderness Preservation System.

1978   Endangered American Wilderness Act establishes or expands many wilderness areas in the western states by designating certain public lands for protection.

1979   Archeological Resources Protection Act (ARPA). Mandates that any work that will disturb new ground be preceded by an archeological review, and that any work such as trail relocation that uncovers archeological resources be halted pending professional site assessment. ARPA applies to historic as well as prehistoric sites and artifacts.

1991   Intermodal Surface Transportation Efficiency Act (ISTEA). A portion of the act provides funding to states for fiscal years 1991–1997 for the construction and maintenance of off-highway recreational trails.

CHAPTER 2

Crew Leadership

A leader who has never been lost on a prairie or in a great forest has not yet been fully trained for his work.

Earle Amos Brooks
A HANDBOOK OF THE
OUTDOORS (NEW YORK:
GEORGE H. DORAN
COMPANY, 1925), P. 231.

PEOPLE BECOME INVOLVED in backcountry projects for many reasons. Some are looking for real, physical work with results that are readily evident. They want to get dirt under their fingernails and sweat on their brows. Others are drawn to conservation efforts as an active form of earth stewardship. They want personal responsibility for a section of trail, a campsite, or an alpine meadow. There are those who join trail crews as a way to get outdoors and enjoy the sun and wind, and even the rain and cold. They revel in the freedom of the backcountry, in being close to nature, and in having a reason to stay out in the hills. Some like the traditional tools and the technical aspects of rustic construction. Others are attracted to backcountry labor by the promise of fun, because their friends are doing it, or because they are eager to meet new people. For many, trail work is a part of their professional responsibilities.

Those who work in the backcountry come from all walks of life. Some have built and repaired trails for years. Others are new to the woods, making up with enthusiasm for their lack of knowledge. Professionals and volunteers, old and young, men and women, members of youth groups, conservation corps, mountain clubs, or of no group at all, they represent a body of tremendous diversity and potential.

Equally rich is the variety of those who manage America's backcountry, including wilderness rangers, private landowners, camp directors, land-management agency administrators, and improvement committees of outdoor recreation organizations. They range in experience and savvy from those who are very seasoned to those who are just beginning to learn the essentials of their jobs.

Crew leaders must meld together the energies of trail workers and the needs of land managers. They must serve as problem solvers, arbitrators, motivators, negotiators, and even visionaries. Add the vagaries of weather, terrain, wildlife, and the other elements of the backcountry, and the challenges facing trail crew leaders become remarkably demanding, varied, and ultimately rewarding.

There is no single way to be a good leader, and some people will find that leadership comes easier to them than to others. But everyone can improve their leadership skills by being aware of how they are interacting with others, and by being willing to learn from positive and negative experiences.

Establishing Leadership Authority

Crew leaders must be exactly that—the leaders of their crew. Even when everyone in a group is about the same age, has about the same level of skill, and enjoys friendships that extend beyond time in the woods, those who are a group's leaders should conduct themselves as leaders. They are the ones who must make ultimate decisions concerning safety. They are the ones to whom the crew will turn for guidance in an emergency. The most effective form of leadership is that which is earned by proving through the leaders' actions that they have in mind the best interests of the group, and that their decisions, even when unpopular, are based on the needs and safety of everyone in the crew.

Backcountry leaders should not let their desire to be crew members rather than the crew leaders allow them to lose control of the group or to be persuaded to make unwise decisions. On the other hand, they should give crew members as much responsibility as each is able to handle. For example, leaders who have directed a youth group's work effort all day may be able to withdraw from overseeing camp activities, especially after everyone has learned the routines of food preparation and cleanup. Hunger will prod a crew into action far more effectively than nagging, and even if supper isn't ready until dusk, leaving to them the decision of when to eat (and perhaps also the choice of menu and how it will be prepared) gives a crew a greater sense of confidence in its abilities.

Effective Leadership

While their styles may vary, effective leaders share the following qualities:

- They insure a safe working environment for their crews and themselves.
- They establish ground rules ahead of time and insist that they are followed.
- They clearly communicate their expectations.
- They retain for themselves the right and responsibility of ultimate decision-making authority.

Leadership as Innovation

In the backcountry, crew leaders must cope with conditions that cannot be controlled, and with equipment that may or may not be exactly suited to the job at hand. Part of the satisfaction of leadership is devising solutions to the problems that present themselves, be it figuring out how to move heavy materials, how to shape a trail, or how to feed a crew when no one remembered to bring fuel for the camp stove. Innovation also extends to crew management—motivating people, teaching them the skills they need, and helping them realize their potential for working efficiently and living well in the outdoors.

While those in charge of a crew must, in some way, establish and maintain a sense of leadership, they need not be expert in every aspect of trail work and backcountry living. Rather than pretending to know everything, leaders can indicate that they are willing to learn along with crew members whenever opportunities for learning arise. That can begin by sharing with one another the wisdom that each person possesses, and by using books to learn together skills such as knot tying, map and compass use, camp cooking, or the identification of plants, wildlife, and constellations.

Leadership as Motivation

If you want people to do good work, give them good work to do. Careful planning and visits to the work site before a project begins will help crew leaders clarify for themselves the nature of the effort, how best to complete the work, and how to provide crew members with a satisfying experience. Having land-management personnel visit the crew during a project can reinforce the importance of the task the crew has undertaken and the value of their work to the environment and the agency.

Variety can also be a great motivator, especially early in a project when participants may not yet have the skill or conditioning to perform a sustained task for a long period of time. Shift people from one kind of work to another, and allow for rest and refreshment. Physically easy jobs such as sharpening and repairing tools can be interspersed with more demanding labors. Some crew leaders have had success using a Polaroid camera to take daily photographs of the work to document progress on the project.

Be flexible. You may have a clear vision of the experience you want for crew members—perhaps that in addition to completing the work, they will come away with a greater respect for natural environments. Everything may turn out exactly as you had hoped, but the greater likelihood is that your group will develop its own ideas of what it wants, and will respond to trail work opportunities in unique and surprising ways.

Timeless Advice on Leadership

Over 2,000 years ago, the Chinese philosopher Sun Tsu wrote that they lead best who seem to lead least. Following that advice, good leaders can provide the means for people to do good work and, at the same time, give them the feeling that "we did it ourselves."

Creating a Safe Work Environment

A key responsibility of a crew leader is to provide people with a work environment that is safe for them both physically and emotionally.

Physical safety is a matter of specifics—training crew members to use tools properly, to use their bodies without injuring themselves, and to know how to cope with backcountry hazards. Leaders must maintain an awareness of their crew's activities and surroundings, and make judgment calls based on enhancing the security of the group. Retreating from an approaching thunderstorm, hanging bear bags in camp, and deciding not to attempt a task that is beyond a crew's abilities are obvious acts of leadership. Equally important to group safety may be coping with crew members whose carelessness endangers others, perhaps even to the point that they must be asked to leave the backcountry.

Emotional safety is a more elusive concept for a trail crew, but in its effects upon the well-being of each person, it is every bit as vital as physical security. By their example and attitudes, leaders should do all they can to develop an atmosphere of trust and conviviality between themselves and their crews, and among group members. Group interactions should be relatively free of negativity, put-downs, or excessive teasing. Leaders must also be aware of gender issues, especially when crews are younger. On the work site, that may be a matter of helping everyone gain a mastery of the tools, and giving crew members of both genders equal roles in completing all aspects of a project. In a long-term camp, it may require frank discussions of the impact upon group dynamics if cliques or couples are becoming exclusive in the ways they share their time.

Estimating Work

Crew leaders must often estimate how much work their groups can accomplish in a given time. For private contractors bidding on projects, accurate estimating translates into hard dollars. For those in charge of volunteers, predictions of reasonable progress can help agency administrators determine larger management plans, and can assist leaders in motivating their crews.

Weather conditions, worker ability levels, availability of tools and materials, and a host of other variables can complicate the process of estimating. Even so, estimating work is an acquired skill that can be mastered. In the beginning, perhaps the best way to get a feel for how long it takes to do a certain task is to pick up a tool and do it yourself a few times.

Visiting a site well in advance of a crew's arrival is another essential part of estimating work. Schedule the visit so that you can go into the field with land-management personnel able to explain the goals of the work and the expectations they have for your crew. If possible, obtain a copy of the project prospectus, log, or other written plans. Copies of agency guidelines or handbooks can also give you a head start on thinking about how best to approach the work. Then, during the visit, find the answers to the following questions:

- How long will it take for the crew to travel to the work site each day from a trailhead or their camp?

- What tools will be needed to do the work, and how will they be transported to the site?
- What building materials will be required (rock, timber, etc.)? Are they available on-site? If materials must be moved some distance, will the crew have wheelbarrows, motorized toters, or rigging gear, and the expertise to use them?
- Will the agency provide any on-site personnel in the form of work supervisors or laborers?
- Will the project site be closed to public use? If not, is the crew likely to lose production time waiting for hikers and other trail users to pass by?
- When the work is complete, how much time will be required to close down the project, clean up the area, carry out tools and gear, and store equipment?
- Are there seasonal patterns of heat, cold, precipitation, or other environmental conditions that could affect production? Will the crew require time to acclimate to a high elevation before being able to work at full strength?
- Can a backcountry crew complete the project safely? If you have concerns about what you see, time estimates become secondary to finding a safe way of doing the work or abandoning the project and locating another that is more appropriate.
- Will the project engage the interest of crew members and leave them with a sense of accomplishment?
- Will crew members at backcountry sites transport their gear and provisions to their camp? Will they be expected to take time out from work to bring in resupplies?
- Can the crew stay in the same camp for the duration of the project, or will they need time to move their gear and set up camp in a new location?
- Is there a backup project for the crew if they finish the primary work ahead of schedule? Is it nearby, or will the crew have to move their camp in order to reach it?

In addition, take into consideration what you know about the age, fitness, experience, and motivation of your crew members. Complex projects or extensive work that must be completed under a tight schedule may be just right for seasoned backcountry crews, but too demanding for inexperienced volunteers.

On the other hand, don't sell crew members short. Where time constraints will allow it and the motivation of a crew is high, inexperienced people can learn a great deal by working their way through projects that stretch their limits and give them opportunities to master and use new skills. Leaders must also honestly assess their own ability to provide effective supervision and to teach the skills their crews must possess in order to finish projects without undue frustration or delay.

The Last Ten Percent

Attention to final details and the cleanup of a site makes a great difference in the ultimate appearance and quality of a work project. Unfortunately, that final ten percent of effort is often neglected. Crew leaders should include time in their work schedule to allow for the last ten percent, and then motivate crews to take pride in giving their work the polish it deserves.

CHAPTER 3

Camping with Work Crews

EVEN CREWS WILDLY ENTHUSED about completing projects cannot work 24 hours a day. Eventually the participants in every rustic work effort must put down their tools so they can eat, sleep, and practice at least a minimum of personal hygiene. For people working in the backcountry on multi-day projects, that usually means establishing a camp.

Volumes have been written about how small groups of backpackers can camp for short periods of time without leaving a trace of their presence. Those techniques are fine as far as they go, but seldom address the unique needs of trail crews requiring long-term camps. The decisions that crew leaders make concerning camp logistics and location will greatly affect the health, happiness, and productivity of the crew, and the quality of the environment in which they are living.

Camp Location

Construction crews generally establish one camp and use it for the duration of a project. Maintenance crews may move their camps as their work progresses, or set up a base camp and then stay in simpler *spike camps* closer to far-flung projects, returning to their main campsite every 3 or 4 days.

Whatever the case, campsite location is most often determined by agency personnel rather than leaders of work crews, though group leaders should examine a site before a crew arrives to insure that it is suitable. A trail crew camp must have access to water. There should be room to prepare and store food, to pitch tents, and to allow people to move about and socialize during their free time. In bear country, there must be sturdy trees from which to hang food, or some other storage arrangement to protect provisions from wildlife.

Use established campsites whenever possible. Minimize impact by selecting a campsite on bare earth or in an area covered with leaves or pine needles. If you must camp on undisturbed ground, do what you can to limit soil compaction, the formation of bootleg trails, and the trampling of plants. Designating trails between areas used for sleeping and cooking will encourage people to stay on a few pathways rather than beating down the rest of the vegetation. Paths can be temporarily delineated with sticks, rocks, or flagging. Some SCA groups have had success shielding the earth beneath tents with geo-textile fabric, a tough material used in the construction of walkways over muddy terrain.

Protect shorelines and water purity by locating camps at least 200 feet from lakes, streams, and wetlands. Select water collection points that are not susceptible to damage, and consider reinforcing a water collection site with stepping stones. In most environments, washing even with biodegradable soap should be done well away from sources of water.

Privacy

If possible, work crew campsites should be placed where they cannot be seen from trails the public may use. Since tents must often be left unattended during the day while the crew is working, screening the camp behind terrain or heavy vegetation can enhance its security. Furthermore, the experience of backcountry visitors will not be marred by suddenly coming upon the tarps, laundry lines, and other paraphernalia of a long-term camp.

Privacy may also be an issue within a camp. Crew members who work as a team all day and then spend part of the evening together cooking meals and

Careful location and layout decisions can minimize the environmental impact and maximize the comfort and safety of a trail crew.

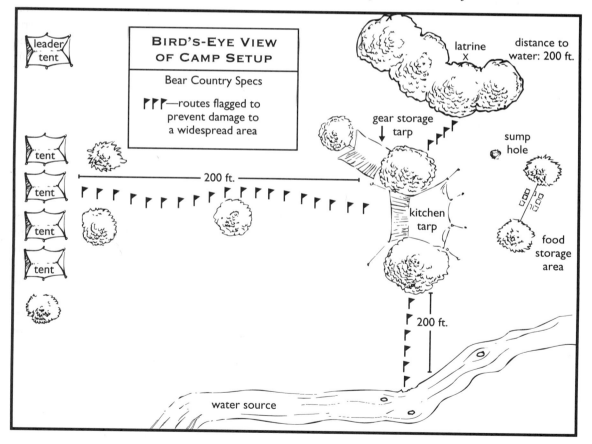

BIRD'S-EYE VIEW OF CAMP SETUP

Bear Country Specs

ГГГ—routes flagged to prevent damage to a widespread area

leader tent

tent
tent
tent
tent

200 ft.

latrine
X

distance to water: 200 ft.

gear storage tarp

sump hole

kitchen tarp

food storage area

200 ft.

water source

cleaning up may crave time alone. Placing the sleeping tents some distance from the center of camp is not only a basic safety measure in bear country, but can also allow people to make their tents a refuge from group activities.

Tarps and Tents

Crews camping in temperate and dry environments may need little shelter other than tents for sleeping and a dining fly to shield the cooking area from afternoon showers. If you expect more rain, take along extra tarps or a wall tent to establish additional dry areas for cooking, eating, and socializing. Crew members can use large pieces of four-mil clear plastic and lengths of cord to fashion a vestibule extending in front of each sleeping tent to provide a sheltered space for changing out of dirty clothes and muddy boots before crawling into bed. A large tent made of insect netting will give crews in mosquito country a bug-free haven where they can do their cooking and eating. Tents and tarps colored to blend with the background can further reduce the visual impact of a camp.

Personal Hygiene

Personal cleanliness in the backcountry will seldom be what people experience at home, but a commonsense approach to hygiene will go a long way toward keeping a crew healthy.

- Wash hands with soap and water after using the latrine and before preparing or eating meals.
- Don't share silverware, cups, or water bottles.
- After meals, thoroughly wash dishes, cooking utensils, and cutting boards with biodegradable soap and a disinfectant.
- Use a cup rather than bare hands to scoop trail mix and other foods out of communal buckets and bags.

As for bathing, some crews will be blessed with a camp near a lake or stream where they can swim every day after work. Those laboring in dry areas may have to settle for washing up in a bucket of water. Showers can sometimes be devised by hanging a bladder bag from a tree branch and letting the water run through a hose fitted with a sprinkler head.

Latrines

If a crew is staying in the same area for more than a few days, digging a trench latrine is appropriate in most backcountry settings. Locate the latrine at least 200 feet from water, trails, and campsites. If there are several inches or more of organic soil, keep the trench shallow so that microorganisms can break down human waste. Sprinkle a little earth in the latrine after each use, extending the length of the trench whenever necessary.

Depending on the ferocity of their environmental leanings and the depth of their adventurous natures, crew members may choose to resolve the problem of toilet paper disposal by relying instead on leaves, pine needles, snow, or other native materials. Otherwise, a crew can keep a paper bag near the latrine for the collection of used toilet paper. Burn each day's bag in a hot campfire or, if you have no open fires, seal it in a plastic bag for eventual transport to the trailhead along with other camp garbage. If aromas might attract bears, hang the bag well out of reach of animals. Do not burn toilet paper in the latrine itself; the danger of igniting a forest fire is too great.

Crew members seeking relief at the work site can wander some distance from the project and use the heels of their boots to dig cat holes a few inches deep. Completely cover the holes after use. Crews working in desert regions or in alpine tundra may need to rely on portable chemical toilets for disposing of human waste without polluting the environment.

Kitchen

A long-term camp will be much more inviting to those who live in it if there are a few amenities to make chores easier. One of the most useful is a kitchen table that will allow cooks to stand upright while they prepare meals. A simple table can be made by lashing poles between two trees, then laying a couple of boards across the poles. The table top could be decking that will later become part of a bridge, or boards brought in specifically for use as a table. Propane or white gas stoves can rest atop the table, on nearby stumps, or on overturned pack boxes. A cutting board and a good selection of kitchen utensils and pots and pans will help cooks prepare the volumes of food required to feed a crew.

Campfires

There are many advantages to having a campfire in a trail crew camp. It can be used for heating water, baking in Dutch ovens and reflector ovens, and completing other cooking tasks, thereby reducing the amount of fuel required for camp stoves. A crew enduring a long siege of cold, rainy weather may need a fire if they hope ever again to wiggle their toes into dry socks. Open fires can make camping easier in territory shared with bears by providing a crew with a convenient way to dispose of food scraps, toilet paper, tampons, and other combustible materials.

On the other hand, fires are often impractical or environmentally unacceptable. Heat can sterilize the soil beneath a fire, and soot will permanently blacken stones that are close to the flames. People collecting firewood may be contributing to ground compaction and the disruption of fragile vegetation. Wood gathered for burning will no longer be available to decompose on the ground and replenish the earth with nutrients. The disposal of ashes can alter the natural chemistry of the soil.

Our table was a large piece of freshly peeled birch-bark, laid wrong-side-up, and our breakfast consisted of hard bread, fried pork, and strong coffee, well sweetened, in which we did not miss the milk.

Henry David Thoreau
THE MAINE WOODS
(BOSTON: TICKNOR & FIELDS, 1864).

I am a woodland fellow, sir, that always loved a great fire.

THE CLOWN IN WILLIAM SHAKESPEARE'S *ALL'S WELL THAT ENDS WELL*, ACT 4, SCENE 5.

Tarps shelter a backcountry kitchen and gear storage area. The sump hole in the foreground is for waste water disposal.

Even where campfires are allowed, crew leaders must still weigh the positive and negative aspects of kindling a blaze, leaning heavily in favor of what is best for the environment. Use existing fire rings whenever possible, or shield the earth with a fire pan raised above the ground. The National Outdoor Leadership School (NOLS) has developed a method of protecting the soil with a fireproof emergency shelter such as those carried by forest fire fighting crews. Lay the shelter flat on the ground, place several inches of mineral soil on top of it, and build a small fire on the soil. After the fire has been extinguished, scatter the ashes and soil, and pack out the shelter.

A Fireless Vision

A fire often serves as the social centerpiece of a campsite, but there are alternatives. Rather than gazing in toward the center of the camp, crews without fires tend to look outward, becoming more aware of their surroundings. The social needs of a group's pyromaniacs can often be satisfied by the glow of a candle or lantern.

Camp Stoves

Camp stoves can be used for all of a crew's cooking and cleanup requirements. Two-burner propane stoves are extremely efficient and safe to use. Propane can be transported into the backcountry in refillable bottles; a tank containing 20 pounds of propane should last two or three weeks for a crew of eight people. Take an extra bottle if campfires are not allowed and all cooking and water heating will be done on the stove. Each crew should have a stove repair kit containing any spare washers or O-rings the stove may require, and an adjustable wrench for attaching and removing the hose leading from the propane tank to the stove. Crews may also want to take along one or two backpacking stoves to add firepower to the kitchen for complicated feasts and to use when trail workers are living out of their packs.

Washing Dishes

Care in washing and sterilizing dishes is an important step in preventing bacteria and viruses from being passed from one crew member to another. Proper procedure will also protect the environment, most notably by keeping dishwater at least 200 feet from any stream, spring, or other source of water.

A thorough cleanup requires three dishpans. The first holds hot, soapy wash water. The second is a hot rinse containing a few drops of chlorine bleach or other germ-killing agent. The third is filled with cold water for a final rinse. Depending upon the crew and the meal, you may wish to add an additional pan with cold water for a pre-wash to get the big chunks off the plates and keep the wash water cleaner longer. Water used for washing and rinsing need not be purified; as dishes dry, germs will die.

Dishes can be air-dried in net hammocks strung between trees near the wash area. Mesh bags or a large tin can with holes punched in the bottom may be more practical for drying and storing silverware and kitchen utensils.

Waste Water Management

Not far from the kitchen, dig a sump hole at least 3 feet deep for disposal of water left over from cooking and from washing dishes. Lay a 3-foot square of wire window screen over the hole to catch food particles as the water is poured through. Clean the screen after each use by shaking food particles into a campfire or a trash bag. Metal screens can be passed rapidly over a campfire to burn any remaining food bits, but will melt if left too long close to the flames.

Garbage Disposal

Purchasing food in bulk will enable crews to reduce the amount of packaging they carry into the backcountry. Careful menu selection and portion size can also minimize the production of garbage. Even so, a trail crew preparing meals will generate a fair amount of refuse. Where fires are appropriate, garbage and trash can be burned by scattering it into the flames a little at a time. Do not burn plastics, as they may give off toxic gases while they combust. Instead, pack them out along with foil, cans, bottles, and any garbage that has not been incinerated.

Garbage may have to be stored for days or even weeks at a backcountry camp before it can be transported to the frontcountry. The most practical storage method is to seal it in plastic buckets with tightly fitted lids and hang them out of reach of wildlife. If the garbage is especially aromatic, hang it away from lines that are suspending food supplies; animals attracted by the smells of the garbage may focus their energies on trying to reach the trash rather than going after the good stuff. Burying refuse is an unacceptable disposal method since animals are likely to dig up garbage and scatter it.

Breaking Camp

As you are preparing to leave a trail crew camp, be sure to:
- Fill sump holes and latrines.
- Collect any bits of plastic, metal, string, paper, and other trash.
- Use restoration techniques to erase signs of trails, tent pads, food preparation areas, latrines, and fire sites.

Food

You don't need to be an epicure to appreciate that the noonday snack on the trail is an important factor in the enjoyment of a day's run. Of course it is possible to lunch on a handful of cold raisins, but for myself I find that the pleasure of the trip, clear through to the end of the day, is enhanced by a satisfying bite along about meridian.

Allen Chamberlain
"A FROST-PROOF NOONDAY SNACK," *OUTING MAGAZINE,* VOL. 61 (OCTOBER 1912-MARCH 1913), P. 447.

Trail work involves hard physical labor, and crews doing it need plenty of good nourishment. Weather and location can also influence the volume and kinds of foods people crave. Crews toiling in chilly weather or at high elevations may need more food with greater volumes of complex carbohydrates than groups laboring in the heat.

Food is also a powerful psychological motivator, particularly when a crew will be in the backcountry for a long time or must endure bad weather. An interesting variety of food and plenty of spices to liven up the typical trail stews and pots of pasta will go a long way toward quelling gastronomical mutiny. Dutch ovens or ovens that fit atop propane stoves allow cooks to bake bread, pies, biscuits, lasagna, enchiladas, and pizzas. A bag of chocolate suddenly materializing in the middle of a chilly, damp day on the trail can perform miracles for the spirits of a despondent group.

FAMILIAR FOOD

Volunteers on trail crews may be new to backcountry living. They may be challenged by tasks they have not done before, and by unusual surroundings. Food that is familiar to them can be greatly reassuring. Cultural backgrounds can also play a role in food preferences, as may vegetarianism or an avoidance of dairy products. Whenever possible, find out before developing menus what foods group members would like to eat. It may be possible to involve the crew in drawing up food lists, shopping for provisions, and preparing them to be packed into the backcountry.

BALANCED NUTRITION

Hard working crews need balanced diets composed of a variety of whole grains, proteins, vegetables, fruits, and fats. If for reasons of storage or preference you bring only a small amount of meat, rely on the complete proteins provided by combinations such as beans and rice or pasta and cheese.

CAMP LOCATION

Crews staying near roads may be able to replenish their camp kitchens frequently with fresh foods. Groups deeper in the backcountry may have to rely on pack animals, helicopters, or their own shoulders to transport provisions. Their food choices may need to be lighter in weight and non-perishable.

BUYING FOOD

Food co-ops and natural food stores are good sources for the bulk ordering of nuts, dried fruits, grains, pastas, rice, and other food staples. Discount warehouses and restaurant supply stores offer bargains on foods ordered in quantity. Grocery stores may also give discounts on large amounts, especially if you place orders well in advance. The catalogues and stores of camping supply companies are good sources of dehydrated and freeze-dried foods, though it is wise to sample small amounts of these highly processed rations before investing in large quantities.

Removing excess packaging will save weight and reduce the amount of trash that must be packed out of the backcountry. Many food staples can be measured into plastic bags, then stowed in the same containers you will use for storage in camp. Wooden pack boxes or square plastic buckets with lids are ideal. Use cord or duct tape to seal the lids on buckets and boxes. If supplies will be delivered to your campsite at different times, indicate which containers should be transported in the first load and which in each resupply. Color coding with tape or markers can help insure that a packer will bring your crew the right containers at the right time.

PACKING FOR HORSES, MULES, OR HELICOPTERS

Horses and mules are used in many parks and forests, particularly in Western states, to transport trail crew gear, tools, and provisions to remote campsites. Packers are usually particular about how loads should be prepared for their livestock to carry. It's a very good idea to have a planning meeting with your packers several days before they disappear into the backcountry with your worldly goods.

Round containers are difficult to pack on animals. Stick with square plastic buckets and heavy-duty boxes. If you have a choice, use long, thin 28-pound propane tanks; they can be strapped on a load more easily than the fatter 38-pound

Never eat anything named Supreme, Surprise, or Delight.
Diane Grua
SCA CREW LEADER

On a rainy day in the mountains, I never met a fresh, hot biscuit I didn't like.
Rod Replogle
U.S. FOREST SERVICE

Supplies and tools for work crews may be moved into the backcountry by pack animals or helicopters.

size. Repackage condiments into plastic bottles and jars to minimize the amount of glass, and protect any glass containers you must take by putting each one in a plastic bag and burying it inside a bucket loaded with flour, rice, beans, or some other food that will act as a cushion.

Depending on their size, pack animals can carry loads of 150 to 200 pounds. As you stow food in buckets or boxes, weigh each one and label it with its weight. The packers can then load these into containers called *panniers,* or wrap them tightly with tarps that, in much of the West, are called *manties.* Secured with rope, panniers or manties of equal weight (usually 50 to 75 pounds) are hung on either side of each animal. Sleeping bags, tents, and other bulky items can be lashed on top of the load. (For information on tying mantie loads, see Chapter 18, "Knots.")

Careful packing is equally important when the mode of transport is a helicopter. Pilots will want each container marked with its weight so that they can make up loads that are within the helicopter's margin of operational safety. Containers are sometimes stowed inside the aircraft, though it is more likely that they will be lifted in a net slung underneath.

Supplying a camp by pack animals or helicopters is timely and efficient as long as everything works according to plan. Unfortunately, schedules may go awry due to bad weather, emergencies elsewhere, or other unforeseeable circumstances. The hard-learned lesson is that if you must rely upon someone else to transport your supplies into the backcountry, be sure that your crew members have enough food and camping gear in their packs to get along on their own for several days until an overdue pack string or helicopter is able to make its delivery.

Camp and Food Management in Bear Country

Trail crews sharing the backcountry with bears must take special precautions to protect themselves, their campsites, and their food supplies. Due to regional differences in the habits of humans and bears, safety practices vary in different parts of the country. Some agencies in Alaska, for example, require that work crews carry firearms. Crews in some other parks are encouraged to have canisters of pepper spray with them. Wherever your crew is stationed, consult local wildlife experts to learn the most effective means for ensuring the safety of workers and bears.

The following guidelines have proven successful in areas where grizzly bears are common, and should be heeded anywhere grizzlies may be suspected. Leaders of crews working in black bear country must judge local situations and deviate from these guidelines only with careful consideration. When in doubt, err in favor of taking too many precautions rather than too few.

PRECAUTIONS WHILE TRAVELING

- The majority of bear attacks upon people occur when bears are startled, are threatened, or are protecting cubs or food. As you hike, reduce the likelihood of surprising a bear by staying alert and scanning the country ahead.
- Travel in groups of three or more; the larger the group, the less the likelihood of a bear incident.
- Make noise to alert bears of your approach. Remember, though, that sound may be muffled by the wind or the rush of a stream.
- Think twice about off-trail travel in grizzly bear country, especially where heavy foliage may reduce your range of vision.
- Avoid hiking or wandering about after dark when bears tend to be more active.

PRECAUTIONS IN CAMP

- Don't camp in an area that shows signs of recent bear disturbance such as new claw marks on trees or fresh scat. Be wary of campsites where fire lays have been dug up, an indication that bears may have become accustomed to finding garbage left by previous campers.
- Sleep in tents rather than in the open. The tent may be enough of a barrier to prevent a wandering bear from investigating you in your sleeping bag.
- Pitch your sleeping tents at least 100 yards from food preparation and storage areas. Situate the tents upwind of the kitchen and any food storage so that prevailing breezes will carry aromas away from, rather than toward, the tents.
- Set up tents in a line rather than a circle so that a bear will not feel trapped if it blunders into your camp at night.
- Have nothing in the tents except sleeping bags and foam pads,

flashlights, and perhaps a book or two. No food or scented items of any kind should ever be taken into a tent used for sleeping.

- Set up a tarp near the kitchen for storing packs and personal gear, and to serve as an area for changing clothes.
- Just before going to bed, change out of clothing that may have picked up odors during the day while you were working, cooking, and eating. Put on a clean sweat suit, long underwear, or other tent clothes that are never worn for anything except sleeping.
- If you must venture out at night, use a flashlight and make plenty of noise to alert any bears to your presence.
- Menstruating women should consider using tampons that can be burned in a hot fire. Where fire is not available, seal used tampons or pads in plastic bags and store them in the bear hang until trash can be packed out of the backcountry.

PRECAUTIONS WITH FOOD AND OTHER "SMELLABLES"

- Bears that have feasted on human food are likely to return for more. Maintain an immaculate camp—no food in tents; dishes washed immediately after meals; tables, cutting boards, and stoves kept clean; food, toilet items, and all other *smellables* stored well out of the reach of animals whenever the crew will be out of camp for even a few minutes.
- Limit the amount of food in camp to that which will be used between resupply runs. This requires prudent planning of menus before the crew goes into the backcountry. Provisions can be divided into boxes keyed to specific resupply opportunities, then stored in the frontcountry until they are needed by the crew.
- Be aware of the appetites of crew members and gauge meal portions so that there are few leftovers.
- Select provisions that give off a minimum of odor—grains, cereals, dried fruits, vegetables, and dehydrated dairy products.
- If food spills on the ground, scrape up as much as you can.
- Burn all your garbage, including food bits screened out of dish water, or stash garbage in a plastic bucket or trash bag and store it on a bear line until it can be packed to a trailhead. When not in use, hang the screen on a bear line.

Bear Lines

Many experienced backpackers are accustomed to hanging their food from trees to keep it away from animals. That is fairly easy to do when the amount of supplies is limited to that carried by hikers enjoying a few days and nights in the woods. A trail crew, however, may need to protect hundreds of pounds of provisions, yet have quick access when they are ready to prepare their meals.

Crews can sometimes use large metal containers called bear boxes to store their food. Where bear boxes are not available, groups can set up a bear line system developed by SCA staff on the Greater Yellowstone Recovery Corps working in grizzly bear territory. With it, a crew of eight to ten people can protect enough provisions for three weeks or more.

BEAR LINE COMPONENTS:

¼-inch wire rope—100 feet

¼-inch cable clamps—12

⅛-inch nylon cord or parachute cord—300 feet

⅜-inch nylon rope—30 feet

Block & tackle—three sets, for tensioning the cable and hoisting food buckets. To save weight, each block can be a plastic and metal sailing pulley with two sheaves (wheels) about 2 inches in diameter. Thread each pair

A food hanging system for bear country

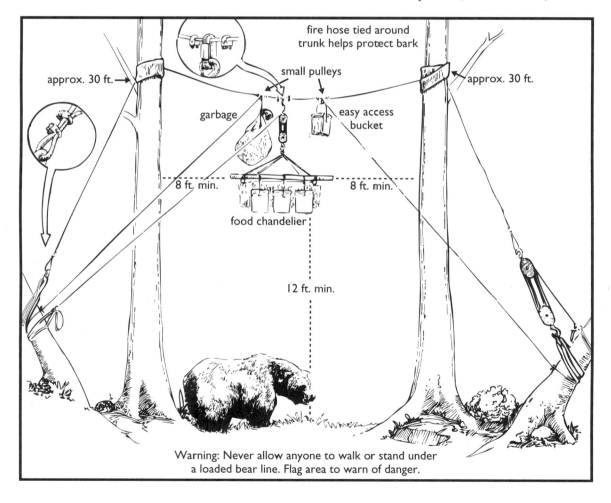

approx. 30 ft.

fire hose tied around trunk helps protect bark

small pulleys

garbage

easy access bucket

approx. 30 ft.

8 ft. min.

8 ft. min.

food chandelier

12 ft. min.

Warning: Never allow anyone to walk or stand under a loaded bear line. Flag area to warn of danger.

of blocks with 125 feet of ⅜-inch braided nylon rope. (For more on block and tackle, tensioning and hoisting, see Chapter 17, "Rigging.")

Small single sheave blocks—2, for hoisting toilet kits

Carabiners—8

2-inch clips—24, for clipping food buckets to the system (Galvanized clips from a hardware store work well.)

Anchor material—two sets of either ¾-inch rope sling 8 feet long, or 2-inch wide nylon webbing sling (loop or eye-and-eye)

1. Form an eye in each end of the wire rope. (See Chapter 17, "Rigging," for details on using cable clamps to make an eye.)
2. Choose two live trees 35 to 40 feet apart and stout enough not to bend under considerable strain. Pass the wire rope over a branch in each tree 25 to 30 feet above the ground. You may be able to elevate the wire rope by tying a rock to a length of parachute cord, tossing the rock over a branch, then using the nylon line to haul the wire rope into place. If you climb the tree to install the wire rope, use the opportunity to place a piece of fire hose or other padding between the rope and the branch to shield the tree bark from abrasion.

    Some Forest Service crews in Southeast Alaska further deter animals from climbing bear hang trees by sheathing each trunk with sections of metal stovepipe.
3. Set a webbing or rope anchor around the base of a nearby stump or tree, then attach one eye of the wire rope to it with a carabiner. Attach the other eye of the wire rope to the power block of a block and tackle. With a carabiner, secure the remaining block to an anchor that has been placed around a second stump or tree. Use the block and tackle to draw the wire rope taut.
4. Toss a parachute cord over the tensioned wire rope. As you let out slack from the block and tackle and use the cord to pull down the middle of the rope, keep your eye on the point on the rope that was centered between the two trees. Fasten a cable clamp at that point.
5. With a carabiner, clip the lead-line block of the second block and tackle next to the cable clamp on the wire rope. Place another cable clamp on the wire rope on the other side of the carabiner to prevent it from sliding.
6. Tension the wire rope again. The power block of the block and tackle suspended from the center of the wire rope should be hanging close to the ground.
7. If you have a modest number of buckets, a half-dozen or so, tie a bowline in the end of an 18-inch cord for each bucket and, at the other end, tie on a small clip. Slip the loops of the bowlines into a carabiner and attach it to the power block. Snap each clip onto a bucket handle, and you will be ready to hoist the buckets into the air.

If you have a larger number of buckets, attaching them directly to the block can become ungainly. Instead, construct a *chandelier* to hold up to sixteen buckets at one time without twisting and tangling. Use square lashings to bind together four poles, each about 4 feet long and 3 to 4 inches in diameter, to form a frame. For each bucket, tie a small clip onto a loop made from a 36-inch length of cord. Use the loops to secure the clips to the frame, spacing 3 or 4 of them along each pole.

8. Knot a 30-foot length of ⅜-inch nylon rope to form a sling, and loop it around the four lashed corners of the frame. Attach the center of the sling to the suspended block, using a carabiner. Haul on the lead line to lift the completed chandelier a few feet off the ground. Snap the bails of the food buckets into the clips, then hoist the chandelier up to the wire rope. Tie off the lead rope to a tree.

Note: A cargo net can be stretched across chandelier to add to carrying capacity

A chandelier provides room for attaching buckets of supplies to a food hanging system.

Bear Line Safety

A chandelier may suspend several hundred pounds of food 12 feet or more above the ground. Although a properly rigged system is almost always reliable, no one should ever walk under a loaded bear line. Mark off the zone beneath the wire rope and chandelier with flagging or cord, and prohibit entry into that area unless the chandelier is on the ground.

HINTS:

- Attach a small block to the wire rope and run a parachute cord through it so that crew members can raise and lower a single bucket containing their toilet articles without having to move the entire chandelier. Prevent that block from sliding along the wire rope by attaching a cable clamp on either side of it.
- Tie one end of a 50-foot parachute cord to the chandelier. Light tension on the cord will prevent the chandelier from twisting while it is being raised and lowered.
- Create additional storage space by lacing a mesh net of parachute cord into the center of the chandelier.
- Use square plastic buckets rather than round ones. Square buckets are more practical for transport into the backcountry by pack animals or helicopter.
- Label the contents of each bucket by using strips of duct tape and a felt-tipped marker. That will allow you to find the supplies you need without

having to search through all the buckets every time you want something. Additional labels on the bottoms of the buckets can be seen while the chandelier is suspended.

- A bucket lid opener, essentially a simple lever, will lessen the annoyance of popping lids off plastic buckets two or three times a day.
- Store the chocolate bars in a bucket under the lentils and split peas where no one but you would ever think to look.

Camp Coolers

Where bears are not a problem, consider embedding a large picnic cooler in the earth in a spot that will be shaded throughout the day. With all but its lid beneath the surface of the soil, the cooler will extend the life of cheese, vegetables, and fruits. A large rock on the closed lid will discourage small animals from getting inside.

A metal or plastic bucket full of perishable food can sometimes be kept cool by setting it partway into a stream in a shaded location. The trick, of course, is to brace it in place so that it does not flood or float away.

BASE CAMP GEAR
- Tents with groundcloths, poles, and stakes
- Kitchen tarp, about 15 x 20 feet
- Pack-storage tarp, 6 x 10 feet
- ⅛-inch nylon cord, 200 feet
- Head lamp with extra batteries and bulbs

Optional Gear:
- Wall tent for foul weather or, where insects are a problem, a large screen tent
- White gas-lantern with extra mantles
- Hammocks
- Bear spray

KITCHEN EQUIPMENT
Basic Gear:
- Propane stove—a 2-burner unit for every six to eight people
- Collapsible oven suitable for use on a propane stove
- Propane tank(s)
- Square plastic buckets with lids, for food storage
- Collapsible water jugs
- Plastic cutting board
- Cookbooks
- Fire grill to hold pots if open fires will be used for cooking or heating water
- Kitchen matches, butane lighters

In permanent camp it is well to sink a barrel in the earth in some dry, shaded place; it will answer for a cellar in which to keep your food cool.

John M. Gould
HOW TO CAMP OUT (NEW YORK: SCRIBNER, ARMSTRONG & CO., 1877), P. 48.

- Hot pads
- Dishtowels
- Plastic containers with lids, for carrying sandwiches to work and for storing leftovers
- Resealable plastic bags

Pots and Pans:
- Pots with lids—18-quart and 13-quart
- Pressure cooker—16-quart
- Large skillet
- Large coffee pot for heating water

Mixing and Serving Utensils:
- Mixing bowls—1 large, 1 small
- Measuring cup
- Measuring spoons
- Spatula
- Rubber scraper
- Slotted spoon
- Wooden spoon
- Ladle
- Kitchen knives
- Wire whisk
- Cheese grater
- 9-inch baking pans—2
- Bread pans—2
- Can opener

Washing and Garbage Disposal:
- Plastic or metal dishpans—4
- Sponges—2 per week
- Scouring pads
- Biodegradable dishwashing liquid
- Bleach—a small container for use in rinse water
- Fine screen mesh for screening food particles out of wash water before dumping
- Plastic garbage bags for storing food waste
- Toilet paper

CHAPTER 4

Safety

SAFETY TAKES PRECEDENCE over all other considerations in the backcountry. No conservation work is worth risking the well-being of people. Given time and ingenuity, every task at project sites and in camp can be accomplished with minimal risk to those being asked to do it.

But even with the best preparation, training, and leadership, bad things still happen in the big woods. A tool slips, an ankle twists, or a log rolls unexpectedly, and a trail crew may suddenly find itself confronted with an emergency. The remoteness of backcountry work sites increases the seriousness of any mishap since a medical team may not be able to reach an accident victim for hours or even days. A work crew must be able to administer initial treatment for an injured person, then care for him until help arrives or evacuate him to a road or helicopter landing area.

First Aid Training

First aid training is essential for those who lead outdoor work groups. If possible, training should be geared to backcountry emergencies. General first aid classes stress caring for someone during the brief wait until an ambulance arrives. Mountaineering and wilderness emergency response courses, on the other hand, teach methods of stabilizing an injured or ill person for longer periods of time, and cover ways that a crew can transport someone to safety.

Emergency Response Plan

Safety is a major consideration during the planning phase of a backcountry project. Crew leaders meeting with land-management agency personnel can gather the information they need in order to respond to emergencies. At a minimum, group leaders should develop an emergency response plan that includes the following:

- The manner in which they should contact help. If by telephone, the locations of the closest phones. If by radio, how to operate the equipment and whom to call.
- Backcountry maps showing the locations of helicopter landing sites.
- Road maps showing the locations of the nearest medical facilities.

Don't cut your foot with the axe. It will not add to the pleasures of camp life.
Jeannette Marks
VACATION CAMPING FOR
GIRLS (NEW YORK:
D. APPLETON &
CO., 1913), P. 222.

When in trouble, when in doubt,
Run in circles, scream and shout.
TRADITIONAL

- The telephone numbers of the nearest hospital, sheriff, and local land-management personnel, including home numbers for emergency calls when offices are closed.
- The steps crew members should take if the victim of an accident is the group's leader. This is especially important when the crew is made up of young or inexperienced trail workers, and in crews with a solo leader.

Emergency Contact Cards

Every SCA program participant fills out three identical Emergency Contact Cards with information that may be critical in case of an accident or illness. One is filed at the SCA's national office, the second goes to the agency administrator in whose area the crew will be working, and the third is kept at the work site by crew leaders.

EMERGENCY CONTACT INFORMATION

Name _____

Social Security Number _____

Address and phone number of person to be contacted in an emergency:

Name _____ Home Phone _____

Street _____ Work Phone _____

City _____ State _____

Zip _____

If you cannot reach them, contact:

Name _____ Home Phone _____

Street _____ Work Phone _____

City _____ State _____ Zip _____

Name _____ Home Phone _____

Street _____ Work Phone _____

City _____ State _____ Zip _____

Medical History

There are few physical conditions that would bar a person from taking part in some form of conservation work. By knowing the medical status of crew participants—asthma, for example, or an allergic reaction to bee stings—a leader can minimize risks to individuals and maximize the quality of their backcountry experience.

Each participant in an SCA backcountry program provides crew leaders with a medical history. Because SCA programs are often distant from participants' homes, the Association also asks that parents of minors sign consent-of-treatment forms so that physicians can administer emergency care.

Safety in the Field

Leaders should always begin a project with the assumption that crew members know nothing about working safely. While you may be pleasantly surprised to discover the breadth of their knowledge, you may also be startled by their faulty beliefs. Unfortunately, accumulated experience does not insure that hands-on wisdom will be well used. Serious injuries among trail crews are too often suffered by veteran workers who have become careless, who are shortcutting safety procedures, or who assume certain principles of safety do not apply to them.

IMAGINE THE "WHAT IF"

Effective backcountry workers strive to make themselves aware of the *what-if* of unfolding events. What if that leaning dead tree comes down while a crew is working under it? What if the anchor of a rigging system pulls loose while it is under tension? What if the crew becomes overheated while working in the afternoon sun? Identifying and defusing potentially dangerous situations or activities is a good way to prevent accidents.

Working defensively also encourages leaders and crew members to expand their vision to take in an entire project area and the changing flow of conditions and activities. This is not to say that leaders must micro-manage every action of every crew member, or that the slightest hint of hazard is grounds for shutting down a work effort. However, group leaders should try to maintain an overall awareness of the site, the work, the people, and the environmental conditions, and make adjustments that will contribute to crew safety.

INVOLVE CREW MEMBERS IN SAFETY

Every person on a trail crew should have the power to bring activities to a stop. Situations sometimes arise where safety is being compromised. The potential danger may be caused by lack of attention, haste, deteriorating weather, weariness, or any of a hundred other factors. The reason is not important. What is vital is that anyone who senses that an unsafe situation is developing, even if he or she cannot say exactly why, can call a momentary halt to the work. Once that has been done, the crew can discuss the issues of concern, identify hazards or dangerous activities, and develop a strategy for dealing with them.

Giving a crew this kind of authority is a sign of mature leadership. It indicates that crew members are being encouraged to think for themselves and for the good of the entire crew, and it shows that leaders are open to suggestions for better ways to conduct the work.

ESTABLISH REASONABLE SAFETY RULES

Most people work best when they understand the parameters within which they can operate. Establish realistic safety guidelines and goals for your crew, and explain the reasons behind them. Safety rules should be simple, clearly defined, and workable. They should apply equally to all participants and crew leaders, and should be followed by everyone all of the time. Crews will be influenced more by what they see their leaders doing than by what they hear them say, so set a good example with your own approach to backcountry labor.

TAILGATE SAFETY TALKS

Agency crews often begin each work day and each new task with a *tailgate safety talk* to review safety issues. You don't have to be sitting on a tailgate to realize that devoting a few minutes to talking over safety concerns will be time very well spent. Open the discussion so that group members can suggest safety improvements, find answers to any work-related questions, and shift into a safe-work mentality before starting the job.

Guidelines for Working Safely

TRAIL CLOSURE

Maintenance crews and trail users sometimes make an uneasy mix. When trail repair involves excavation, movement of materials, or other potential hazards, it may be wise to close a route to the public until the work is done. Where closure is unnecessary or impossible, crews should still take steps to protect the safety of trail users. That may involve keeping the trail clear of extra tools and gear, piling building materials off the tread, and having someone escort travelers through the disrupted area. A crew encountering horseback riders or pack strings should step downhill off the trail and stand quietly while the horses pass.

Many trail users are unaccustomed to seeing a maintenance crew at work. They may appreciate having someone from the crew explain the work to them and point out the importance of caring for the trails they are using. Simple courtesy on the part of the crew can make interactions with the public extremely positive.

SPACING AND COMMUNICATION

Sufficient spacing between workers will give them room to swing tools without whacking their neighbors. On some crews, each person speaks of "working

inside my dime"—a phrase referring to a 10-foot minimum separation between people. While that is good advice, projects such as rock wall construction require that people work closer together. Awareness, rather than specific spacing distances, is the key to safety.

Workers moving through a project site should let others know that they wish to pass by, then wait for some acknowledgment before stepping within the zone in which tools are being swung. Reinforce the fact of your presence by placing a hand on each person's shoulder or back as you pass by.

FOOTING

Loose rock, downed branches, or other material underfoot can be hazardous, especially on steep hillsides. Before you begin working, be sure you have a stable place to stand.

BODY MECHANICS

The body is a tool that should not be abused, either in the short run or the long term. Inexperienced crew members can be overly enthusiastic about toting big rocks or logs by themselves, and while they may manage it once or twice, they can also become so sore that they may be able to do little for the rest of the project. Those who intend to spend years working in the backcountry must be especially diligent about not hurting themselves. Staying in good physical condition during the off-season can be a valuable injury preventative, as can stretching before beginning a work day and using your brain at least as much as your brawn.

Crew leaders should spend time early in a project discussing the basics of body mechanics, perhaps as part of tailgate safety talks. This is also a good opportunity to establish signals and procedures for lifting and carrying in groups of two or more.

Learn the mechanics of lifting without injury.

Working Smart

Stay within your limits when working with any tool. Legend holds that John Henry, the steel drivin' man, swung a sledge in each hand with such ferocity that he managed to work himself to death. It was certainly an admirable effort, but if Mr. Henry had set for himself a more reasonable goal than beating a steam engine, he could have accomplished a satisfactory piece of labor and still had the energy to go home at the end of the day and enjoy supper with his sweetie.

Factors Affecting Safety

Many factors can have an impact upon the safety of each person and upon a work crew as a whole. Some can be controlled, while others must be confronted, endured, or simply avoided. Among the most important are these:

NUTRITIONAL NEEDS

Hungry people have more on their minds than their work. They may feel weak, shaky, distracted, and short-tempered, and that can set the scene for an accident. Have a nutritious lunch, and make available plenty of wholesome snacks, such as nuts and fruit, that crew members can eat whenever they are hungry. A good breakfast will lay an energy base for the day. A nourishing supper will provide hard-working bodies with the long-term fuel they need.

Water is also vital to the comfort and health of a crew. As a general rule, workers should drink water frequently enough for their urine to remain clear. Each person should carry several quarts of water to a project site, and more if the weather is hot or humid. Canteens can be replenished from lakes or streams if steps are taken to purify the water. (For more on backcountry food considerations, see Chapter 3, "Camping with Trail Crews.")

WEATHER

Enduring difficult weather is sometimes as great a triumph as completing a work effort. Whatever the situation, planning ahead will help a crew get through hard times more easily.

Discuss the dangers of hypothermia with your crew—how to recognize it, how to prevent it, and how to deal with it if it appears to be happening. Crews working in warm or hot climates should also review the prevention and treatment of heat illness. Consider shifting the work schedule to take advantage of the cooler hours early in the morning.

Rain is a work-site hazard since footing may become slippery and crew members may find it harder to hold onto tools. Bulky rain gear can limit motion, and water on glasses or safety goggles will restrict visibility. If weather conditions begin to compromise the safety of a crew, call it a day and retire to someplace warm and dry.

ALTITUDE

The ambitious schedules of the first days of many trail crews going into mountainous terrain may allow little opportunity for participants to adjust completely to high elevations. People coming from sea level may suddenly find themselves at elevations well above 6,000 feet, and it is not uncommon for trail crews in the Rocky Mountains to pitch their tents as high as 10,000 feet.

As air becomes thinner and the amount of oxygen entering the lungs lessens, the body must compensate by making more red blood cells. This acclimatization process takes about 1 day per thousand feet of elevation gain. Aggravating the problem are the dryness of mountain air, which can lead to dehydration, and a lack of appetite. Sleep may also be more difficult.

Leaders should allow crew members as much time as possible to adapt to high elevations, and encourage everyone to drink plenty of water and eat a diet high in carbohydrates. Altitude headaches sometimes respond favorably to aspirin, while descending will usually result in immediate relief.

Serious altitude sickness and altitude-induced pulmonary or cerebral edema rarely occur below 10,000 feet. However, if crew members show symptoms of chronic or serious altitude sickness, get them to a lower elevation and seek medical help.

VEGETATION

During visits to a work site before a project begins, agency personnel and others familiar with the plants of the area can point out poison ivy, poison oak, nettles, and other problematic vegetation. Washing within ten minutes of contact with poisonous plants may prevent the irritating agents from bonding to the skin. The dangers inherent in cactus, brambles, and other spiny plants are more obvious.

LIGHTNING

Trail crews in open country and at higher elevations must keep a cautious eye on the weather. Avoid lightning by evacuating exposed work sites well in advance of approaching storms. Move away from high ground, off the crests of ridges, and away from solitary trees or pinnacles. Stay clear of metal tools, rigging systems, and wire rope. If possible, seek shelter in a forest.

Ground currents from lightning can flash over the earth's surface along the easiest paths of electrical conduction—wet rock, water-filled cracks and crevices, natural fissures, and even wet rope. They may make caves and the open space beneath overhanging cliffs and boulders especially dangerous.

If you are unable to make a timely retreat, put on your rain gear and sit out in the open. Insulate yourself from ground currents by crouching on your pack, a coiled rope, or a foam sleeping pad. Crew members should spread out rather than huddling close together.

TIME OF DAY

A prime time for accidents to occur is just after lunch when muscles are stiff and workers are not yet refocused on their tasks. Doing some stretching and perhaps reviewing the morning's accomplishments will help a crew shift back into a mindset for safe work.

Late in the afternoon, people will begin to tire and their attention may wander. Food and fluids can sometimes revive a lethargic crew. You may also be able to reinvigorate workers by having them trade tools and jobs with one another. Sometimes touring the project and discussing what has been finished and what remains to be done will energize a group by giving them the satisfaction of seeing what they have accomplished.

However, if weariness and inattention threaten to compromise safety, it may be best to store the tools, hike back to camp, and cook a big supper. There is little to be gained by forcing people to continue working at a task for which they have neither the energy nor the interest, especially when a change of pace and perhaps even a day away from the project site will restore their enthusiasm.

Personal Equipment and Clothing for Backcountry Work

Clothing for trail work should enhance the comfort of a crew. While hard hats, goggles, and other gear can improve worker safety, they will not protect against ignorance or inattention. Safety ultimately comes from the person using the gear, not from the gear itself.

- ❑ Shirt
- ❑ Long pants or jeans
- ❑ Boots or sturdy shoes
- ❑ Gloves for protection and/or warmth
- ❑ Bandanna
- ❑ Rain gear
- ❑ Sweater or jacket
- ❑ Hat for shade, warmth, or to keep rain off glasses
- ❑ Water
- ❑ Food
- ❑ Sun screen
- ❑ Insect repellent
- ❑ Hard hat (depending on the project)
- ❑ Goggles (depending on the project)
- ❑ Ear protection (depending on the project)

BOOTS

Sturdy leather boots are essential for most trail work. Lugged soles provide traction and stable footing. In addition to shielding your feet from the minor insults and abuses suffered during the course of a backcountry day, leather boots can also minimize injuries from the misdirected blow of an axe or a dropped rock. Lightweight boots made with nylon fabric do not offer the margin of safety required by crews swinging tools or moving heavy materials.

Some crews prefer the extra protection of steel-toed boots. Others, including High Sierra crews specializing in rock work, prefer the comfort of boots without steel toes, relying on their good judgment and skill in moving of stones to spare their feet from injury. The bottom line is to use whatever leather boots you find most comfortable, and then work with enough care to keep your feet out of harm's way.

GLOVES

Leather is the material of choice for work gloves, though they can become slick when wet. The woven nylon/polyester gloves prominent in the woods of the Pacific Northwest are inexpensive, and the rubber bead covering them provides a secure grip regardless of the weather.

To Use a Hat as a Drinking-Cup.—The brim is folded upward against the sides of the crown and held there with one hand across the crown.

The end of the brim nearest the thumb and forefinger is then dipped into the water and the other end submerged later, allowing the brim to fill. The water is taken from the end most convenient, usually the one first dipped into the water.

Jay L. B. Taylor
HANDBOOK FOR RANGERS & WOODSMEN (NEW YORK: JOHN WILEY & SONS, INC., 1917), P. 2.

HARD HATS

Hard hats will protect workers from the obvious hazards of falling branches and stones. More frequent are the situations when a worker bending down is bonked on the head by the handle of a tool in someone else's hands.

While hard hats protect the outside of workers' heads, wearing them also affects what happens inside those skulls. When trail crews put on their hard hats, they shift into the mentality of the working hours of the day.

Metal hard hats have all but disappeared from the backcountry, replaced by impact-resistant plastic that will not conduct electricity. The broad-brimmed style favored in logging country shields the back of the neck from rain as well as bark, twigs, and other falling debris. A chin strap will hold the hat on your head when you are leaning over to tie your boot laces or sprinting to outrun a falling tree.

SAFETY GOGGLES

Safety goggles must be worn whenever grit, sawdust, or rock chips pose a hazard to the eyes. Eye protection must also be used by anyone operating a chain saw, a power rock drill, or any other tools that may strike rock or metal.

The goggles commonly found at rustic work projects are an inexpensive design featuring a plastic lens across the front and an elastic band to hold the goggles in place. They tend to become scratched, and will fog up when users perspire. Goggles with wire mesh rather than a plastic lens will solve those problems, though they do not provide the clearest vision. People who devote a great deal of time to trail work may want to get their own goggles or prescription safety glasses with side shields.

EAR PROTECTION

Sponge earplugs or muffler-type ear protectors are standard wear for anyone working around chain saws, rock drills, or other motorized equipment.

First Aid Kit

Every backcountry work group must have a first aid kit on site. When crew members will be working some distance from one another, a first aid kit should accompany each portion of the group. A well-marked fanny pack is a good choice for holding first aid supplies.

Work-site first aid kits are intended to aid in the immediate response to injuries. Once a victim has been stabilized, longer-term treatment of injuries or illnesses can be conducted with supplies contained in a more extensive medical kit kept at camp.

Work-Site First Aid Kit—Sample Contents

Adhesive bandages	1 dozen
4 × 4-inch sterile gauze pads	1 per person
	6 more in kit
Triangular bandages	4 to 6
Roll gauze (2-inch and 3-inch)	2 rolls
Adhesive first aid tape	1 roll
Elastic athletic wrap	1
Plastic syringe, no needle	
(10 cc or larger, for irrigating wounds)	1
Tweezers	1
Small scissors	1
Moleskin (for blister treatment)	a lot
Aspirin	1 tin
Anti-bacterial ointment	1 tube
Latex gloves	2 to 3 pair
Soap	small bar
Antiseptic swabs	12

Liability

Leaders responsible for crews working on private or public lands may have questions about their legal liability. In general, Good Samaritan laws will protect them from litigation if they are taking reasonable steps, within their levels of first aid training, to aid the victim of an accident or an illness.

Most first aid training does not qualify crew leaders to administer prescription drugs. Whenever possible, you should let each person make the decision about whether to take drugs that have been prescribed specifically for him. However, in life-threatening situations, make the best decisions you can under the circumstances to save the life of the victim. A case of acute anaphylactic shock, for example, may require injecting epinephrine from a bee-sting kit. There will be plenty of time later to sort out any legal ramifications of having done the best you could at the moment.

Many organizations carry liability policies to protect leaders who conduct themselves reasonably, and accident insurance for leaders and crews. Group insurance policies may require that an injured individual's personal insurance pays as much as possible, leaving the organization's policy to handle any outstanding costs. A person may need to be a member in good standing in order to qualify for that organization's insurance coverage. Group policies vary on whether they cover illnesses.

Federal, state, and local land-management agencies usually insure the activities of volunteers involved in sanctioned activities, but certain requirements and limitations may apply. Some resource areas, for example, expect volunteers to fill out forms making them Volunteers in the Parks (VIPs).

Trail Clothing and the Geography of Fashion

Almost any durable clothing will get a trail worker through a day in the field. Beyond that, however, experienced trail crews in different regions of the country can often be identified by their choices of attire:

Pacific Northwest—Blue and white pin-striped hickory work shirt, black pants (often accessorized with suspenders), full-brim hard hat, and White logging boots.

High Sierra—Shirts from government agencies or conservation corps, bluejeans, high-topped Redwing boots.

Southwest—At Philmont Scout Ranch, crews wear bib overalls over the official Boy Scout uniform.

Rocky Mountains—Carhartt pants and vests, plaid western shirts, and cowboy hats or baseball caps.

New England—Army surplus wool pants or shorts, gaiters, cotton or wool shirts emblazoned with the trail club emblems. Limmer boots may be virtually mandatory.

Southeast and South—T-shirts, boots, jeans or other durable pants, shin guards, and plenty of bug dope.

CHAPTER 5

Tools

FOR ALL ITS COMPLEXITY AND WONDER, the human body's capacity for accomplishing work is not without limits. People of average strength can scoot a rock along the ground, can lift the end of a fair-sized log, and can haul buckets of water and armloads of brush. With that power alone, a crew can tackle the most basic backcountry labor, at least until the sandwiches run out and the cookies are gone.

The facility of the human mind, however, is virtually infinite, especially when it comes to figuring out easier ways for the body to get things done. Whenever confronted with physical labor, use your intelligence to do as much of the heavy lifting as possible. Short of simply persuading somebody else to do it, that means using tools and mechanical advantage to augment the strength and endurance of your muscles.

Tools are made,
But born are hands.
William Blake

How Tools Work—Mechanical Advantage

Over 4,000 years ago, the massive blocks of stone used to construct the great pyramids of Egypt were moved into position with the aid of levers, ramps, and winches. Those three simple devices—the lever, the incline plane, and the wheel—are the basic components of all tools, from axes to space shuttles.

In the backcountry where equipment powered by gasoline or electric engines is the exception rather than the rule, enhancing human strength with mechanical advantage is essential for the efficient completion of construction and maintenance projects. Use of mechanical advantage may also increase the safety with which work can be done.

Mechanical advantage increases the effect of force by transmitting it through a lever, a wheel or an incline plane. One of the first lessons in basic physics introduces the following equation for determining mechanical advantage:

$$\text{Mechanical Advantage} = \frac{\text{distance the input force travels}}{\text{distance the output force travels}}$$

In other words, the greater the distance a machine part travels in relation to the distance a load moves, the greater the mechanical advantage.

LEVER

Levers appear in many forms at backcountry work sites. A rock bar used to pry up a stone is a lever. A shovel often acts as a lever, too, and so do peavies and cant hooks. The handle on a winch or GripHoist is a lever, as is the toothpick you're likely to wish you had after eating a trail lunch of celery sticks, peanut butter, and cold fried chicken.

Here are two ways to determine the mechanical advantage of a lever:
- Compare the length of the lever on either side of the fulcrum.
- Compare how far the ends of the lever travel.

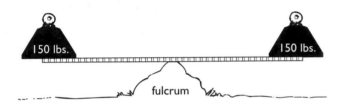

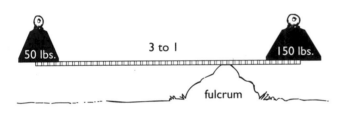

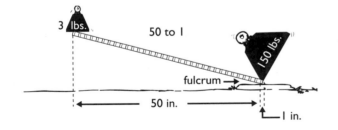

For example, balance a rock bar across a fulcrum as though the bar were a playground teeter-totter. Have someone stand on one end to serve as the load. Push down the free end of the bar 6 inches, and notice that the load rises 6 inches. When the lever is equally long on either side of the fulcrum, each pound of downward pressure on one end causes a pound of upward pressure at the other end. The ratio is 1:1, and there is no mechanical advantage. If the load weighs 150 pounds, you must push down with 150 pounds of force in order to lift it.

Move the fulcrum so that it is three-fourths of the way from the free end of the bar. That leaves one-fourth of the length of the bar between the fulcrum and the weight to be lifted. The ratio of bar length on each side of the fulcrum is three to one (3:1).

When the free end is pushed down 3 feet, the load rises 1 foot. The ratio of the distances the ends move, and thus the mechanical advantage, is 3:1. Each pound of downward force will lift three pounds at the other end of the bar.

The bevel near the end of a typical rock bar can be used as a fulcrum, leaving only 1 inch of the bar on the lifting side of the fulcrum and nearly 50 inches of bar on the other side. Jam the beveled end under a rock and push down on the free end. The free end will travel about 50 inches for each inch of lift created on the short side of the fulcrum. Thus, the mechanical advantage is 50:1. A downward force of just 3 pounds will lift a load of 150 pounds.

INCLINE PLANE

A trail crew uses many incline planes:

- Bits of axes, Pulaskis, splitting mauls, and grub hoes
- Blades of pocket knives
- Chisels and wood planes
- Wedges for splitting wood and rock, and for felling trees
- Drill bits and augers (in these tools, the incline planes are spiral rather than straight)

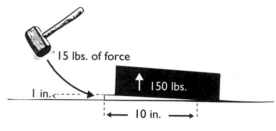

The mechanical advantage of an incline plane can be figured by comparing its thickness, or *rise,* to its length, or *run.* A wedge that is 10 inches long and 1 inch thick at its thickest point has a ratio of 10:1. If you were to use a sledgehammer to drive that wedge under a slab of granite or into the saw cut in a log, the wedge would magnify the force of the hammer blows tenfold. The thin incline plane that forms a knife blade may have a mechanical advantage of 30:1 or greater, while the mechanical advantage of a splitting maul may be only 4:1 or less.

WHEEL

In addition to wheelbarrows and to logs used as rollers, one of the most effective applications of wheels in backcountry work is their integration into pulleys for block and tackle systems. (For details on using block and tackle and ways to figure its mechanical advantage, see Chapter 17, "Rigging.")

Sources for Tools

Crews working on public lands often find the tools they need in the equipment caches and maintenance shops of land-management agencies. Some conservation organizations have assembled their own collections of tools. Individuals interested in trail work may want to augment those caches with tools of their own.

Tools can be purchased from hardware stores and suppliers of forestry gear, or searched out in used equipment outlets, at garage sales, and in the dusty corners of barns and sheds. Finding used tools is by far the most satisfying method of equipping a crew, for in addition to the likelihood that you will pay a reasonable price, you will also be getting tools infused with the history of having been used by other hands.

Marking Your Tools

Tools owned by agencies and conservation groups frequently have a touch of spray paint on them, the color selected to indicate ownership. Mark your own tools so that they can be easily identified, choosing a color other than the red and orange that are most often used to mark tools reserved for fighting fires.

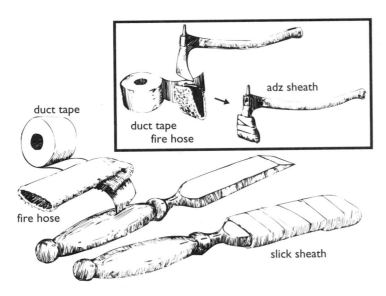

Tool sheaths can be made from old fire hose.

Sheaths

Tools with cutting edges should be sheathed whenever they are being transported or stored. Sheaths protect workers from injury and insure that sharpened edges will stay that way when the tools are not in use.

The leather or plastic sheaths that guard new tools have a habit of disappearing. Fashion replacement sheaths for axes, Pulaskis, McLeods, slicks and many other tools by cutting pieces of old fire hose to size, doubling them over the bits of the tools, and holding them in shape with wraps of duct tape. Lengths of split garden hose can serve as sheaths for bow saws, bush saws, and draw knives; secure them to the tools with cord or tape. Use strips of inner tube and duct tape to fabricate sheaths for small tools such as chisels.

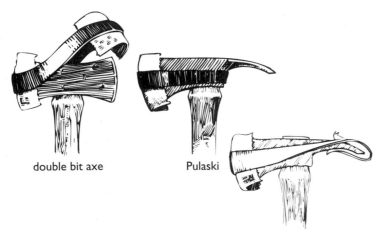

Use duct tape or slices of inner tube to hold sheaths in place.

Transporting Tools

The goal of tool carrying, whether through the backcountry or just a few yards across a project site, is to do it in such a way that you injure neither yourself nor anyone else. Most tools should be carried at your side with the cutting edge turned down and away from your body in your downslope hand. When people stumble, they tend to fall toward a hillside; it is easier to cast away a tool if it is already on your downhill side.

Do not carry tools on your shoulder, a practice that may place a cutting edge or heavy tool head close to your neck. There are several exceptions to this safety rule. Because of their weight and the absence of honed edges, rock bars and sledgehammers are sometimes carried on the shoulder, especially if the crew must travel long distances. A chain saw that has been sheathed and allowed to cool down after use can also be hoisted onto a shoulder with the bar forward and engine situated so that the little dribbles of oil will go down the back of your shirt.

The other exception may also be the least obvious—the crosscut saw. Sheath the blade, then balance the saw flat on your shoulder with the teeth turned away from your neck. Control the position of the saw by grasping the handle at arm's length in front of you. Removing the saw's other handle will prevent it from snagging tree branches.

For long carries, many tools can be stowed in knapsacks, lashed to backpack frames, or loaded on horses or mules. Mattocks, picks, and grub hoes have removable handles for easy packing.

Backcountry Tool Cache

The remote locations and extended duration of much conservation work often require that tools be stored on-site for a number of days or weeks. Take the time to set up a storage area where tools can be protected from the elements and easily inventoried to lessen the likelihood of loss. A tool cache can be as simple as two trees with a pole lashed between them for the tools to lean against, and a tarp pitched over it to shed the rain. Establish the cache away from trails and camp activities.

TOOL CACHE

Before work commences, make a list of the tools at your disposal. Use the list when the project is complete to be sure you carry out of the backcountry all the tools you brought in. Some trail crews assign one person to hand out the tools each morning, count them as they are returned, and oversee their storage and maintenance.

Long-term Tool Storage

At the end of a project there is often a temptation to toss tools through the door of a storeroom and beat a path for home, especially if a crew has been in the woods for a long time. However, the work isn't really done until the tools have been cleaned, repaired, sharpened, and hung or stacked in the cache.

A film of oil rubbed on the metal surfaces of tools will protect them from rust. Preserve wooden handles with linseed oil by either rubbing it onto the handles or placing it in shallow holes drilled into their knob ends. Axes, Pulaskis, and other handled tools should be stored by hanging them from racks. Leaning them against a wall for the winter can warp the handles.

Proper long-term storage will extend the working lives of valuable tools. Crews that follow you into the area will appreciate finding the tools ready for them to use.

The Right Tool for the Job

Equipment caches do not always contain exactly the right tools for the work at hand, but with a bit of ingenuity, crews can often make do with what is available. Pulaskis, for instance, are designed specifically for fighting forest fires, not for trail work, but in the absence of mattocks, crews can use Pulaskis to grub out trail. Likewise, a finely sharpened Pulaski can perform many of the same timber-shaping tasks as an adz.

While crew leaders teaching backcountry skills should emphasize the importance of selecting the correct tool in order to achieve maximum results with a minimum of effort, they can also point out that necessity is the mother of invention, and that some tools can be substituted for others without greatly reducing their effectiveness.

Trail Clearing Tools

LOPPERS

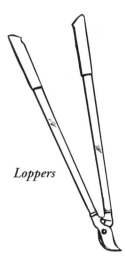

Loppers

A pair of loppers is actually two levers sharing a bolt as a common fulcrum. The long length of the handles compared with the short length of the jaws results in a mechanical advantage of 18:1 or more. Loppers are almost essential for trail corridor brushing that involves clipping vegetation flush with the ground and nipping small branches close to the trunks of trees.

If you have a choice, select heavy-duty loppers rather than the garden variety. Look for metal handles, or wooden handles attached to the blades with metal sleeves. The cutting blade of a pair of loppers can be honed with a file. Lightly oil the joint of the jaws and keep the bolt tight enough for the tool to cut cleanly.

WEED WHIP

Swung back and forth with both hands, the weed whip is used to clear trail corridors of succulent vegetation. The beveled edges of the serrated blade can be sharpened with a file. When installing a weed whip blade, turn the flat face of the blade toward the ground and the bevel toward the handle. Screws holding the double-edged blade in place are notorious for working loose, so check them often.

MACHETE

In the dense vegetation of Southern states and in the heavy forests of Southeastern Alaska, trail surveyors and crews brushing out new routes often use machetes to clear the way. The machete is most effectively wielded with a vertical stroke rather than the low, horizontal swing required to hew vegetation at ground level. However, it should not be used to hack branches from trailside trees, as that may strip the bark from tree trunks.

SANDVIK

Sandvik and *Swedish Safety Brush Axe* are brand names of a machete-like tool with a short, replaceable blade. Because it has a smaller blade, the tool may be safer than a machete, but like the machete, the Sandvik can leave a mess when used to remove branches from trees.

Timber Tools

AXES

Much has been written, sometimes in verse and sometimes in rhyme, and always knee-deep in sweet, sticky sentiment, about The Woodsman's Ax. But the fact remains that the durned thing weighs from two to six pounds all the time, raises blisters most of the time, and lops off a foot or two once in so often.

C. L. Gilman
"SQUAW WOOD" *OUTING MAGAZINE,* VOL. 64
(APRIL-SEPTEMBER, 1914), PP. 190–191.

No tool is as strongly identified with backcountry life and work as the axe. For centuries it has gone into the forests with Native Americans, travelers, settlers, and work crews. Over the last 200 years, American axes have been manufactured

Weed Whip

Sandvik

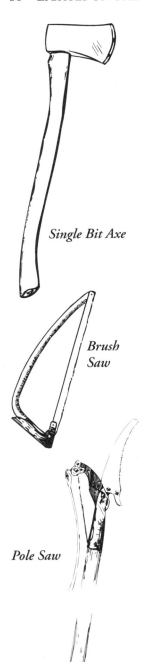

Single Bit Axe

Brush Saw

Pole Saw

in dozens of shapes for both general and specific applications. The axes you are most likely to find in tool caches will fall into one of three categories:

Double bit axe. The double bit has been the hallmark of generations of timber workers. Traditionally, one bit is sharpened to a fine taper to make deep cuts for felling trees and chopping through logs. The other bit, used for limbing branches from downed trees, is honed with a stouter edge that is not so likely to bind in the wood. Many timber workers believe that the balanced weight of the head and the straight shape of the handle make the double bit more accurate and powerful than other axes.

Single bit axe. Single bit axes are the mainstay of many trail crews, in part because an axe with one bit somehow seems twice as safe as an axe with two. However, those same crews are likely to use Pulaskis with hardly a thought for the fact that it, too, is a double-bladed tool.

The single bit axe differs from the double bit not only in the shape of its head, but also by the fact that its handle is curved. While the single bit axe handle gives the appearance of greater comfort and ease of use, a curved handle requires more wood than does a straight handle. That results in a handle that is less limber, less powerful, and provides less cushioning to the hands with each blow. Some experts also argue that the hand position required by the curved handle decreases the accuracy of the single bit axe.

Three-quarter axe. The three-quarter axe is a smaller version of a full-sized single bit axe. It is lighter and less bulky for packing, and easier to use in close quarters. Despite its size, the three-quarter axe is neither a toy nor a learning tool, demanding as much caution in its use as do axes more imposing in appearance.

HAND SAWS

Brush Saw and Bow Saw. A brush saw with an 18- to 21-inch blade is a fine tool for clearing small branches from trees and cutting underbrush out of a trail corridor.

With blades up to 36 inches in length, bow saws are unwieldy for brushing projects, especially those requiring horizontal cutting. They are better suited for the vertical cuts involved in clearing modest-sized logs from trails and bucking firewood in camp.

The thin, flexible blades of brush and bow saws are difficult to sharpen but easy to replace. If you expect your saws will see serious use, pack along several spare blades. Remove a dull blade by pulling back the lever on the saw frame to release the blade tension, then slipping the blade ends free of restraining pins. Position the new blade and snap the lever back against the frame.

Pole Saw. Pole saws enable crews to prune branches that would otherwise be out of reach. The simplest of these tools consists of a cutting blade bolted onto a long pole. Some models also have built-in loppers that can be operated from the ground with a rope. Another useful feature is a pole that will disassemble into several pieces for carrying.

Trail Tread Tools

PULASKI

Many tools have been in their present form for centuries, but the Pulaski is a relative upstart in the world of wilderness work. It is also a tool with a hero behind it.

Edward Pulaski was a District Ranger on the Coeur d'Alene National Forest in the early days of the Forest Service when crews battling wildfires were often equipped with axes for cutting branches and shovels for digging fire lines. It could be an awkward combination, since a fire fighter had to lay down one tool in order to use the other.

In 1910, a massive blaze swept through Pulaski's district. Trapped by flames on a ridge above Wallace, Idaho, Pulaski rescued his contingent of forty fire fighters by leading them into a mine tunnel. The men suffered terribly from the heat and lack of oxygen, but Pulaski and thirty-five others survived the ordeal.

In the years following the fire, Pulaski toyed with ideas for making back-country fire fighters more efficient. Using his skill as a blacksmith, he twisted one blade of a double-bit axe ninety degrees to form an adz, retempered the metal, and had the prototype of the combination cutting/digging tool that would come to bear his name. Throughout the Western states, the Pulaski soon became the tool preferred by backcountry fire crews, a fact that is still true today.

The modest weight and multiple uses that make the Pulaski an efficient implement for fighting fires also make it a tool preferred by many trail crews for grubbing tread, chopping roots, removing slough and berm, and loosening compacted soil. Pulaskis can be sharpened to adz timbers for bridges, turnpikes, water bars, and puncheon. A sharpened Pulaski should be marked with spray paint or a strip of duct tape around its handle to discourage anyone from mistakenly dulling a timber-work Pulaski by using it for digging.

Pulaski

McLEOD

McLeods are another part of the tradition of forest work of the western United States, though their appearance in other regions of the country is rare. The McLeod was originally intended for raking fire lines with the teeth and for cutting branches and sod with the sharpened edge. Trail workers have found the tool to be equally useful for moving dry soil, duff, and talus, for finish work on treads, and for shaping a trail's backslope. The tines also lend themselves to scoring soil in preparation for seeding.

FIRE RAKE

The McLeod's Eastern counterpart is the fire rake. The triangular tines, similar to the cutters on a bar mower, can be honed with a file. The fire rake is lighter in weight than the McLeod. It is better for clearing duff from trail corridors than it is for shaping tread or backslopes.

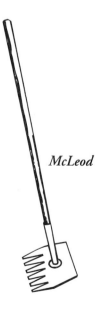

McLeod

Grub Hoe

Top: *Long-handled Shovel*
Middle: *D-handled Shovel*
Bottom: *Fire Shovel*

GRUB HOE, HAZEL HOE, ADZ HOE

These sturdy hoes are made for excavating trail in fine to medium-rocky soil. They are also excellent for removing sod and muskeg by scoring the turf and peeling up squares of organic matter. Hazel hoes and adz hoes are fitted with square, curved handles, while a grub hoe uses a straight pick or mattock handle. The handles of all three can be removed to facilitate packing or replacement.

SHOVEL

Shovels show up on more backcountry project sites than any other tool, and while they are rugged, they are not indestructible. A shovel is best used for moving loosened earth. The handle can break if it is forced back while the scoop is embedded in hard ground or the shovel is used as a lever to pry rocks.

A broken shovel can be rehandled, though it is a difficult task to accomplish in the field. In the shop, knock out the rivet that secures the handle to the scoop. Remove the remaining wood, fit in the new handle, drill it to receive a replacement rivet, and drive the rivet home.

Shovelling earth at a pace that can be sustained for a long period of time is a skill that requires some native talent and a little practice. Use a minimum of effort and motion to throw each scoop of soil so that the material stays in a fairly compact mass and lands where you aim it. One trick is to swing the shovel and then drop the scoop out from under the load rather than letting the load scatter off the scoop. Another is to use your thigh as a fulcrum under the shovel handle to help lift the load and start it on its way.

Shovels are also used to smooth the tread of a trail. By bracing the shovel handle against the inside of your knee as you scrape the tread, you may be able to accomplish the work by using the strength of your legs rather than the muscles of your arms and back.

Long-handled shovel. Long-handled shovels permit crews to work without leaning over all the time. Their length can make them difficult to haul into the backcountry on livestock or lashed to pack frames, and workers may find it easiest simply to carry them to a project site by hand.

D-handled shovel. As its name implies, this shovel has a handle topped by a D-shaped handpiece. It is designed more for scooping than for digging, or for use in close quarters such as the excavation of a deep ditch or the foundations of a bridge.

Fire shovel. Trail crews often find fire shovels in the tool caches of land-management agencies, especially in the western United States. Fire shovels have handles midway in length between their long-handled and D-handled cousins, though the scoop of the fire shovel is set at a sharper angle than are those of the other two. The handle length and shape of the scoop aid fire fighters in flinging earth onto a blaze, and the sharpened edge of the scoop helps them knock down branches and cut through the soil. Of shovel types available, they are the least practical for trail work.

PICKS AND MATTOCKS

Picks and mattocks are the heavy hitters of tread work. Users can pry rocks with them without breaking their stout handles. The adzes of mattocks are great for loosening compacted soil. The blade of a cutter mattock is meant for chopping through roots.

The head of a pick or mattock features a large eye to accommodate a handle that can be removed for ease of packing, storage, or repair. To install a handle, slide it into the eye and jamb-tighten it by striking the head-bearing end against a stump, a rock, or hard ground. Remove the handle by holding the head and banging the heel of the handle against a solid surface. Be sure to keep your face and costly dental work clear of the handle's potential trajectory as it pops free of the head.

Trail crews in the eastern United States often drive a screw into the handle of a pick or mattock just beneath the head to prevent it from slipping down while the tool is in use. The screw is placed parallel with the tool head rather than in the side of the handle where it might split the wood. In the West, where it is more common to dismantle tools in order to lash them onto pack animals or backpacks, placing screws in handles is a rare practice. The configuration of a particular pick or mattock determines its identity and the uses for which it is most appropriate:

PICK

The points at the ends of a pick head are made for chipping into rock and loosening compacted earth. The points are beveled and can be honed, though the well-used picks found in tool caches usually have points worn down so far they will defy most efforts to sharpen them.

In average hard ground the workman will find that from twelve to fifteen blows per minute with a pick, mattock, or hoe will constitute a reasonable rate of speed in labor for him to maintain throughout an eight-hour day.

Jay L. B. Taylor
HANDBOOK FOR RANGERS &
WOODSMEN (NEW YORK:
JOHN WILEY & SONS, INC.,
1917), P. 63.

Left: *Pick*
Middle: *Pick Mattock*
Right: *Cutter Mattock*

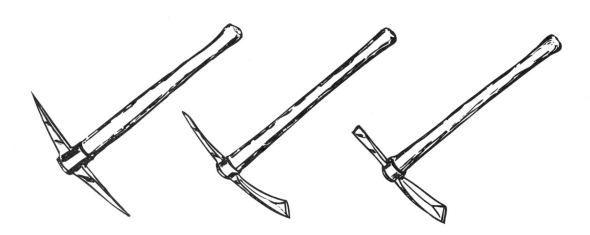

PICK MATTOCK

Combine a pick with an adz and you have one of the best tools for grubbing in hard soils and rocky terrain. The pick on a mattock is squared rather than beveled, and while the adz is sometimes sharpened, the pick seldom is.

CUTTER MATTOCK

The head of a cutter mattock couples an adz with a stout axe blade. The cutter mattock works well when a grubbing project requires chopping through many roots or vines.

Why Tool Handles Can (or Can't) Be Removed

The handles of picks, mattocks, and grub hoes are so easy to remove and replace that you may wonder why other tools are not made that way. To accommodate a removable handle, the eye must be quite large. In addition, a portion of the handle must extend above the eye to insure a tight jamb-fit of the head.

Axes, Pulaskis, and similar tools meant for timber work have heads thin enough to fit inside the deepening cuts they are making in a log or tree trunk. The eyes of these tools are simply too narrow and the handles trimmed too closely for removable handles to be practical.

Rock Tools

ROCK BAR

The rock bar of choice for trail work is about 4 feet in length, weighs 16 to 18 pounds, and has a beveled end. The length is ideal for moving both large and small rocks, and the bevel can be used as a fulcrum when tremendous mechanical advantage is required. The steel of these bars is very stiff, allowing only a minimum of give while the tool is in use.

Larger bars, sometimes 6 feet or more in length, often have a flat blade on one end for shaping the bottoms of fence post holes, and a round disk at the other end for tamping soil around the post itself. These digging and tamping bars are too long and too springy to be used for rock work. Another common bar is nearly 6 feet long and has a square, pointed end. It is unwieldy to carry, and the lack of a bevel makes it difficult to slip the point under large stones.

HAMMERS

Hammers can be distinguished from one another by their sizes and by the shapes of their heads. Almost every hammer head has a slightly rounded striking face, often with the edges beveled to reduce chipping. If the surface opposite the striking face is not identical, it is called a *peen*. A *ball peen hammer*, for example, has a striking face backed by a rounded peen for shaping sheet metal.

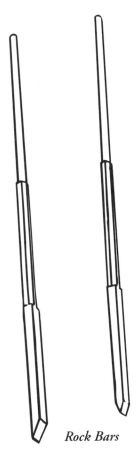

Rock Bars

Hammer heads are tempered during manufacture to withstand impact, though that hardness can also make them brittle. Never strike one tempered steel face against another, such as one hammer against another hammer, or a hammer against the butt of an axe. If a tempered face strikes a surface that is equally hard or harder, it may splinter off a shard of steel.

Single Jack. The hammer used in one-person rock drilling operations has a head weighing 3 to 4 pounds, is double-faced, and is mounted on a short, stout handle that gives a driller maximum control. The single jack can also be used to drive cold chisels, sets of wedges and feathers, and bridge spikes.

Double Jack. A double jack hammer has a full-length handle and a double-faced head weighing 6 to 8 pounds. It takes its name from its historic use by pairs of rock drillers. Double jack drilling requires great skill, since the person holding the drill is at the mercy of the accuracy of the person swinging the hammer. Today, double jacks are most often used in trail work as all-purpose sledgehammers. (For more on hand-drilling, see Chapter 12, "Building with Rock.")

Straight Peen and Cross Peen. Hammers for shaping rock may have a wedge-shaped peen. Vertically oriented, it is a *straight peen,* while a horizontal wedge is a *cross peen.* Straight peen hammers are safer to use because they throw chips of rock off to either side of a worker, while a cross peen may direct chips toward a worker's face and body.

Sledge. Sledgehammers have heads weighing 6 to 12 pounds, the poundage often imprinted on the side of the head. Hammers of 8 to 10 pounds are the most useful on trail projects because they have the heft to crush rock and drive wedges, yet are not too heavy to be used for long periods of time.

Slide one hand out toward the head of the sledge as you lift it overhead, then bring your hands together. The hammer head should be dropped as much as swung, for it is the weight of the head traveling through a wide arc that creates the force of impact. Swinging a hammer hard does more damage to the swinger, in the long run, than to the rock.

Take care in aiming a sledgehammer. If the handle rather than the head hits the edge of a rock or the end of a spike, the handle is likely to splinter, or the head may snap off. Since accuracy is too often in short supply, a good preventative to broken hammers is a rubber collar snugged around the handle just below the head to cushion the shock of any errant blows. The collar can be pounded onto the handle with a single jack hammer.

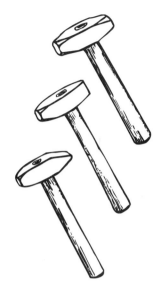

Top: *Single Jack Hammer*
Middle: *Straight Peen Hammer*
Bottom: *Cross Peen Hammer*

Wood Structure Tools

BROAD AXE

Broad axes are big, heavy, and relatively rare. The head of the broad axe is beveled to allow it to be used for a single purpose—cutting with the grain to hew a flat face in a log. The bent handle can be inserted into the head from either

Broad Axe

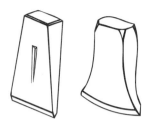

Wedges

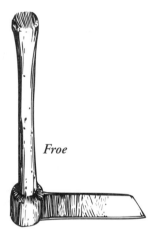

Froe

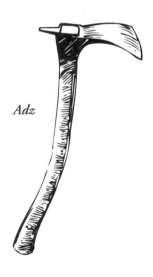

Adz

direction, making the tool left-handed or right-handed. Historically, broad axes were used to hew railroad ties and the beams for timber-frame structures.

FELLING WEDGE

Felling wedges are driven into saw cuts, or *kerfs,* to hold them open and prevent pinching of the saw blade, or to influence the direction a tree will fall. Since they must fit into the kerf rather than simply breaking wood apart, wedges for felling are thinner and sometimes longer than splitting wedges. Wedges made of plastic or soft aluminum will not tear up the teeth of a chain saw or nick the back of a crosscut.

SPLITTING WEDGE

Wedges for splitting firewood or for laying open logs to build walkways are usually made of soft steel or aluminum. They are thick and heavy, and are used in groups of two or more. If a splitting operation requires more wedges than you have on hand, fashion wooden facsimiles called *gluts* and fit them into the growing split in a log to hold it open as you move the wedges further along the timber. Over time, the butts of metal wedges may mushroom out from the blows of a sledge. Use a grinder or a file to keep your wedges trimmed. (For more on log splitting, see Chapter 14, "Building with Timber.")

FROE

A close relative of the wedge, the froe splits puncheon and shingles from rounds of wood, particularly cedar. Drive the froe with blows from a mallet made of wood or aluminum/magnesium alloy, *never* with a steel hammer or the butt of an axe. The handle of a froe can be used as a lever to break apart the wood as the blade is driven deep into the round.

ADZ

Adzes are wood shaving tools found in many shapes and sizes, from the shipwrights' adz curved to fit corners of boat frames, to the lipped adz ideal for timber structures. The adz is used in backcountry work to smooth the surfaces of timbers for puncheon, boardwalks, and bridges. The process begins by *scoring* the wood—making a series of parallel saw cuts down to the level of the intended surface. A worker then stands over the timber and uses small, even strokes of the adz to break out the wood between the saw cuts and then to plane away the remainder of the excess wood. Some experts find the adz most effective when used across the grain, while others go with the grain. An adz must be swung with great control, the upper hand staying locked in place close to the body.

For fine adzing, the blade skims so closely to the surface of the wood that it will sometimes miss all together. Expert timber workers, some sporting nicknames such as Tommy No-Toes, tilt one foot up on its heel so that misguided adz strokes will be stopped by the sole of the shoe rather than by its contents.

Mere mortals are well advised to wear metal or plastic toe-caps over their boots. (For more on laying out and completing adz work, see Chapter 15, "Bridge Construction.")

CHISELS AND SLICKS

Chisels have many uses in shaping timber. They can be driven with a wooden mallet or pushed by hand. The metal rings around the handles of many chisels protect them from splitting under the impact of a mallet.

A slick is a chisel suffering delusions of grandeur. The width of the cutting edge can range from 1 inch to 3 inches or more. It can make quick work of smoothing the surfaces of adzed logs or clearing wood from large dovetail notches. When shopping for a slick, look for one with a handle socket bent slightly upward so that knuckles wrapped around the handle can clear the surface of the wood.

Do not drive a slick with a mallet. The size of the tool and the strength of your arms are all you need. Grasp the handle in both hands and slide the cutting edge along the surface of the wood, or work the tool with one hand on the handle and the other on top of the blade.

Chisels

The beveled edges of chisels and slicks should be kept razor sharp. Hone them with a fine whetstone, leaving the flat underside of the blade untouched so that it will glide across the wood.

LOG CARRIER

Log carriers, known in some parts of the country as *Swede hooks* or *tongs,* are used in pairs to lift and move logs. Larger logs may require three or four carriers. The handle of a standard carrier is long enough to allow one or two people to lift on each side of a log.

The points on the hooks of log carriers need to be sharp enough to dig into the wood. Dull points can be touched up with a file, though don't make them so sharp that they present an unnecessary hazard to workers. For ease of transport, secure the hooks to the handle with duct tape or cord.

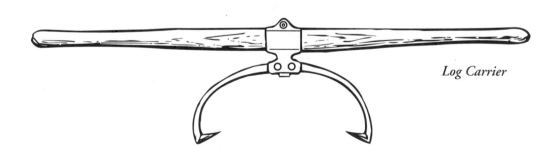

Log Carrier

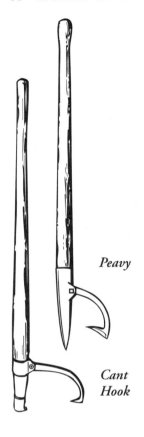

Peavy

Cant Hook

Log Dogs

Drawknife

Hand Auger

CANT HOOKS AND PEAVIES

With its hinged, hooked arm, a cant hook provides tremendous leverage for maneuvering logs. The peavy, named in the 1870s for inventor Joseph Peavy of New Hampshire, is a cant hook with a pike on the end rather than a metal cap. The pike creates added length and leverage, and can be used to pry logs apart. Slide a cant hook or peavy across a log until the hook catches in the wood, then lift the handle to hold or turn the timber. Two peavies or cant hooks can be used as a makeshift log carrier by positioning one on either side of a log.

LOG DOG

Log dogs are angles of steel pounded into two logs to anchor them together and stabilize them while they are being worked. Lengths of rebar can be hammered into shape and the ends sharpened to form log dogs.

HAND AUGER

Use a hand auger for boring large-diameter holes such as those needed to accommodate wooden dowels, and for removing waste wood from the mortises of mortise and tenon joints. The handle is detachable.

Only the inside cutting edge of an auger bit should be filed; filing the outside may narrow the guides and cause the tool to bind in the wood. Use a special file designed to sharpen the cutting edges without damaging portions of the bit you do not want to hone.

Bark Removal Tools

DRAWKNIFE

Drawknives come in sizes from 12 to 18 inches in width, and may be straight or curved. The beveled blade can be turned up or down, depending upon the task at hand. Position yourself by straddling a log and then, as the tool's name implies, pulling the drawknife toward yourself to remove the bark or shave the wood.

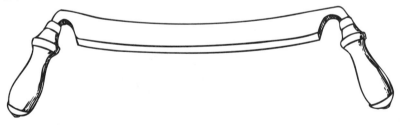

BARKING SPUD

Along with drawknives, barking spuds are the safest tools for removing bark. The spud is used on green bark while the drawknife is better for bark that has become dry, tight, and hard.

Hoisting Tools

RATCHET WINCH

A ratchet winch is useful for moving rocks and logs and for pulling stumps. The winch must be properly anchored. Although tempting, do not wrap the winch cable around the load to be moved; that will almost surely damage the cable. Instead, secure the load with a sling or choker and attach that to the cable hook.

Many ratchet winches have a small block riding on the cable. Connect the block to the load, double the cable back and connect the hook to an anchor, and you will have a 2:1 mechanical advantage that will double the pulling power of the winch.

When you are through using a ratchet winch, maintain tension on the cable as you crank it in. Regularly inspect the cable for damage and wear, just as you would any wire rope. (For more on anchors, blocks, and care of cable, see Chapter 17, "Rigging.")

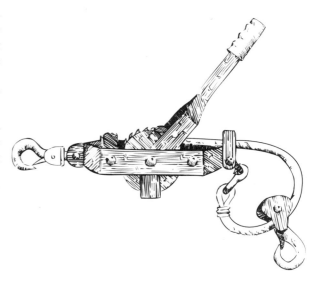

Ratchet Winch

GRIPHOIST

GripHoist is the brand name for a compact, lightweight tool capable of dragging tremendous weights or putting tension on wire rope in rigging systems designed for moving rock, timber, and other building materials. The machine consists of a metal body with a cable running through it. A lever on the Grip-Hoist allows a worker to crank the cable through the machine with a mechanical advantage of 30:1 or more. As the lever moves forward, a set of grippers inside the GripHoist clenches the cable and pulls it a few inches. Moving the lever backwards causes a second set of grippers to clamp the cable and pull, while the first set relaxes its hold and moves into position for the next grasp.

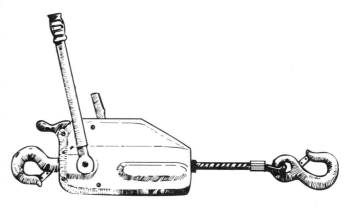

GripHoist

If too much pressure is placed on the GripHoist handle, shear pins in the hub of the lever assembly will break, protecting the machine from damage and workers from injury. Replacement pins are often stored inside the handle. The best way to prevent the pins from breaking is to remember how the lever felt the last time the pins sheared, and, if it begins to feel that way again, immediately reduce the pressure on the handle.

The GripHoist cable is designed to resist being crushed by the grippers. Keep the cable clean as it enters the GripHoist to prevent it from dragging grit into the mechanism. Remove the cable from the GripHoist when the work is done, and roll it onto a storage spool. Never coil the cable or otherwise allow it to become twisted or kinked.

GripHoist and Ratchet Winch Safety

Ratchet winches and GripHoists must be used only within the rated Working Load Limits imprinted somewhere on the body of each machine. For guidance on what to do with that knowledge, see the discussion of Safe Working Load in Chapter 17, "Rigging."

Protecting Tool Handles from Breakage

Tools are built to withstand strain placed on them in certain directions, but they can be quite fragile when stressed from other angles. Prying rocks with a shovel or pounding stakes with the side of an axe can easily lead to damage. Use tools for the tasks they were designed to accomplish, and only in the manner they were meant to be used.

Handles may become brittle if they dry out. Maintain them by sanding lightly and rubbing linseed oil into the wood. Prevent them from warping by hanging tools in storage racks rather than leaning them against a wall.

Figuring the Mechanical Advantage of GripHoists and Ratchet Winches

To determine the mechanical advantage of a GripHoist or ratchet winch, measure how far the end of the handle travels in its arc (for example, about 30 inches). Measure how far the cable moves with each swing of the handle (say, 1 inch). The ratio of the two measurements indicates the mechanical advantage (in this example, 30:1).

Tightening Loose Tool Heads

In dry weather, handle wood may shrink enough that the head of a tool will loosen. A temporary solution is to soak the head end of the tool overnight in a stream or a bucket of water. The wood in the handle should swell enough to get you through the next day's work.

You may be able to fix a persistently loose tool head by driving a wooden or steel wedge into the wood in the eye. If that doesn't solve the problem, re-handle the tool.

Rehandling Tools

Rehandling is most easily accomplished in a maintenance shop where you have access to a full range of repair tools and a radio playing country-western music. Unfortunately, handles loosen or break in the field, not in the shop. A well-equipped rehandling kit will allow you to fix many of your tools in camp and return them to duty as soon as possible, but you'll have to do the singing yourself.

REHANDLING KIT
- Pliers
- Wood rasp
- Tool-head wedges (plastic or wood, and steel)
- Coping saw
- Hack saw
- Hammer
- Punch
- Brace and bit
- Vise (optional, but useful in established camps)
- Lag screws (for securing the vise to a stump)

STEPS FOR REHANDLING A TOOL
1. Saw the broken handle from the head.
2. Secure the head in a vise if one is available, or brace the head with its eye over a notch in a log. Drive the handle wood from the tool eye with a hammer and punch, working from the bottom of the head toward the top. A punch that approximates the shape of the eye will yield the best results by allowing you to knock out the wood in one piece. Drilling out some of the wood with a brace and bit may loosen the wood enough so that it can be driven free. Select an old bit for this task, since it can be dulled if it rubs against the metal head.

   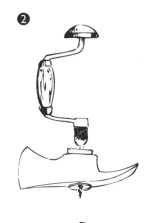

   Manufacturers have turned increasingly to the use of plastic wedges and epoxy glue to secure wooden handles in new tools. Unlike the handle carefully shaped by a backcountry worker to fit tightly into a particular tool head, a machine-shaped handle is slightly undersized so that it will slip easily into the eye of a tool. Plastic wedges are inserted, and epoxy is used to fill any remaining space between the handle and the sides of the eye.

   To remove such a handle from a tool, cut the wood flush with the head. Place the head in a pot of boiling water for half an hour to soften the epoxy, then drive out the wood with a punch.

> Never put a tool head in a fire to burn out handle wood. The wood may disappear, but so will the temper of the metal, making the tool brittle and dangerous to use.

3. Select the new handle. Those commercially available are most often made of hickory or ash, with hickory being preferable. The wood should be free of knots. When viewed from the butt end, the grain of a good handle is tight, straight, and parallel with the plane of the tool head.

   Properly fitted, the tool head will rest snugly on the shoulder of the handle. Begin by pushing the head onto the handle to see how far it will go. Remove it and use a wood rasp to shape the handle to better receive the head. Continue the process of trial fittings and rasping until the head can be pushed by hand about halfway to its final position.

4. When you are confident the handle is correctly shaped, you're ready to hang the head, the most curious and entertaining act in tool repair. Push the head onto the handle as far as it will go, then hold the tool by the handle with the head down, suspended above the ground. Strike the butt of the handle squarely with a wooden mallet or an old mattock handle. The force of the blows will draw the head evenly onto the handle.

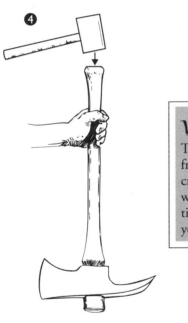

Why Handles Have Shoulders

The shoulder on a handle serves two purposes. It prevents the tool head from sliding too far down, and it absorbs and directs the shock wave created when the head strikes its target. Broken wood fibers or curls of wood caused by insufficient attention to rasping can weaken the transition from the tool head to the shoulder of the handle. Take all the time you need to shape the handle for a proper fit.

5. Cut the excess handle wood flush with the top of the head and hammer a wooden wedge into the slot. (You may have better luck by cutting off just one side of the excess wood, and then using the remaining side to support and guide the wedge while it is being driven.) Widen the slot a little with a chisel in order to get the wedge started. The wedges packaged with new handles are usually made of soft wood that will compress when driven into the handle and then expand to create constant outward pressure against the tool head, though a strong case can also be made for using hardwood wedges that will retain their shape. Any wooden wedge

may split as it is being hammered into the handle. When the pieces of the wedge will go no deeper, saw or rasp the top of the wedge flush with the head.

6. Drive one or two small steel wedges diagonally across the wooden wedge to expand the handle wood lengthwise in the eye of the tool. Steel wedges can be sharpened with a flat file to facilitate driving them into the wood.

7. Finally, sand the handle and rub the wood with linseed oil. Clear shellac applied at the factory makes a handle look clean and shiny in a hardware store, but also prevents the wood from breathing. Over time, a handle with shellac on it may become brittle. Removing the finish and occasionally applying linseed oil will extend the life of the handle and increase the efficiency with which it can be used.

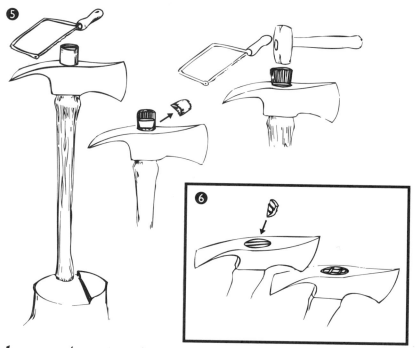

Sharpening Tools

Tools can be used most safely and efficiently when they are sharp. People who sharpen their own tools better understand how a tool is meant to be used, and that can increase their effectiveness when they are working. When they realize the labor that goes into sharpening a tool, they are also likely to take good care of it so it will not soon need to be sharpened again. Most sharpening of backcountry tools is done with files or sharpening stones.

FILES

Files are distinguished from one another by length, name, cut, and coarseness:

Length. File length is measured in inches and does not include the tang.

Name. The name of a file is determined by its shape or by its historic uses—flat, half round, mill, machinist, etc.

Cut. The shape and alignment of the teeth determine a file's cut:

- *Single Cut*—Parallel teeth set at an angle for creating a smooth finish and keen edges.
- *Double Cut*—A second set of teeth is stamped into the file at an angle to the first, creating a tool that removes material quickly but leaves a rough finish.
- *Rasp Cut*—Each tooth is individually stamped into the file. Rasps make an extremely rough cut for fast removal of wood, leather, and metal.
- *Curved Cut*—The crescent shape of teeth in a curved cut file is meant for unusual applications such as smoothing the surface of aluminum and steel sheets.

Coarseness. In addition to its cut, a file's capacity to remove material is determined by the number of teeth per inch. Some files are intended to shave off lots of metal with each pass, while others put a fine finish on the work. File classifications, in decreasing order of coarseness, are:

- *Coarse Cut*
- *Bastard Cut*
- *Second Cut*
- *Smooth Cut*

FILES FOR TRAIL CREWS

The all-purpose files of choice for sharpening most backcountry tools are *mill bastard files* ranging in length from 6 to 12 inches. Mill files take their name from their traditional use for sharpening saws in lumber mills. They have a single cut and come in many styles, including shapes specifically for axes, crosscut saws, and chain saws.

Checking the Sharpness of a File

Examined under bright light, a sharp file will have no shine. Bent or broken teeth will reflect the light and give a dull file a silvery sheen.

STORING FILES

Rust and rough handling will badly damage the teeth of files. Don't stack them together or pack them where they might rub against one another. Instead, wrap each file in a heavy cloth or store each in a piece of plastic tubing or rubber hose. Keep them absolutely dry. When a file is not in use, a thin coating of light machine oil will help protect the metal from rust.

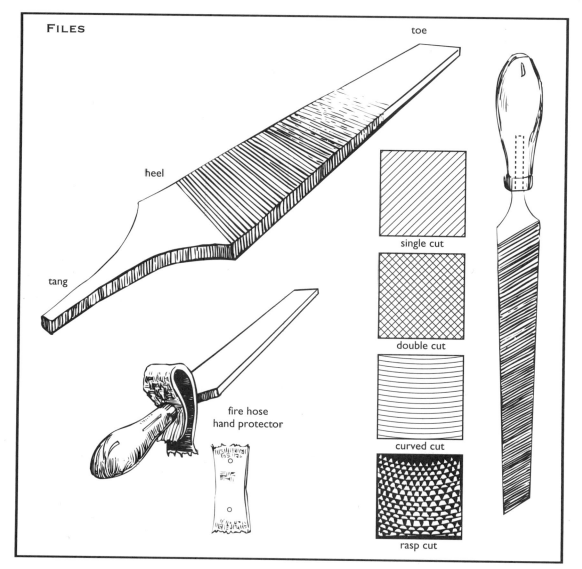

FILES

toe

heel

tang

single cut

double cut

curved cut

rasp cut

fire hose
hand protector

SHARPENING WITH A FILE

There are three chief considerations when using a file to sharpen a tool:

- Protect yourself from injury.
- Protect the file from damage.
- Hone an edge appropriate for the job the tool will be asked to do.

Every file you use should be fitted with a *knuckle guard* and a *handle,* and your hands should be further protected with leather gloves. The knuckle guard can be made from a 4-inch square of fire hose, inner tube, leather, or plywood. Cut a hole in the center and fit it over the tang of the file, then push the handle in place. If you do not have a handle that is matched to a particular file, try using a 6-inch length of wood such as straight maple, or a corncob.

PULASKI SHARPENING

Sharpen bevel side ONLY.

Danger!

Correct

Sharpen by moving a file into *the bit of a tool. Pulling a file backwards over a bit will damage the file and leave the tool little improved.*

The tool to be sharpened must be held motionless. A tool with two edges, such as a double bit axe or a Pulaski, can be driven into a stump while you sharpen the free bit. Shovels can be laid flat on the ground and held with the weight of your foot while you file into the edge of the scoop. Other tools may not be so accommodating, but most can be clamped into a vise, if you have one. In the field, have a partner brace a tool against a log or on a stump while you use the file.

The teeth of a file are always raked away from the tang. They cut only when the file is moving toward the point. The file must be lifted on the return stroke; dragging a file backwards across a blade will damage the teeth.

File *into* the edge of a tool, using long, even strokes and just enough pressure for the file to cut throughout each pass. Filing in the other direction can bend over the keen edge of a blade and leave a burr. Tap the file on a block of wood after every few strokes to clear the teeth of metal flakes, or use a *file card* to brush them away.

Sharpen both sides of the bits of hewing tools such as axes. File only the angled side of beveled bits such as adzes, draw knives, and weed whips, holding the file so that your strokes recreate the original slope of the bevel.

Tools that have been dulled by striking rocks may be difficult to sharpen because of nicks and gouges in the cutting edges, and because impact against stones can harden the temper of the metal. Trying to sharpen such a surface can ruin the teeth of a file. Instead, employ the narrow edge of a file to remove the hardened metal, then use the face of the file for final sharpening. Minimize the extent of work-hardened surfaces by filing tools frequently.

SHARPENING STONES

Use whetstones to restore the keen edges of tools such as pocketknives, chisels, and slicks, and to put the finishing touches on the bits of other tools after they have been filed. Natural whetstones are made from stone, particularly novacu-lite quarried in northwestern Arkansas; thus the term Arkansas Stone. Other sharpening stones are made by compressing aluminum oxide or silicon carbide grit to form stones of uniform quality. In recent years, manufacturers have also marketed efficient sharpening bars made of metal or ceramic.

Sharpening stones come in various hardnesses. The harder the stone, the finer the edge it will put on a tool. Softer stones are used for coarser and faster honing, either of tools that don't require a razor-sharp edge, or to sharpen a tool to the point that the honing can be completed with a hard stone. Compressed grit stones may have a hard sharpening surface on one side and a coarser face on the other.

Some trail crews advocate preparing a new stone for use by soaking it over-night in light oil. Each time it is to be used, they put a few more drops of oil on the surface to suspend bits of grit and metal produced by the sharpening process until they can be wiped away with a cloth. Stones that have become so clogged with grit that they no longer sharpen well can be restored by soaking them in kerosene and then cleaning their surfaces with a wire brush. Other trail workers prefer to use water rather than oil on their stones. Metal and ceramic sharpening bars should be lubricated, used, and cleaned according to the in-structions provided with each bar.

To sharpen, hold the edge of the tool at the correct angle against the face of the stone, then move the stone into the blade as you would a file. Check the sharpness of an edge by looking at it under bright light. Light will gleam off dull areas, while a sharp edge will have no spots flat enough to reflect light.

SHARPENING WHEELS AND ELECTRIC GRINDERS

Sharpening wheels turned by hand or with a foot pedal can rough-sharpen tool edges. Water dripping onto the wheel from above or picked up by the surface of the wheel as it passes through a container below will wash away grit and keep the wheel cool.

Electric grinders rotate at such high speeds that the heat they create against metal can destroy the temper of tools. Use electric grinders sparingly, if at all.

SHARPENING KIT
- Files with handles and knuckle guards
- File card
- Whetstones of assorted hardness
- Metal or ceramic sharpening bars (optional)
- Light machine oil
- Cleaning rags

CHAPTER 6

Crosscuts and Chain Saws

From the origins of Russia to those of the United States; from the primitive forests of 10th-century Kiev to the virgin lands of the equally harsh New World colonies of the 17th century; and from the pyramids of Egypt to Portland stone of Dorset in England, the saw has been a creative influence in the economic and social history of the world.

P. d'A. Jones and E. N. Simons
STORY OF THE SAW
(LONDON: JAMES COND
LTD., 1961), P. 73.

THE PRIMITIVE SKILLS AWARD, granted by the U.S. Forest Service to crews using traditional methods for completing exceptional backcountry projects, is a belt buckle featuring a pack string on a wilderness trail. Among the tools featured on the buckle is a crosscut saw. This is a fitting tribute to the crosscut, for it has long been at the center of much rustic work.

There is no buckle engraved with a chain saw, no "Technologically Advanced Skills Award," although there could be. Many modern crews are very good at using chain saws for addressing a wide range of trail projects.

Perhaps someday there will be an award that shows a crosscut and a chain saw. It would celebrate the best qualities of each, and honor a crew not only for knowing how to operate both kinds of saws effectively, but also for understanding when each is appropriate for a given task.

Crosscut Saws

Next to the axe, the crosscut saw is the wilderness tool steeped in the richest traditions. The sheer size of the crosscut lends itself to legend, as does its central role in felling the forests of the American frontier.

Backcountry use of crosscut saws in the twentieth century has gone from boom to bust and a little way back again. Until mid-century, crosscut saws were the primary tool of the logging industry and of crews clearing trails and building rustic structures. With the appearance of gasoline-powered chain saws, crosscuts rapidly fell out of favor.

The Wilderness Act of 1964 limited the use of motorized equipment in federally administered wilderness areas. Work crews could no longer rely on power saws for building and maintaining wilderness trails and bridges. The crosscut came out of retirement and is enjoying a renaissance as a workhorse of wilderness work.

Crosscut saws of the highest quality are no longer being manufactured in this country, nor are many of the tools required for their sharpening and care. Among woodcraft devotees, the collecting of saws and sharpening tools has become a serious hobby. Many old saws suffered the indignity of having pastoral scenes painted on them so that they could be hung on the walls of smoky cafes in economically depressed logging towns. While the art was usually quite bad, the paint has protected the saws from rust. Scour off the flowered fields, snowy peaks, weathered barns, and the moose and deer, and underneath you may find a vintage crosscut in perfect condition.

If your projects call for the use of crosscuts, the saws you use will probably come from the cache of an agency or conservation organization. A basic understanding of saws will help you select the best of those at your disposal, and allow you to transport, store, and use them efficiently.

Crosscut saws are of two types—*bucking* and *felling*. Bucking saws, intended for cutting through downed timber, are heavier, stiffer, and have a straight back. The weight helps the teeth sink into the wood, and the stiffness allows a bucking saw to be used by one person. Felling saws are lighter and have a curved back, making them easier to manage while cutting horizontally through a tree trunk. The felling saw's thinner profile allows sawyers to drive wedges behind the blade to hold open the kerf and prevent a tree from settling onto the moving saw.

Bucking and felling saws can be either *straight ground,* meaning the blade has been ground to the same thickness throughout; or *crescent, taper,* or *segment ground,* resulting in a saw that is thicker at the teeth and narrower toward the back. A crescent ground saw is less likely to bind in a kerf than is a straight ground saw. If a saw has a taper, you should be able to see it. The manufacturer's emblem engraved in the center of the saw may indicate how the saw was ground. If the trademark also says *Simonds, Disston,* or *Atkins,* you have a saw made by one of the best-known manufacturers, though many other saw makers also produced quality blades. Over years of use, the company logos on many saws have worn away, leaving their genealogy to speculation.

Saw lengths vary according to the uses for which they are intended. The ends of two-person saws are identical, and the blades are typically about 6 feet in

Crosscuts for felling trees are narrower and more flexible than saws for cutting, or bucking, *downed timber.*

felling crosscut

bucking crosscut

The difference between the work of one of these (dull) saws and one in proper order is about the same as that between a hole bored by a sharp auger and one gnawed by rats.

H. W. Holly
THE ART OF SAW-FILING, SCIENTIFICALLY TREATED AND EXPLAINED ON PHILOSOPHICAL PRINCIPLES, 5TH ED. (NEW YORK: JOHN WILEY & SONS, 1902. FIRST ED., 1864), P. 12.

length, though saws for felling old-growth cedar and fir in the Pacific Northwest and redwoods in California can be as long as 16 feet. One-person crosscuts, recognizable by the D-shaped wooden handle and a blade that narrows toward the far end, are 3 to 6 feet in length.

RECOGNIZING A SHARP CROSSCUT SAW

A well-tuned saw will make quick work of most cutting jobs, turning out long, well-formed shavings rather than sawdust. The tips of the teeth should come to sharp points that are angular or somewhat almond shaped. Sight along the edge of a sharp saw and you will see that the teeth are *set*—bent a little off center, alternately left and right—so that they will score two parallel lines through the wood fibers. The rakers, slightly shorter than the tips of the teeth, act as small chisels scooping out the wood between the scored lines. They may be bent over, or *swaged,* to accentuate their chiseling action. The most common crosscut saw tooth patterns are the *lance tooth* (common in the West for cutting softwoods) and *champion* (used in the East for hardwoods and timber that is frozen).

A crosscut must be free of rust if it is to work well. Scour tarnished blades with a griddle brick such as those used to clean restaurant stoves. Tree pitch can be removed with kerosene and a rag. Kinks, bends, and broken teeth will also reduce a saw's effectiveness and ease of use.

Sharpening crosscut saws is an art that demands time and patience to master. It also requires a collection of jigs, jointers, gauges, files, and hammers, and a special vise to hold the saw. The authoritative step-by-step guide to saw sharpening and repair is *The Crosscut Saw Manual,* written by Warren Miller and published by the U.S. Forest Service (U.S. Government Printing Office: 1988-593-748).

If it is transported, stored, and used correctly, a saw in serviceable condition should last through a season of backcountry use without further sharpening.

CROSSCUT SHEATHS

Make a crosscut sheath by splitting open a piece of fire hose the length of the saw. Punch holes spaced at 1-foot intervals along the hose and tie cords through them. To place the sheath on the saw, open the hose and roll it up, inside out. Place the coiled hose at one end of the saw and unroll it over the teeth. As it assumes its original shape, the hose will sheath the blade. Use the cords to tie the sheath in place. If backcountry conditions are wet, prevent rust

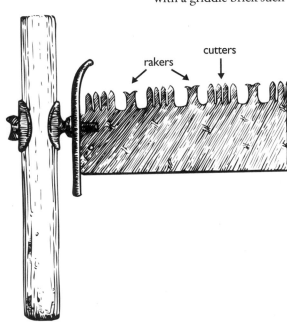

Cutter teeth *cut two parallel lines in a log.* **Rakers** *rake out the wood in between.*

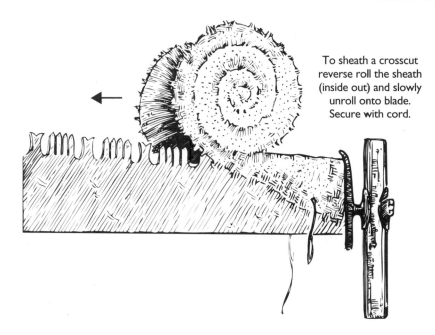

To sheath a crosscut reverse roll the sheath (inside out) and slowly unroll onto blade. Secure with cord.

A protective sheath for a crosscut saw can be made of split fire hose tied in place with parachute cord.

from forming by wiping the saw and the inside of the fire hose with an oily rag before sheathing the blade.

CARRYING CROSSCUTS

Transporting a crosscut saw is seldom an easy matter. A sheathed saw can be carried on your shoulder with the teeth turned away from your head. Removing the rear handle before shouldering the saw will keep it from being lost, will minimize the bouncing of the blade, and will prevent the handle from snagging on brush. You may also have success tying the ends of a cord to the ends of the saw, placing the cord over your shoulder, and toting the saw suspended horizontally at waist level. For long-distance carrying, bend the crosscut over a backpack or over the panniers of a pack animal, and tie it in place.

SCA crew leaders traveling to work projects by commercial airliner sometimes use a thin wooden case to hold several saw blades. The case slips into a ski bag, and the bag can be checked as luggage.

STORING CROSSCUT SAWS

At a work site, store a crosscut where it will stay out of harm's way. Hang it securely against a tree trunk, or place it under a fallen log with the teeth toward the log.

For winter storage, clean the saw, protect it from rust with a thin film of heavy oil, and stow it unsheathed in a dry place so that it is either lying flat and

Sawing with a two-person crosscut requires cooperation, patience, and rhythm.

supported along its entire length, or hanging vertically—*not* leaning against a wall where it could develop a permanent bend. Or paint a pastoral scene on it and nail it above the counter of your neighborhood cafe.

USING CROSSCUTS

While one-person crosscut saws are straightforward in their operation, two-person sawing demands cooperation. The power to move a saw through a cut is generated by pulling on the saw, not by pushing. Use your legs and shoulders as well as your arms to accomplish the work.

Grit is the mortal enemy of a sharp saw. A few passes of the teeth through dirty tree bark or into the earth beneath a log can spoil hours of careful filing. Use an axe or drawknife to remove bark from the vicinity of the intended cut. Clear the immediate area of underbrush and branches so they will not snag the saw or be pulled by the teeth into the kerf.

Before bucking a fallen log, try to predict how the timber will react as the cut is made. Tension and compression will affect the movement and force of log sections as they come apart. It may be necessary to follow the blade into the kerf with wedges, to undercut the log, or to support part of the log with another timber or a rock to keep the kerf from closing and trapping the saw.

There must also be enough clearance to complete the cut without allowing the blade to touch the ground, even if you must dig under the log to create the room you need. Place a chunk of wood or large piece of bark beneath the log to shield the saw from the ground when the blade breaks through. No matter how much time these preventative measures require, they are quick and easy compared with the effort of freeing a trapped saw from a log or resharpening dulled teeth.

Gadgets called *underbuckers* were developed in the heyday of crosscut sawing to brace the blade under a log as it was used to complete an undercut. Almost as effective is the handle of an axe driven horizontally into the log. The back of the saw blade rides on the axe handle as the sawyer guides the teeth upward into the log.

Sappy green wood can cause a buildup of pitch on a saw. If tree sap is slow-

UNDERBUCKING

fulcrum

ing your work, an occasional application of kerosene from a squirt bottle should dilute the pitch and keep the blade clean. Some sawyers mix a little 30-weight oil with the kerosene in the belief that it will lubricate the saw at the same time.

As to the big thing, sawing, it is something beautiful when you are working rhythmically together—at times you forget what you are doing and get lost in abstractions of motion and power. But when sawing isn't rhythmical, even for a short time, it becomes a kind of mental illness—maybe even something more deeply disturbing than that.

NORMAN MACLEAN
A RIVER RUNS THROUGH IT
(UNIVERSITY OF CHICAGO PRESS, 1976), P. 113.

An axe may be used as an underbucker *to position the saw for cutting upward into a log.*

Shorter bucking saws, 6 feet or less, may be the most versatile saws for trail work. They can be used for felling trees as well as bucking, and can be managed by either one person or two. Running a saw solo may be necessary when a log can be safely approached from only one side. Finishing the last few strokes of a cut by removing one handle and using just the tip of the blade may also keep the sawyer safer and reduce wear and tear on the saw.

(For general guidelines on cutting down trees and sawing up logs, see Chapter 13, "Felling and Bucking.")

Chain Saws

For centuries, axes and crosscut saws were the only tools available for felling and bucking trees. The development of a practical motorized saw is relatively recent, but the speed and ease of use of chain saws have all but swept crosscuts from the woods.

Beginning in the mid-1800s, inventors patented all sorts of sawing contraptions fabricated from steel plates, pulleys, and hinged sections of band saw blades. However, a practical power source remained elusive until the 1920s when a German named Andreas Stihl, the inventor of a gasoline-powered washing machine, bolted a bar and cutting chain onto one of his washing machine motors. The new saw was so heavy that it had to be disassembled before it could be moved. Even so, Andreas Stihl's creation was the prototype of all chain saws to come.

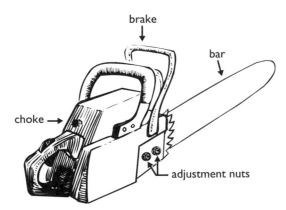

The approach of World War II accelerated chain saw development, especially in Germany where manpower shortages caused by military conscription were affecting timber harvesting. After the war, McCulloch, Homelite, and Stihl all had saws on the market, though the machines weighed close to fifty pounds and still lacked an efficient chain.

Enter the timber beetle, *Ergates spiculatus.* In 1947, American forester Joe Cox noticed that as timber beetle larvae chew their way through wood, they rely on raised protrusions on their jaws to gauge the size of each bite. Cox incorporated that concept into a chain by alternating rakers with the cutting teeth along a chain. The rakers controlled the depth of the bite of each tooth. A final improvement was made by another forester, John Gray, who produced a chain that combined a cutter and a raker in each tooth—the Oregon chain found today in power saws throughout the world.

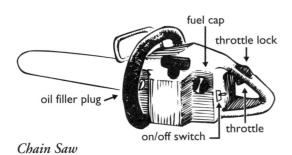

Chain Saw

Other advances in chain saw technology have increased the safety and reliability of the machines. Features to look for in modern saws include:

- Chain brake—causes the chain to stop turning if the saw kicks back toward the operator.
- Antivibration mounts between the engine and the handles—increase the control and lessen the fatigue of sawyers.
- Throttle lock-out button—prevents a saw from operating unless the sawyer is grasping the throttle handle.

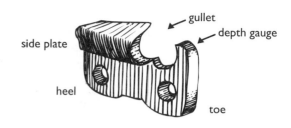

A link in a modern chain saw chain features both a cutting edge and a gauge to control the depth of the bite.

WOODS WEAR

Proper clothing is a major consideration in any timber cutting operation. Hard hats, safety goggles, and hearing protection must be worn at all times. Best of all is a sawyer's hard hat with attached ear protectors and a flip-down wire face screen.

Chain saw chaps are required by many land-management agencies. Chaps are filled with heavy fiber padding and/or Kevlar, a material used in bulletproof vests. If a running chain hits a sawyer's leg, the Kevlar can shield him from injury while the fiber binds the chain and brings it to a stop before it reaches flesh. Some chain saw crews also wear baseball catcher shin guards.

Lug-soled boots are adequate for most timber operations, though they can slip on barkless or wet logs. Calks (pronounced "corks") are traditional logger boots featuring a pattern of short nails in the soles. They give the maximum "stick-on" power on logs, provided the wearer remembers to knock the bark loose from the calks once in a while. Calks are rare outside the timber-harvesting profession, though trail workers doing extensive cutting in large windfalls may want to wear them. Slip-on calks—a sort of timber crampon—are sometimes popular among foresters fighting wildfires.

Professional loggers may *stag* their pants by cutting them off well above the ankle. Without the double-stitched hem, stagged pant legs are less likely to catch on a limb or underbrush while a sawyer is hurrying for safety, and will more easily tear free if they are snagged. Although trail crews seldom go so far as to stag their pants, the clothing of anyone using a chain saw should not be baggy or hang loose in such a way that it could be snagged by brush or by the chain itself.

CHAIN SAW MAINTENANCE

A chain saw operator must carry into the woods the gear required to keep the saw running. Other than the fuel and oil, most of the following items can be stowed in a fanny pack:

- ❏ Fuel (pre-mixed gas and oil)
- ❏ Chain oil

❑ Bar tool, or *scrench,* a combination screwdriver and wrench sized to fit the saw's nuts, screws, and spark plug
❑ Plastic or aluminum wedges
❑ Single-bit axe or single-jack hammer to drive wedges
❑ Extra starter cord
❑ Chain file
❑ 6-inch mill bastard file and a raker gauge for lowering rakers
❑ Chain filing jig (may be kept in camp)
❑ Extra spark plug
❑ Extra chain
❑ Extra bar nuts (2)
❑ Extra caps for gas and oil ports
❑ Fire extinguisher
❑ Shovel (optional)

Safe Chain Saw Use

It is not the purpose or intent of this book to provide a complete discussion of chain saw maintenance, use, or timber-cutting techniques. What follows is, rather, a brief overview of key safety and usage issues. DO NOT assume that by merely reading this section you will have the knowledge to begin using a chain saw. Every person who intends to use a chain saw must receive adequate training by a qualified instructor.

STARTING A CHAIN SAW

Before starting any chain saw, read the operator's manual. Familiarize yourself with the instructions for the safe use of the saw, and follow them to the letter.

In general, starting a chain saw will involve these steps:

Check the Fuel. Chain saws are powered by two-cycle engines. Among other things, that means that the gasoline used in the saw must always be mixed with a special lubricating oil. Manufacturers' guidelines will indicate the ratio for mixing gas and oil, ranging from 16:1 for some models up to 50:1 for others. To eliminate confusion, the fuel container holding the oil/gas mixture should be clearly marked, and the correct amount of oil added to the gasoline every time the container is refilled. It is also a good idea to engrave on the saw engine the proper ratio for mixing gas and oil.

Never attempt to refuel a hot saw, since gas spilling on hot surfaces may ignite.

Check the Bar Oil. Add bar oil every time you refuel the saw. Bar oil lubricates the bar and chain when the saw is running. Without it, the bar may heat and warp, and the chain will invent all manner of unspeakable things to do to itself. Saw manufacturers sell special bar oil, though many sawyers feel that clean motor oil is as effective and much less expensive.

Some saws have an automatic oiler that keeps the chain lubricated, while others have a thumb button that must be depressed frequently to pump oil onto the bar. A few models of saws feature both.

Check the Chain. The sharpness of a chain is difficult to determine by looking at the teeth, but will be almost instantly evident once you begin using the saw. However, a visual examination of the chain can turn up broken teeth, damaged links, worn rivets, or other indications that the saw may be unsafe.

The chain on a saw should be loose enough to move easily, but not so loose that it sags below the bar. Modern bars with a roller nose or sprocket nose require that the chain be tighter than older hard-tip bars. As a general rule, you should be able lift a chain far enough that a few of the guide links will just clear the slot in the bar.

To adjust the chain, loosen the nuts holding the bar against the side of the engine. Maintain upward pressure on the bar tip as you turn the adjusting screw on the engine housing to extend or draw in the bar until the chain is properly tensioned, then retighten the nuts.

Check the Air Filter. The working environment of a chain saw is full of dust, wood chips, and a mist of bar oil. The air filter prevents those contaminants from entering the engine.

Check the air filter each time you refuel the saw. Most manufacturers suggest washing the filter with soap and water, a task that can be done in the backcountry with the help of a plastic bag. Washing the filter with gasoline can also be effective, though any oil mixed into the gas can leave a residue on the filter that will attract dust.

Starting the Saw. Place the saw on the ground in an area free of leaves, pine needles, or other flammable material. Turn the ON/OFF switch to ON. Depress and lock open the throttle trigger. Always open the choke of a cold saw engine, but do not choke a saw that has been running.

Holding the saw steady with one hand, pull the starter cord with the other. If the engine starts, immediately depress the throttle to release the catch and give you control over the speed of the saw, then close the choke. Allow the saw to idle for 30 seconds before beginning to cut with it.

If the saw does not start after a number of attempts, figure out why. Flooding is the most common culprit, indicated by the strong smell of gas. One way to deal with a flooded saw is to leave it alone for 20 minutes, then try starting it with no throttle. If you don't have that kind of patience, set the switch to OFF, open the choke, leave the throttle closed, and pull the starter cord a dozen times or more to dry out the engine.

When flooding is not the problem, remember that in order to operate, an engine must have fuel, air, and a spark. Investigate the obvious:
- Is there fuel in the tank? If not, fill it.
- Is the air filter clean? If not, clean it.
- Is there a spark? Find out by removing the spark plug, leaving the wire attached to the plug's top. Ground the plug by touching its base to the

engine as you pull the starter cord, and watch for a spark to jump the gap on the plug. If there is no spark or the spark is weak, scrape carbon buildup from the gap surfaces with a pocketknife, check the wiring for wear, and inspect the connection of the wire to the top of the plug. Finally, consider installing a new plug.

When fuel, air, and a spark are all present but the saw still refuses to start, your options will be dictated by your sense of pride, your mechanical know-how, and the distance you must travel to swap the finicky saw for one in operating condition.

CUTTING WITH A CHAIN SAW

Most chain saw cutting is done with the underside of the bar. The motion of the teeth creates a steady pull *toward* the cut, keeping the body of the saw tight against the log.

If the top of the bar or the bar tip comes in contact with a log while the saw is running, the rotation of the chain can push the bar away from the log and back toward the operator. While a sawyer may cut with the top of the bar, as when making an undercut, doing so requires a strong grip and stiff arms to prevent the motion of the chain from pushing the saw in directions the sawyer does not intend. If the top or tip of the bar hits something when the sawyer is not prepared for it, the bar may kick back violently, placing the sawyer in extreme peril.

Most modern saws are equipped with a *chain brake* that features a lever curving over the top of the saw just ahead of the upper hand grip. A saw kicking back will force the lever against the sawyer's hand. That, in turn, tightens a metal band around the saw's clutch assembly and freezes the motion of the chain before it can hit the sawyer in the body or face.

Operators using chain saws must always observe the following safety guidelines:
- Maintain a tight grip on the saw, and wrap your thumbs around the handles. Lock your elbow to control potential kickback.
- Keep the bar pointed away from yourself, and position your head and body to the side of the saw, out of the path the blade will take if it kicks back.
- Do not use the saw to make cuts above waist level.
- Release the throttle at the first hint of trouble.
- Never walk with a saw while the engine is running.

BOUND CHAIN REMOVAL

Even with the best planning, a kerf being cut into a log may close on a chain saw bar and trap it. Once you've hit the OFF switch and given the saw and your temper a few minutes to cool, there are several alternatives for freeing the bar:
- If the log is not too large, lift it slightly with a pole or rock bar. Bigger timber can be lifted with a jack to release pressure on the cut and free the saw.

- Try freeing a blade trapped in a large log by driving wedges horizontally into either side of the kerf at points just above the blade.
- Unbolt and remove the saw engine from the bar and chain. You may be able to work the bar out of the log, then free the chain with short tugs.
- Start over again with another chain saw, but take care not to allow the same compression that pinched the first saw to trap the second.
- Use an axe to chop the saw out of the tree.

BROKEN CHAIN

Never allow anyone to stand directly opposite a running saw. While it is highly unusual for a saw chain to break, it could happen. The sawyer is in a fairly safe position behind the saw, but anyone standing in front of the saw may be in danger.

CHAPTER 7

Measuring Distances, Grades, and Heights

BACKCOUNTRY MEASURING IS A SKILL embedded in the lore of the wilderness. Native Americans based much of their measurement systems upon natural phenomena—the height of the sun, the speed of a walker, the span of a hand. Surveyors sent out to quantify the continent were equipped with basic instruments to plot imaginary lines of boundary and contour that would bring an element of order (often as imaginary as the lines) to wild territory.

Trail crews today can greatly increase their efficiency and the pleasure of their work if, in addition to being skilled with a tape measure and level, they master backcountry methods for estimating and measuring distances, grades, heights, and widths.

Measuring Distances by Pacing

In ancient times, distances were often determined by the length of a person's stride. Knowing how to pace is a valuable skill in our day, too, since it allows a trail worker to estimate distances simply by walking.

Developing an accurate measuring pace is a learned skill. Use a tape measure or measuring wheel to mark off a hundred-foot distance on flat ground. Beginning at one end, walk to the other with a normal stride, counting your steps as you go, then divide 100 by the number of steps.

Early forestry manuals make the distinction between a *step* (count every time either foot strikes ground) and a *pace* (two steps—count only when left foot strikes ground). Some strides are easier to calculate in paces, others in steps.

MEASURING 100 FEET WITH STEPS AND PACES

Number of *steps*	Length of *step*	Length of *pace* (two steps)
50	2 feet	4 feet
40	2.5 feet	5 feet
33	3 feet	6 feet

If your stride falls in between these distances, try slightly extending or shortening each step you take. Practice should allow you to fall into your *measuring stride* whenever you need it.

Did you ever go on a walk into the hills without learning something new? Many a time a camping trip or a new vision of the outdoors has changed a foolish boy into a wise man, or a thoughtless girl into an unselfish woman. Woodcraft begets wisdom.

Earle Amos Brooks
A HANDBOOK OF THE OUTDOORS (NEW YORK: GEORGE H. DORAN COMPANY, 1925), P. 100.

The Body as Measuring Instrument

The measurement we call a *foot* takes both its name and its approximate dimension from the human foot. If you know the length of your own foot (it may not be exactly 12 inches), you can use it to measure everything from the widths of trails to the lengths of water bars.

Spend a little time in the company of a ruler and you can find a variety of body parts in addition to your foot that will lend themselves to use as measuring devices. Perhaps a finger bone is an inch, the span of your outstretched hand from the tip of your thumb to the tip of your little finger is half a foot, from elbow to wrist is a foot, and the span of your outstretched arms is 2 yards.

Making Measurements with Work Tools

Some measurements must be made repeatedly in the course of completing a project—the width of new trail tread, for example, or the depth of holes being dug for planting saplings. Save time by marking convenient measurements on the tools you will be using. A wrap of duct tape around the handle 24 inches or 36 inches below the head of a mattock or grub hoe will allow a worker to lay the tool across a trail to see if the tread is wide enough. A small notch cut in a shovel handle or scratched on the blade can indicate when a hole is deep enough.

Measuring Steepness

Percent of grade refers to the relationship between horizontal distance and vertical gain. It is a simple way for determining the steepness of hillsides, trail tread, backslope, and downslope. It can also be used to measure the heights of trees and widths of rivers, and to level bridge sills. Percent of grade often appears in construction specifications issued by land-management agencies to designate the maximum allowable steepness for new trail construction or reroutes.

Percent of grade results from the following equation:

$$\text{Percent of grade} = \frac{\text{rise}}{\text{run}}$$

Rise equals the vertical gain.

Run equals the horizontal distance over which the rise is attained.

For example, the grade of a trail that is rising at a rate of 2 vertical feet for every 100 feet of horizontal distance can be determined this way:

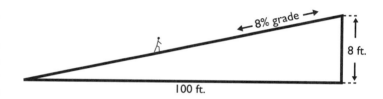

$$\text{Percent of grade} = \frac{2 \text{ feet (rise)}}{100 \text{ feet (run)}}$$

Divide the run into the rise, and you'll discover the prevailing grade of the trail is 2 percent.

The grade of a slope that gains 8 feet of elevation over a horizontal run of 100 feet can be calculated like this:

$$\text{Percent of grade} = \frac{8 \text{ feet (rise)}}{100 \text{ feet (run)}}$$

Dividing the run into the rise reveals a grade of 8 percent.

A simple rule of thumb may help you visualize the abstract relationship between rise and run: *Over a 100-foot run, each foot of rise equals a prevailing grade of 1 percent.*

Measuring Grade

Measuring the steepness of an existing trail or laying out a new route at a prevailing grade is virtually impossible without the aid of a surveying instrument. The tool most frequently used today for measuring trail grade is the *slope inclinometer,* commonly known as a *clinometer* (clin-AH-meter). It is a direct descendant of the *Abney level,* an ingenious combination of protractor, bubble level, and sighting tube developed in the mid-1800s by Captain William Abney of the School of Military Engineering at Chatham, England. The Abney level was used throughout all land-management agencies until its gradual replacement in the 1970s by the clinometer.

A clinometer is a very simple instrument, little more than a weighted disk turning freely inside a housing. The diameter of the disk is calibrated in increments that, when viewed through an eye hole in the housing, render accurate slope readings. The clinometer makes most of the same measurements as an Abney level, but it is easier to use and less likely to fall out of adjustment.

Abney Levels and Topography Maps

Modern contour maps are computer-generated by the U.S. Geological Survey from information provided primarily from aerial photographs. Before that technology existed, however, the collection of raw data was done by teams of surveyors equipped with Abney levels and specially calibrated steel tape measures. The leader moved up a slope pulling one end of a steel tape. A second surveyor held the other end and used an Abney level to take readings on the grades between them, then ran the numbers through a set of equations to determine elevation gain and horizontal distance. Results plotted on a page could be connected to form contour lines that revealed the topography of an area.

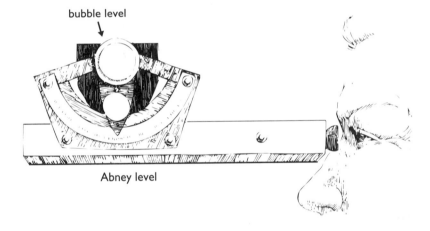

bubble level

Abney level

The Abney level was the workhorse of backcountry surveying from the late 1800s until its replacement in recent decades by the clinometer.

USING A CLINOMETER

Hold the clinometer in your right hand with the eye hole toward you and the lanyard ring hanging down. Most clinometers are illuminated by natural light entering a glass window over the calibrated disk. Grasp the instrument in such a way that your hand does not shade the glass or block the vision of either eye.

While you look through the eye hole with your right eye, keep your left eye open and gaze out at the terrain in front of you. You should be able to see the clinometer scales superimposed upon the landscape. If you have trouble simultaneously seeing the scales in the clinometer and the world beyond, try looking through the instrument with your left eye while you use your right to gaze at the land.

Watch the scales in the clinometer move as you tilt your head and the instrument up and down. Tilt your head and the instrument far enough, and at the end of the scales you will find an indication of how each scale is calibrated. The scale of greatest importance for trail work is the *percent scale,* marked on the clinometer with the percent symbol. Most clinometers feature a second scale

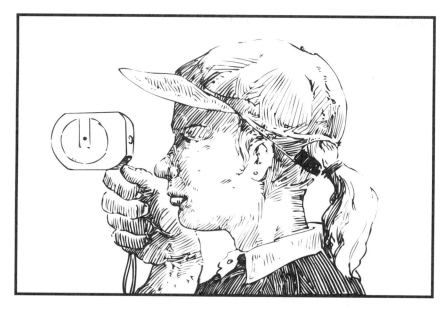

By sighting through a clinometer with both eyes open, the incremental scales inside the instrument and the landscape beyond it will both be visible.

alongside the first, either *chains* for measuring the heights of trees, or, more commonly, *degrees*. Mistaking the degree or chain scale for the percent scale will result in faulty grade readings and trail locations that are badly misaligned. For the purposes of general trail work, ignore those scales and make sure that you are always reading the percent scale.

As you sight through the clinometer with both eyes open, notice the horizontal cross hair that appears to extend across the scale and out onto the landscape. You can measure the percent of grade from your eyes to any landscape feature you can see by simply placing the cross hair on the feature and then reading the clinometer's percent scale. The plus and minus signs interspersed along the percent scale will help you determine whether a grade in question is rising or falling.

For example, as it touches the center of a rock on the ground in front of you, the cross hair may also fall across the *-10 percent* gradation on the clinometer scale. That means that a straight line extending from your eyes to the middle of the rock is descending at a prevailing grade of *10 percent.*

The grade you are measuring will *always* begin at your eyes and extend in a perfectly straight line to any and every point touched by the cross hair. How, then, can you accurately measure a slope that is under your feet rather than even with your eyes?

An effective technique involves using a partner as a human survey staff. Stand face-to-face on a surface known to be level, such as the floor of a ranger station, and look through the clinometer at your partner. Tilt your head and the instrument until the cross hair is at zero percent, then note where the cross hair touches—the center of your partner's chin, perhaps, or the top of the hat. That is your eye level on your partner, and that will be the *target point* you can use in the field for measuring slopes.

You can also use a tall hiking stick or other pole as a survey staff by tying a piece of flagging on it at your eye level. Your partner can hold the stick upright while you use the flagging as your target point.

To measure the grade of a slope, have your partner walk about 20 feet away, then turn to face you. Look through the clinometer and tilt it until the cross hair intersects the target point—the top of the hat, the chin, the flagging on a hiking stick, or whatever. With the line still on the target point, note the reading in the clinometer where the cross hair touches the percent scale. That number is the percent of grade from your eye to the target point on your partner. Because both your eye and the target point are the same height above the ground, the percent indicated by the clinometer is also the prevailing percent of grade of the ground slope extending from beneath your feet to beneath the feet of your partner.

Laying Out a Line at a Prevailing Grade

A key step in surveying many new trail locations is marking a route that climbs or descends at a predetermined grade. The percent of grade is often established

Surveying a trail at a prevailing grade is most easily done by two people, one to handle the clinometer and the other to act as a target of a known height.

by agency specifications. Considerations used to determine grade guidelines include the erosive quality of the soil, special requirements of expected users, and factors of comfort and challenge to be built into the route. For example, many guidelines for barrier-free trails require that the tread be no steeper than 3 percent, while specifications for a wilderness pathway may limit the prevailing grade to 10 percent, with allowable short stretches of 15 percent.

(For more on determining the appropriate grade for a trail, see Chapter 8, "Trail Survey and Design.")

To lay out a line at a prevailing grade, you'll need a clinometer, a partner upon whom you have determined your eye-level target point, and flagging tape, wire pin flags, or wooden stakes.

Stand at the beginning of the route and send your partner 10 to 20 feet in front of you. Sight through the clinometer to the target point on your partner and read the percent of grade. If it is less than the steepness indicated in the specifications, have your partner sidestep up the slope. If the percent of grade you are reading is greater than called for, instruct your partner to sidestep down the slope. Continue directing the movements of your partner until the cross hair lines up with both the target point and the intended percent of grade indicated in the clinometer. Your partner can mark that spot with a wire flag or wooden stake, or can tie a piece of flagging tape to a nearby branch.

Walk to your partner's position and ask him to move forward about the same distance along the potential route of the trail. Repeat the clinometer readings and have your partner mark the prevailing grade with another wire flag, wooden stake, or flagging. Continue in the same manner until you have completed the line.

If you each have a clinometer, your partner can sight back on you while you are making your readings. Your grade measurements should be in agreement at each point of stake or flagging placement. You can also speed the survey process by taking a reading on your partner and then walking past him as he is marking his location. He can then simply turn around and take the second clinometer reading, using you as a target. During the time you are flagging that spot, he can leapfrog ahead and be in position to serve as the target when you are ready to take the next clinometer reading.

Surveying a grade when you are working alone is more difficult, but it can be done. At the beginning of a proposed trail, tie a piece of flagging around a tree branch at your eye level. Walk a short distance up a potential route, then turn and take a clinometer reading on the flagging. Move sideways up or down the slope until the clinometer reading matches the prevailing grade called for in the specifications. Tie a second ribbon at eye level on a branch or around a tree. Move further along the route, repeating the process of shooting grades back at the flagging until you have marked the entire location.

Using Flagging

- Choose a color of flagging that contrasts with the natural background. Yellow ribbon can disappear in a field of brown leaves, green can blend into spring and summer vegetation, and red or pink tree blossoms will swallow up flagging of similar shades. Dark flagging is difficult to see in the dim light of cloudy days and late afternoons. Fluorescent or multicolored striped ribbon may give the best results.
- Select a flagging color that is not being used by the land-management agency for other purposes. In some areas, for example, pink flagging is used only to mark archeological sites and yellow indicates locations of endangered plant species.
- Put a loop of flagging around a branch, tuck the tails of the flagging through the loop, and pull it snug. This *lark's head knot* or *cow hitch* holds the flagging securely, but also makes it easy to remove for reuse.
- Use a square knot to secure flagging around a tree trunk. Place the knot on the side of the tree facing the proposed trail. Where the route changes direction, as in a switchback, tie several pieces of flagging around a tree to indicate the turning point.
- Whether around branches or tree trunks, tie flagging at your eye level. That will help you relocate the exact place you were standing when you were shooting the grade.
- Remove all flagging after it has served its purpose.

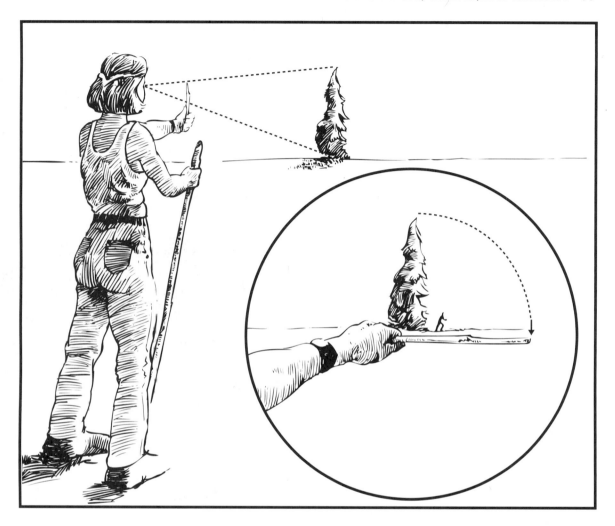

Measuring Heights

Stick Method

The ability to measure heights can help you determine whether a tree is of sufficient size for a timber project, where it will land when it falls, and if there is enough clearance for the tree to come down.

MEASURING TREE HEIGHTS—STICK METHOD

Standing some distance from the tree, hold a straight stick at arm's length and sight along it so that the top appears to touch the crown of the tree while your thumb is in line with the tree's base. Swing the stick down in the same arc the tree would take if it were falling at a right angle from your vantage point. With your thumb still appearing to touch the base of the tree, again sight along the

Stacking Method

end of the stick and note where it seems to be touching the ground—that is, the place where the top of the tree would be resting had it actually fallen. Discover the tree's height by pacing the distance between that point and the base of the tree.

MEASURING TREE HEIGHTS—STACKING METHOD

Have someone whose height you know stand at the base of the tree. Walk 50 to 100 feet away, then hold a straight stick at arm's length so that the end of the stick appears to touch your partner's head and your thumb is in line with his feet. Consider that to be one *person unit* of height measurement.

Keeping your arm straight, use the stick to stack person units on top of each other all the way to the top of the tree. If your partner is 6 feet tall and you can stack nine person units between the ground and the loftiest leaves, the height of the tree is 6 feet **x** 9 feet, or about 54 feet.

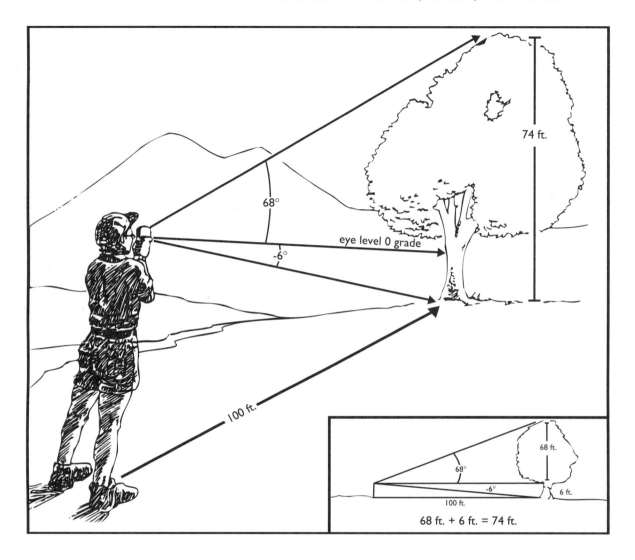

MEASURING TREE HEIGHTS—CLINOMETER METHOD

Clinometer Method

Measuring tree heights with a clinometer relies on the basic equation for figuring percent of grade:

$$\text{Percent of grade} = \frac{\text{rise}}{\text{run}}$$

Pace off 100 feet from the base of a tree. Using the percent scale of the clinometer, take one reading to the top of the tree and a second reading to the tree's base.

- ■ If one reading is positive and the other negative, disregard the plus or minus signs and *add* the numbers.
- ■ If both readings are positive or both are negative, again disregard the plus or minus signs, but *subtract* the smaller number from the larger.

The result represents the height of the tree in feet.

Taking the readings from a distance of 100 feet is convenient because at 100 feet, 1 percent of grade equals 1 foot of rise. If, for example, the reading to the top of the tree is +68 percent and the reading to the base of the tree is -6 percent, adding the two without regard to the plus or minus signs equals 74 percent. One percent of grade equals one foot of rise; thus the tree is 74 feet high.

Foresters using percent clinometers often measure smaller trees by pacing off 50 feet from a tree, shooting the grades, then determining the height of the tree by halving the combination of the grades. Clinometers calibrated for use with steel tapes marked in chains require a measurement distance of 66 feet.

Of course, with a percent clinometer you can measure tree height from any convenient distance, not just 50 feet or 100 feet, by factoring that distance into the equation as the run:

$$\text{Percent of grade} = \frac{\text{rise}}{\text{run}}$$

To obtain tree height, combine the clinometer readings shot at the crown and base of the tree and multiply that result by the number of feet you are standing from the tree. For example, the height of a tree with combined clinometer readings of 70 percent shot at a distance of 80 feet from the base of the trunk can be figured this way:

.70 **x** 80 feet = 56 feet of total tree height

Measuring Widths

The capability of a clinometer to measure widths can be illustrated with a somewhat fanciful scenario that involves bridging an imaginary river. The river in question is full of alligators, sharks, endangered aquatic flora and, if you wish, an exceedingly angry platypus. Your crew is charged with the task of spanning the river with a foot log. To determine how long the log should be, you must measure the width of the river even though you cannot reach the other side until the foot log is in place.

Standing on one bank, take a clinometer reading across the river, using the far bank as the target point. Now find some relatively flat ground on your side of the river, look through the clinometer again with the cross hair intersecting the same reading as when you were sighting the target point, and note the spot on the ground in front of you that the cross hair touches. Pace the distance to that spot, and you will know the approximate width of the river.

Checking Abney Levels and Clinometers for Accuracy

A clinometer is unlikely to fall out of adjustment unless it is dropped or otherwise abused. Check a clinometer's accuracy by taking shots with it between two trees about thirty feet apart. Tie a piece of flagging around one tree at your eye level. Walk to the other tree and tie flagging around it, also at your eye level. Holding the clinometer next to that flagging, shoot the grade back to the flagging on the first tree. Return to the first tree and take a reading on the flagging around the second tree. The two readings should be the same, except one will be a positive grade and the other a negative (or both will be zero). A difference of one or two percent may be a matter of your technique rather than the instrument's calibration. However, if the difference is greater than that, or if more care in taking readings cannot erase the deviation, you should suspect that the clinometer is out of adjustment.

Unfortunately, there is no way to adjust a clinometer other than returning it to the manufacturer for replacement or repair. On the other hand, Abney levels that have drifted out of alignment can be adjusted by sighting on flags in the same way you would check a clinometer, then tightening or loosening the screws holding the bubble tube until your readings in each direction are the same.

CHAPTER 8

Trail Survey and Design

THE IMAGE HAS ADVENTUROUS APPEAL—surveyors going on foot into the backcountry to explore the terrain, gain a close sense of the folds of the earth, and then lay out the route for a new trail that will lie lightly on the land.

But beyond the romance of surveying is a hard, cold truth. Failure to plan thoroughly new trails and trail relocations results in more problems, expense, and ultimate frustration than any other aspect of trail work. Proper surveying can lead to projects that are a joy to construct and a pleasure to use. But if surveying is hasty and sloppy, or if it is not done at all, the trail will reflect it. As the 1915 manual *Trail Construction on the National Forests* points out, "Mistakes in location seldom can be corrected after the trail is constructed. Future generations of men and horses must pay for incompetence or carelessness shown in the preliminary work" (p. 9).

On the other hand, the manual also suggests that surveying is a skill that can be mastered by any who will give it their time and attention. "Trail locating is a fascinating problem, full of interest and satisfaction to the man who successfully solves it. . . . The essentials are good judgment, experience, and hard work" (p. 10).

On public lands, surveying is usually done by agency personnel or by private contractors who mark the route and generate records detailing the work to be done. Those logs, along with copies of the agency's specifications for trail maintenance and construction, are the guidelines that leaders use to direct work crews.

Even though crew leaders may not be involved in the initial design of a project, a knowledge of surveying techniques is an important asset for any backcountry worker. Trail crews can see a project with fresh eyes, and since they consider the route from the point of view of doing the labor, they may notice ways to improve the location that the surveyors have overlooked. In many cases, small adjustments will allow a crew to bypass rocks, trees, and other obstacles without sacrificing the prevailing grade or quality of the trail. Basic surveying methods will also enable leaders of maintenance crews to design the best possible reroutes for replacing short sections of inappropriate or hopelessly damaged trail.

Survey Logs

Used both for new trail construction and for maintenance monitoring, survey logs provide a practical method for recording the points on a route that require the attention of work crews.

Each entry in the log represents one *station*—a location on the trail that has been marked with a wooden stake or, in some cases, flagging tied to a branch. The *station location,* written in a standard format used throughout the agencies, gives the distance in feet between that station and the beginning of the trail. The numbers to the right of the plus sign indicate feet, while numerals on the left stand for hundreds of feet. Thus, a log entry of *00 + 49* refers to a point on the trail 49 feet from the trailhead. A log entry of *02 + 75* signifies a point 275 feet from the trail's beginning. The *station description* contains information about the tasks to be completed at that station or between that station and the next. The station location code and an abbreviated work description should also be written on each stake or strip of flagging. Grease pencils work best for writing on wood, particularly in wet weather. Use a felt-tipped marker to write on flagging and wire pin flags.

Accurately measured distances are important for preparing useful trail logs. In open country or where a trail already exists, a measuring wheel is sufficiently precise to provide the information needed for a log. A 50-foot measuring tape may be the best device for measuring proposed trail locations through areas of dense trees, undergrowth, and irregular terrain.

TYPICAL TRAIL MAINTENANCE LOG

Trail Name _____

Date of Survey _____

Name of Surveyor _____

Station Location	Station Description
00 + 00	Trailhead
00 + 25	Saw out 24-inch log across trail
00 + 65	Install water bar
01 + 22	Begin puncheon
01 + 40	End puncheon
01 + 85	Install water bar—ditch right
02 + 15	Begin slough removal
02 + 30	End slough removal

Maintenance Surveys

Good maintenance depends upon good information. By knowing the conditions of the trails in their areas, land managers can make the most efficient use of human resources for the upkeep of those pathways. Long-term monitoring also allows managers to evaluate changes in trail conditions from one year to the next.

Bad weather is the most revealing time to do maintenance surveys. Surveyors can better locate the sources of water that is affecting trails and determine the best ways to channel it off the tread. Muddy water flowing along a trail may indicate that significant erosion is occurring, while clear water may suggest that the soil has stabilized.

One person can conduct an efficient maintenance survey, quickly covering long distances and producing an accurate log of necessary work for trail upkeep and repair. Such a survey requires the following equipment:

- Measuring wheel
- Stakes, flagging, and/or wire pin flags
- Hammer
- Grease pencils and/or felt-tip markers
- Handheld tape recorder

Measuring Wheel

Set the wheel's odometer at zero and begin rolling the wheel from the trailhead. At the first point of concern—a water bar in need of cleaning, for example—turn on the tape recorder and dictate the odometer reading and a description of the problem and its solution. Next, write on a wooden stake or piece of flagging the distance and a brief description of the work to be accomplished. Drive the stake alongside the tread or tie the flagging near the trail, then roll the wheel further along the route and repeat the recording and staking process each time you come to a location that requires maintenance.

When you return to your camp or office, prepare the final log by writing out the station locations and work descriptions as you play back the tape. You will find this method of log creation much easier than trying to write it in the field, especially if the weather is wet or windy.

Calibrating Measuring Wheels

Using a wheel that measures incorrectly is worse than having no wheel at all, since you may not realize that the readings are faulty. Regularly inspect a wheel for any damage that might affect the calibration, such as a pin out of alignment or a warped rim. Better yet, frequently check the wheel by using it to measure a known distance.

Hip Chains

Survey crews in some parts of the country use a measuring device called a hip chain. It is a container that fits on a surveyor's belt, pays out string as he walks, and meters the length of the string. It can be more accurate than a wheel because the string doesn't react to every bump and dip on the trail. On the other hand, the hip chain leaves a piece of string in the woods, measures best in straight lines, and creates no end of difficulty if the string breaks. Reserve the hip chain for use in heavy brush where neither a wheel nor a tape measure is practical.

New Construction Surveys

No step in the process of constructing a new trail is more important than surveying a detailed, carefully considered route. A well-surveyed trail that is badly constructed can later be brought up to standard. A poorly surveyed trail, even though built by expert crews, will forever suffer from the initial failure to plan it properly.

Surveying for new construction should always be completed well before a crew goes into the field. Depending on the size of the project, it may take several days or weeks to lay out and log the work. *New construction should never begin until a route has been completely surveyed!* Surveyors trying to keep ahead of a busy construction crew will find their options for adjusting the trail location become increasingly limited each time a shovel breaks new ground. The results will invariably be awkward grades, flawed switchbacks, missed opportunities, and assorted other foolishness that timely surveying could easily have avoided.

Guidelines for Good Trail Location

Good trail design will result in a route that can be used and enjoyed for decades to come. Invest enough time to do the job right, keeping these pointers in mind:

- Complete archeological, biological, or environmental impact statements, if necessary. Requirements vary depending on the area and the land-management authority.
- Take advantage of south-facing slopes. A trail that catches sunshine during much of the day will lose its snow load earlier in the spring and dry out after storms more quickly than a shaded route. Vegetation may also be less dense on sunny, drier slopes, making construction and long-term maintenance easier.
- Stay on ground that drains well and will hold a tread.
- Consider future maintenance. Siting a trail through heavy brush, loose rock, avalanche chutes, or wet ground will cause future trail crews to think less than kindly of you.

- Bypass large trees or rocks that would otherwise require removal. Given a choice, put the trail on the uphill side of a large tree. The tree will help stabilize the trail by holding the tread in place. Excavating tread near the downhill side of a tree often requires removal of roots and undermining of the tree.
- Contour the route into and out of drainages so that flowing water will stay in the drainage rather than diverting onto the trail.
- Incorporate gentle undulations into the basic tread design to facilitate drainage and enhance aesthetic appeal.
- Place switchbacks and climbing turns on the rounded faces of ridges.
- Skirt through the trees at the edges of meadows rather than cutting across open spaces.
- Route the trail to take travelers to scenic overviews, natural features, and other points of interest.
- Do not intrude on areas critical for wildlife grazing, nesting, or other seasonal activities. Keep trail users and livestock away from lakeshores and stream banks.
- Be sensitive to plant communities, locating the trail to minimize disruption of fragile or endangered species.
- Design trails so that they rely as little as possible upon bridges, turnpikes, puncheon, or other structures. Building them can consume a great deal of time. If they are not regularly maintained, wooden structures can deteriorate to the point of being dangerous. Structures also impose an obvious human element upon the landscape that may be out of place in a natural environment.

Seven Steps to Good Surveying

- Study printed resources.
- Explore the territory.
- Identify control points.
- Plot potential grade.
- Lay out a preliminary flag line.
- Survey subsequent flag lines.
- Stake the final route location and generate a construction log.

STUDY PRINTED RESOURCES

Maps are often the most useful printed materials providing information about an area. With them, you can study elevation contours, identify landmarks, and gain a sense of the general lay of the land between the beginning and ending points of a proposed trail.

Aerial photos may also be available. Seen through a stereoscopic viewer, they can give a three-dimensional appearance to the terrain. Also seek out any descriptive reports about the area written by previous surveyors or by historians, archeologists, botanists, or biologists. Each can add to your understanding of the region.

EXPLORE THE TERRITORY

Perhaps no step in the surveying process is more vital than lacing up your boots, sticking a map, compass, and perhaps an altimeter in your pockets, loading a lunch into your pack, and tramping all over the area through which a new trail will pass. Exploring the territory will give you a feel for the terrain, for the locations and shapes of water courses, outcroppings, and viewpoints, and for the types of vegetation, varieties of soil and rock, and amounts of sunlight and shade.

In forested regions, the best time to conduct explorations and surveying may be in the spring before foliage blocks your views, or in the autumn after the leaves have fallen. But whatever the season, there is simply no substitute for getting into the field and wandering about until you are very familiar with the place.

LOCATE CONTROL POINTS

During your explorations, identify the proposed trail's major *control points*— the points that the route is almost certain to touch. The trailhead and the final

Explore the backcountry to find the **control points** *a proposed trail must pass. Connecting the control points with a line at an acceptable grade will reveal a potential route for the trail.*

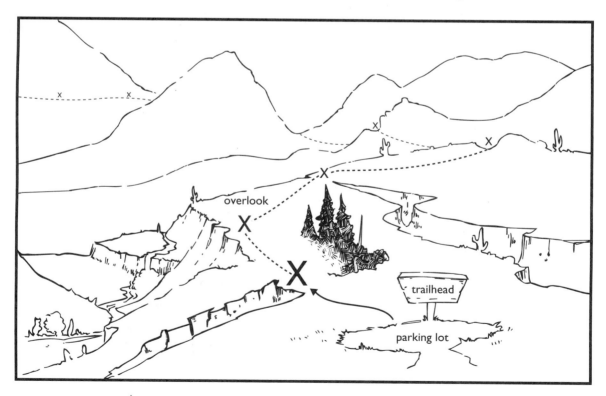

destination are control points, as may be a mountain pass, the base of a rock out-cropping, an opening between dense stands of trees, the edge of a meadow, a scenic overlook, and a stream crossing shallow enough for wading. Pencil in each control point on a topographic map. Plotting the trail route will then be a matter of linking together the control points with a survey line at a prevailing grade—a grand-scale connect-the-dots puzzle played out across the landscape.

Global Positioning Systems

Recent advances in portable global positioning systems (GPS) hold great promise for trail surveyors, especially those laying out routes through complex terrain. Using satellites as reference points, GPS allows survey-ors to pinpoint their locations to within a few yards. That information will help them plot control points on maps with great accuracy.

PLOT POTENTIAL TRAIL GRADES

One of the most time-consuming steps in finding an ideal location for a new trail can be determining the appropriate *prevailing grade,* or steepness, for each segment of the route. Surveyors who wait until they go into the field to figure the grade may find themselves with little idea where to begin.

It doesn't have to be that hard. With a topography map and a pair of divid-ers, you can do much of the initial grade work without leaving your chair. In the process, you may also discover new possibilities for the route that could result in a better location for the trail.

For a full description of percent of grade, see Chapter VII, "Measuring Distances, Grades, and Heights." As a reminder, the equation for determining percent of grade is this:

$$\text{Percent of grade} = \frac{\text{rise}}{\text{run}}$$

Follow these steps to discover a workable grade for a segment of new trail:
1. In the lower margin of the area's topographic map, locate the *contour in-terval* denoting the vertical distance between contour lines. Insert that number in the equation as the *rise.*
2. Select a potential percent of grade that does not exceed the maximum allowed in the specifications for the proposed trail. Insert that number in the equation as the *percent of grade.*
3. Solve for *run* by dividing *rise* by *percent of grade.*
4. In the map margin, find the bar scale that is divided into feet. Use it as a reference to spread the divider points to the length of the run in your equation.

Any other feature of construction may be im-proved from month to month or from year to year, but if the grade is not properly established the trail must in time be abandoned. Thus not only may time and money be wasted, but the trail while in use will be unsatisfactory.

TRAIL CONSTRUCTION ON THE NATIONAL FORESTS (U.S. FOREST SERVICE, 1915), P. 11.

5. That done, set one point of the dividers on the map contour line where the proposed trail will begin. Swing the dividers around in the direction the trail will probably take, and rest the other point on the next higher contour line (if you expect the trail will climb) or on the next lower contour line (if you presume the trail will descend). The gap between the points of the dividers represents on the map the approximate location of a route climbing or descending at your selected percent of grade.

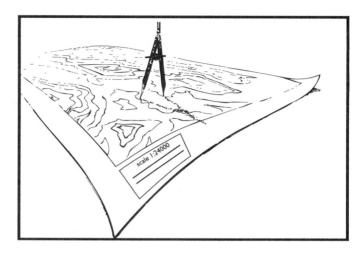

Plot a potential trail location on a map by setting dividers to represent a prevailing grade, then "walk" the dividers from one contour line to the next.

SAMPLE EQUATIONS OF COMMON PERCENTS AND CONTOUR INTERVALS

Percent of Grade	Rise, in feet (Map Contour Interval)	Run, in feet
16	80	500
16	40	250
16	20	125
12	80	666
12	40	333
12	20	166
10	80	800
10	40	400
10	20	200
8	80	1,000
8	40	500
8	20	250
6	80	1,333
6	40	667
6	20	333
4	80	2,000
4	40	1,000
4	20	500

Here is another way to think about it. At an 8 percent grade, a trail will rise a total of 8 feet in elevation for every 100 feet of run. If the interval between a map's contour lines is 40 feet, an 8 percent trail must have a run of 500 feet (40 = .08 × 500) to rise from one contour line to the next.

Walk the dividers from the trailhead to the first control point, steadily climbing or descending by always placing the free point of the dividers on the appropriate adjacent contour line. If the dividers come close to the mark on your map that represents the first control point (or the end of the trail, if there are no intervening control points), you'll know that the percent of grade you have chosen is the reading to use when you begin the actual surveying in the field. If, however, the dividers pass well below or above the first control point, you should set them for different percents of grade and keep plotting possible routes on the map until you hit upon the one that works.

When you are satisfied that you have discovered a potentially workable route between the trailhead and the first control point, pencil it lightly on the map. Repeat the process of testing grades with the dividers to connect that control point with the next, and so on until you have plotted the entire location of the trail. The grade may vary between each pair of control points.

Where the terrain is steep, you may not be able to plot a line that reaches a control point even with the dividers set for the greatest grade allowed by the area's land-management specifications. Use the dividers to test every other option—contouring the trail around the head of a valley, say, or swinging behind a hillside to gain elevation.

As a last resort, design one or more switchbacks to allow the trail to gain or lose sufficient elevation. Study the map for the best place to put a switchback, ideally on the rounded face of a ridge. When a divider point reaches that area, swing the other point almost 180 degrees to reverse the direction of the route. Make the trail segments leading to and from each switchback as long as possible to lessen the number of turns that must be built. A minimum of switchbacks will reduce the temptation for hikers to take shortcuts down the slope.

You can also use the dividers to measure the length of any route that is drawn on a map. Since you know from the bar in the margin the horizontal distance represented by the width of the dividers (a half-inch equals 200 feet, for example), simply count the number of times the dividers are turned in the course of plotting the trail, then multiply that number by the feet (40 turns of the dividers x 200 feet equals an approximate trail length of 8,000 feet).

Practicing Plotting

Even if you don't intend to build a new trail, plotting routes with a map and dividers can be good practice and great fun. Participants in SCA high school trail crews sometimes use plotting as a way of applying their book-learned math knowledge to the practical tasks of designing potential trails, or of determining the prevailing grades of existing routes and then comparing their computations with clinometer readings in the field.

LAY OUT A PRELIMINARY FLAG LINE

The preliminary flag line roughly transfers a potential trail route from the map to the ground. Its purpose is twofold; to test the potential prevailing grade, and to identify additional control points that did not present themselves while you were exploring the territory.

Beginning at the trailhead, establish an initial flag line at a selected prevailing grade. (Follow the basic survey method explained in "Using A Clinometer," found in Chapter 8, "Measuring Distances, Grades, and Heights.") Use the grades you determined with the map and dividers, or make your best guess of a grade that falls within the specifications. As you survey, change the grade slightly to work around significant obstacles, but don't waste time fine-tuning the location.

If your initial flag line takes you directly to the first control point, you will have strong evidence that you've hit upon the correct prevailing grade for that leg of the route. On the other hand, a flag line that comes in well above or below its intended destination probably means that the estimated grade was too steep or too shallow.

Continue connecting the control points with the initial flag line until it extends from the trailhead to the final destination. Note the accuracy of the grade estimate between each pair of control points, and also record any discoveries of conditions that may have an impact on the final location of the trail.

SURVEY SUBSEQUENT FLAG LINES

Based on the knowledge gained from the initial flag line, survey the route again, marking the second location with flagging of a different color. Deviate from the first flag line wherever a different grade will result in a better trail location, but always stay within the maximum grade allowed by the project specifications. Keep at it until you have a flag line that answers the questions of grade to connect the control points from one end of the trail to the other. In rugged terrain, that may take three, four, or even more flag lines of different colors, each placed to try out a different grade.

As you survey, gently adjust the prevailing grade of the flag line to bypass obstacles that could slow construction. For example, a route shot at 8 percent may lead into a rock outcropping. Building a tread past the rock would require constructing a retaining wall or using explosives to blast a shelf for the trail. But by backing up 100 feet and reshooting the grade at 9 percent or 10 percent, you may be able to lift the flag line just above the rock to a location better for tread construction. Reducing the grade to 6 or 7 percent for 100 feet beyond the rock will bring the route back in line with its prevailing grade.

Agency specifications for trail steepness usually give a maximum *prevailing grade* (8 percent, say), and then an exception given in both percent and distance (for example, "Up to 15 percent for pitches of no more than 100 feet"). Avoid the temptation of resorting to that steeper grade to jog abruptly around an obstacle rather than backing up far enough to use a much smaller change in grade to ease the trail above or below the same obstacle. Be patient and adjust the flag line properly so that changes in grade are gradual and the smooth flow of the route is maintained.

Even the best trail locations will sometimes require that a construction crew build through a rock slide, remove a large tree, span a bog, construct a bridge, or complete some other rustic structure. If alternative solutions have been examined and found wanting, then survey the best route you can find through the obstacle and let the crew do the rest. It is better for workers to build the trail correctly and in the right place the first time, rather than having to return to reconstruct or relocate the route.

While this much care in locating flag lines may seem excessive (as well as resulting in a rainbow of flagging ribbons to be removed when you are done), hours spent surveying can save weeks of construction time. Since a properly located pathway is also easier to maintain, correctly surveying a proposed route may save additional months of labor over the lifetime of the trail.

Grade Dip

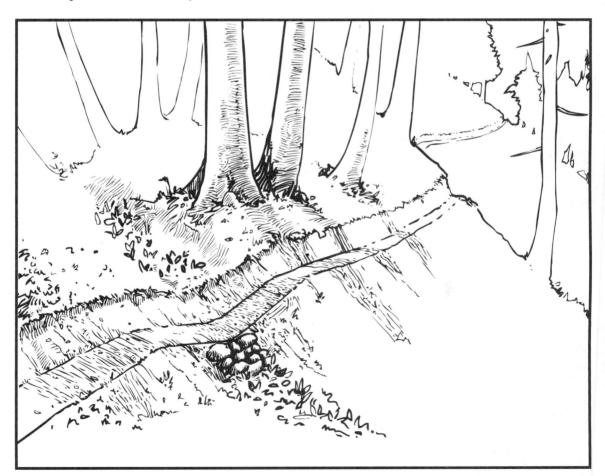

Grade Dips

The final flag line may incorporate grade dips to help protect the trail from erosion and eliminate the need to install water bars. Survey a grade dip by reversing the prevailing grade of the trail for just enough distance to establish in the tread a 1-foot rise, or *freeboard,* that will divert water off the route before it can cause erosion. Grade dips are most effective and least noticeable when they are built into new trail rather than into existing pathways. The spacing of grade dips depends upon the steepness of the trail, the expected frequency of water, and the stability of the soil. (For more on grade dips, see Chapter 10, "Drainage.")

STAKE THE FINAL ROUTE LOCATION AND CREATE A CONSTRUCTION LOG

After establishing a flag line that resolves the problems of determining the prevailing grade, connecting control points, and avoiding obstacles, perform a final survey of the route, this time marking it with wooden stakes and developing a log to record the details of the proposed project. Reshoot the grade with a clinometer as you go, making any last refinements in the location. Inscribe the stakes with distance and construction information, noting the same details in a written log or on a tape recording to be transcribed later.

In most parts of the nation, wooden stakes provide as much permanence as possible for a route location. The stakes will outlast flagging tied to branches or pin flags pushed into the ground, especially if construction is delayed by a season or more, or if deer are inclined to treat themselves to flagging *hors d'oeuvres.* The exception is some desert terrain where termites can destroy wooden stakes. Surveyors in those areas rely instead upon metal pins.

Surveyors vary on their preference of stake location:

Center Staking. Placing each stake in the center of the survey line.

Advantage: Center staking may give surveyors the most accurate vision of the flow of the trail.

Disadvantage: As construction reaches each stake, it must be removed to allow excavation.

Outside Edge Staking. Placing each stake on the outside edge of the intended tread. This is sometimes called *grade staking.*

Advantage: Each stake indicates the exact level of the eventual tread. Stakes can stay in place during excavation.

Disadvantage: Determining where to begin cutting the inside edge of the tread may be more difficult than with other forms of staking.

Inside Edge Staking. Placing stakes over the expected inside edge of the tread. This kind of staking is rarely done unless in conjunction with other forms.

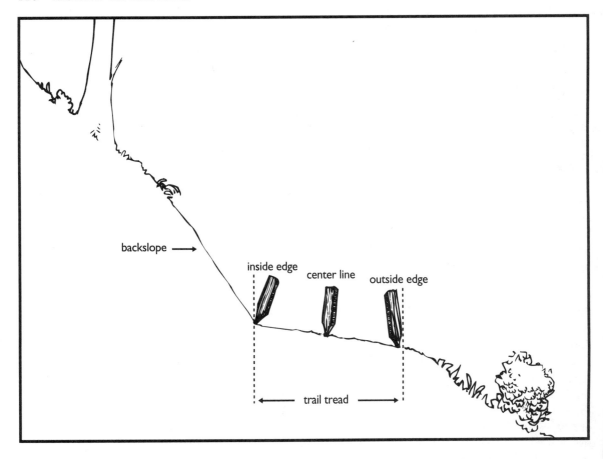

backslope

inside edge

center line

outside edge

trail tread

Final marking of a potential trail can be done with wooden stakes placed on the inside, outside, or center of the route, or a combination of all three.

Advantage: Crews can more readily see where to begin tread excavation.

Disadvantage: Stakes may be disrupted early in the digging process.

Combination Staking. Placing stakes at the center, the outside edge, and the inside edge of a proposed tread.

Advantage: This is ideal staking for showing all aspects of an intended route, especially for crews of beginning trail builders.

Disadvantage: Combination staking consumes three times as many stakes as other methods.

CHAPTER 9

Trail Construction

CONSTRUCTING NEW TRAIL can be among the most satisfying projects that a crew can undertake. Workers laying a pathway across the terrain are creating from nothing a linear structure that will give pleasure to backcountry travelers and protect the environment for years to come. The opportunity to build a new trail can offer people the chance to leave their legacy upon the land in a most positive and useful way.

Building new trail also carries with it the responsibility to do it right. The scar that a construction crew cuts into the landscape will be there for decades. Once a tread has been dug out and the soil compacted, it becomes very difficult to adjust the location or, if the route must be abandoned, to fully restore the area to its previous condition and appearance.

Good trail construction begins with crew leaders becoming familiar with all aspects of the trail design, layout, and project specifications. Taking time to do this is especially important if the leaders were not involved in the survey of the route. While members of a group may become absorbed with the short pieces of trail each of them is building, crew leaders must maintain an overall perspective of the project so that they can blend together these often isolated efforts and assure the smooth flow of the new trail.

Trail construction should never begin until the route has been thoroughly surveyed. Starting excavation without a complete understanding of where the trail will go almost always results in a disappointing outcome. (For more on planning and laying out trails, see Chapter 8, "Trail Survey and Design.")

New construction can be divided into three distinct phases:
- Brushing and clearing
- Excavating
- Finishing

Brushing and Clearing

The first step in building a new trail is the clearing of a *travel corridor* of the dimensions called for in the project specifications. The corridor for hiking trails usually extends 3 to 4 feet to each side of the trail centerline and 8 feet up from the proposed tread. Trails intended for stock use may require a 10 foot x 10 foot

Local conditions so completely govern the work of trail construction as to make a set of definite rules impracticable, but nevertheless certain general rules can always be followed with more or less success, and it is felt that a few suggestions concerning the actual work in the field will not be out of place.

Jay L. B. Taylor
HANDBOOK FOR RANGERS & WOODSMEN (NEW YORK: JOHN WILEY & SONS, INC., 1917), PP. 52–53.

corridor to provide vertical clearance for riders in the saddle and horizontal leeway for loads on pack animals.

Trees that must be removed to make way for tread should be cut off at waist height. Later, as workers dig them out during the excavation phase, the extended stumps will provide leverage for pulling the roots free of the earth. Trees within the clearance corridor but not growing in the tread itself may be cut flush with the surface of the ground, leaving their root systems intact to continue stabilizing the earth around them.

Stump Removal

The tribulations of stump removal will try your patience as do few other tasks in trail work. When you match your intelligence to that of a stump, though, chances are better than even that you will be at a slight advantage. Granted, the stump has nothing to think about except how to stay firmly situated in the center of your trail, but a bit of cleverness on your part may persuade even the most tenacious root ball to ease its grip and go away.

It is often possible to excavate the soil and rocks from around the roots, then chop through them with a cutter mattock. If you have rigging anchored to the base of a nearby tree, you can attach a winch or block and tackle to the stump and generate a great deal of pull.

Large trees should be removed only after careful consideration. In many cases, a slight adjustment of the survey line for a distance of 50 feet or more may realign the tread so that it misses a large tree all together, but discuss possible options with land-management personnel before changing a surveyed route. Whenever a sizeable tree must be felled, think about using the trunk as material for water bars, retaining walls, bridges, and other rustic structures. (For more on adjusting stake lines, see Chapter 8, "Trail Survey and Design.")

Brush saws are ideal for cutting back tree branches that extend into the corridor. Trim the branches close to the trunk so as not to leave protruding *hat racks* that could snag hikers or riders. Undercutting each branch before sawing through it from above will prevent the limb from stripping bark off the trunk as it falls. Use a pole saw to drop overhead branches.

Cutting a few branches from the side opposite the trail may improve the appearance of a tree that has been pruned. However, removing branches from a small tree may leave it looking scraggly. In those cases, it is probably better to remove the whole thing.

In some regions, crews find it best to clear away ground cover down to bare soil before constructing trail tread. Workers in other areas have found that leaving the duff on a trail can retard erosion. In all cases, brush, duff, and ground litter that have been removed should be scattered out of sight of the trail. Accelerate natural decomposition by sawing large branches into pieces that will lie flat on the ground.

Complete all the brushing and clearing before beginning the next construction phase, and you will be better able to visualize the actual location of the trail route. Problems that did not appear during surveying may become apparent as you walk the trail corridor and study the exact placement of the intended tread. Even though brushing can involve extensive removal of trees and undergrowth, vegetation will grow back if you decide that some of the proposed trail and its corridor should be rerouted or abandoned before construction.

Brushing is work for saws and loppers. A shovel, however, signals the start of excavation. Once digging begins, you are at long last fully committed to the surveyed trail location.

Excavation

Building trail across flat or gently rolling terrain may require little more than brushing a travel corridor and then using stones laid at the edges of the proposed tread to guide hikers along the route of the new trail. Over time, the user impact will beat a tread into the earth, and the rocks can be removed. This method minimizes the disturbance of protective ground cover and allows the trail to be created with the least disruption to the soil.

As terrain becomes steeper, however, it is increasingly likely that the new trail will travel along the side of a slope, and that will require excavation to shape a shelf, or *bench,* to hold the trail. The surveying work completed prior to the

Trail Structure Terms

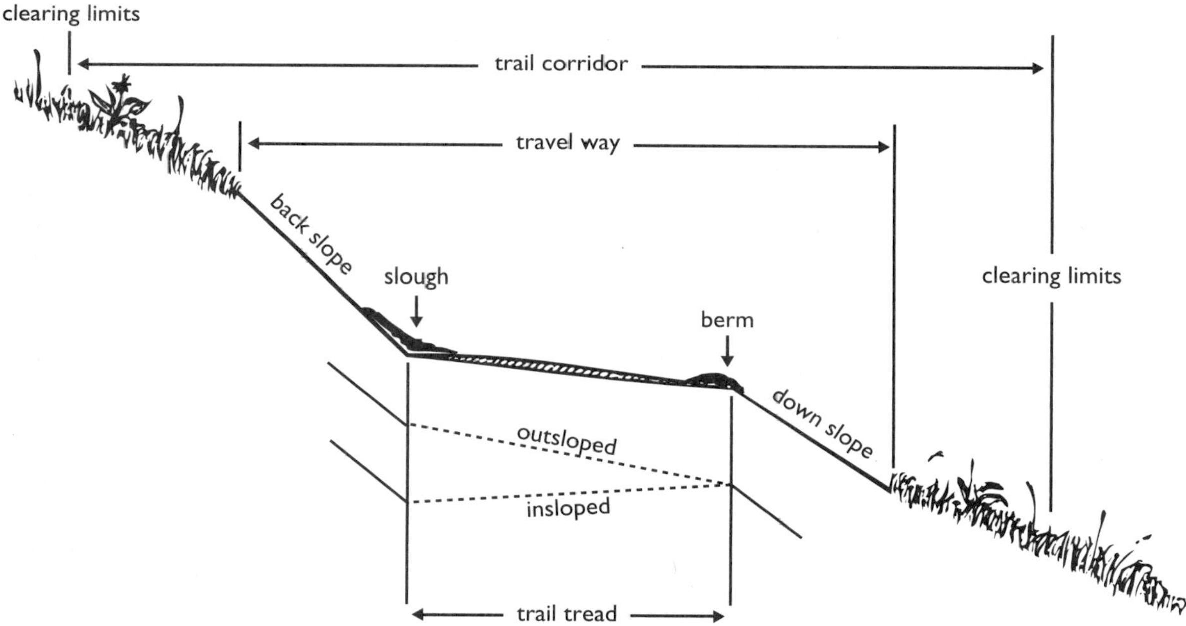

clearing limits

trail corridor

travel way

back slope

slough

berm

clearing limits

down slope

outsloped

insloped

trail tread

commencement of construction should have resulted in a series of wooden stakes marking the trail location. Depending on the method chosen by the surveyors, the stakes will mark the center of the trail, the outside edge of the tread, the point at which the backslope and tread meet, or a combination of all three. It is essential that trail builders understand which staking method was used during the survey process.

While each stake shows the tread location at the point where the stake is driven into the ground, it may not be so obvious exactly where the tread should be built in the gaps between pairs of stakes. Placing pin flags between the wooden stakes at intervals of 5 feet or less will give a very clear indication of the flow of the proposed tread. Since they are easy to move, a row of pin flags can be adjusted to produce the most appropriate line for the trail. This is especially valuable when locating the trail through drainages and switchbacks, and around other terrain contours. Marking trail segments with pin flags is also an effective way to help inexperienced crew members envision the new route.

Scratch a line in the earth to mark the inside edge of the tread. Workers using that line as a guide can dig down with mattocks, grub hoes, McLeods, Pulaskis and shovels until they have removed enough soil to form a tread of the correct width. It should be a *full bench cut,* meaning the entire width of the tread is on solid, undisturbed mineral earth.

Loose soil should almost never be piled at the edge of the trail in an effort to widen the tread. Trail that has been widened with free-standing fill material has an outside face that is much steeper than the prevailing grade of the slope on which it rests. That, in addition to the fact that the soil will never be as compacted as undisturbed earth, usually causes these ill-conceived tread extenders to be washed away or to slide out from under the feet of hikers and horses.

One way to dispose of excavated soil is to stockpile it for later use in restoration sites or as fill behind retaining walls and in turnpikes. Where stockpiling is impractical, you may be able to fling loose earth downhill as far as possible, or use wheelbarrows or buckets to transport the soil to a better disposal location.

Project specifications will call for a tread of a particular width—usually 18 inches, 24 inches, or 36 inches. Try to build the tread a couple of inches wider than called for. Silt building up on the inside edge of the tread and some inevitable crumbling of the outside edge will narrow the trail, eliminating that 2-inch cushion and leaving a tread of the specified width.

After a section of tread has been grubbed out, shape the backslope. Some construction specifications suggest equations for figuring the angle of the backslope in relation to the angle of the prevailing grade of the hillside, but they all boil down to this—build the backslope by removing any material above the trail that would otherwise fall down onto the tread in the course of the first few years of snowmelt and rain. McLeods and fire rakes work well for pulling soil, rock, and duff from the backslope onto the tread where it can be scooped up with shovels and removed.

TYPICAL TRAIL CONSTRUCTION LOG

Trail Name _____

Date of Survey _____

Name of Surveyor _____

Location	Grade	Station Description
00 + 00	8%	Begin full-bench construction 24-inch tread.
00 + 15	8%	Remove 3 small trees.
00 + 82	7%	Begin rock retaining wall.
00 + 97	7%	End rock retaining wall.
01 + 45	8%	Begin turnpike.
01 + 66	6%	End turnpike.
01 + 90	10%	Increase grade to approach switchback.
02 + 75	10%	Begin ramp of rock retaining wall leading into switchback.
02 + 87	10%	Turning point of switchback. Construct level turning platform with 6-foot radius measured from the turning point.
02 + 87	10%	Begin upper leg of switchback, insloped and ditched.
03 + 12	10%	End insloping. Return to outsloped tread.
03 + 05	8%	Return to prevailing grade.

Finishing

With the tread roughed out and the backslope in shape, a crew can finish a section of new trail by smoothing the tread and creating the outslope. They can also install any bridges, retaining walls, turnpikes, and other structures required for the completion of the trail.

Most sidehill trails are *outsloped,* or slightly tilted, so that water flowing onto them will run across the tread and down the hillside. The amount of the tilt is small—specifications usually call for an outslope grade of only a few percent. That is a slight enough pitch that hikers, bikers, and horseback riders will be unlikely to notice it. Insure proper drainage by keeping the edge of the trail clear of berm, logs, rocks, or other barriers.

The tendency among inexperienced crews is to build tread with too much outslope. If, as you stand in the center of a trail, you can feel the tread listing beneath you, there is more outslope than necessary. A crew that attempts to build a tread that has no tilt at all will probably end up with just about the right outslope.

If you have an orange in your lunch bag, you can get an idea of the effectiveness of an outslope. Roll the orange down the trail. Rather than staying on a straight course, it should gradually curve across the tread. Another technique for measuring outslope is to lay a board across the trail, place a clinometer upon it, and take the reading off the side of the instrument. Remember to convert the degrees shown on the side of the clinometer into percent of grade. (For more on using clinometers, see Chapter 7, "Measuring Distances, Grades, and Heights." For more on trail structures, refer to Chapter 10, "Trail Drainage"; Chapter 11, "Building with Rock"; Chapter 14, "Building with Timber"; and Chapter 15, "Bridge Construction.")

Advantages and Disadvantages of Partial Construction

Some crews do the initial tread excavation, put in essential structures, then open a new trail corridor for a season of use. The idea is that hikers using the route, especially one that crosses open ground or wanders through flat forests, will indicate by their footsteps where the tread should be. The crew can return later to put the finishing touches on the pathway.

The drawback to this approach is that funding for the crew may dry up before the trail is finished, or that volunteer workers may lose interest or move on to other projects. It is often wiser to complete as much work as possible the first time a crew is in the field, rather than halting construction short of completion with the hope that a second crew can later be dispatched to the trail.

Switchbacks and Climbing Turns

Switchbacks involve trail-building artistry of the highest order. They are difficult to construct correctly. They are also subject to more abuse, and they require more maintenance, than other sections of trail. Switchbacks should be incorporated into a route only as a last resort, and then with serious forethought as to their location and execution.

It is important to understand the difference between a switchback and a climbing turn so that you don't try to build one when you intend to construct the other. A climbing turn is just that—a trail that gradually reverses direction on a hillside by making a wide, ascending curve. The grade of the tread in the turn must not be significantly greater than the prevailing grade of the trail leading into and out of the turn. Climbing turns work only on fairly gentle slopes—ideally 15 percent or less. Like switchbacks, they are best placed on the rounded face of a ridge.

Because a climbing turn is much easier to build than is a switchback, it may be tempting to force climbing turns onto hillsides steeper than 15 percent. It simply can't be done. Instead of a pathway that bends gradually, imposing a climbing turn on steep terrain will almost always result in the upper and lower legs of the trail being joined by a short, very steep pitch that lies directly in the fall line. Unless the turn is hardened with rock or timber steps, it will very likely suffer significant erosion.

Climbing Turn

By contrast, the upper and lower legs of a switchback intersect sharply, then lead out onto a flat, semicircular *turning platform* large enough for trail users to make a comfortable change of direction. Project specifications should indicate how large to make the platform, depending upon whether it will be used by hikers, horses, bicycles, wheelchairs, or some other form of passage.

The turning platform can sometimes be excavated directly into the hillside. More often, though, at least part of the platform will be held in place by using rock or timber to construct a retaining wall. The wall tapers down to blend into the lower leg of the trail.

Switchback

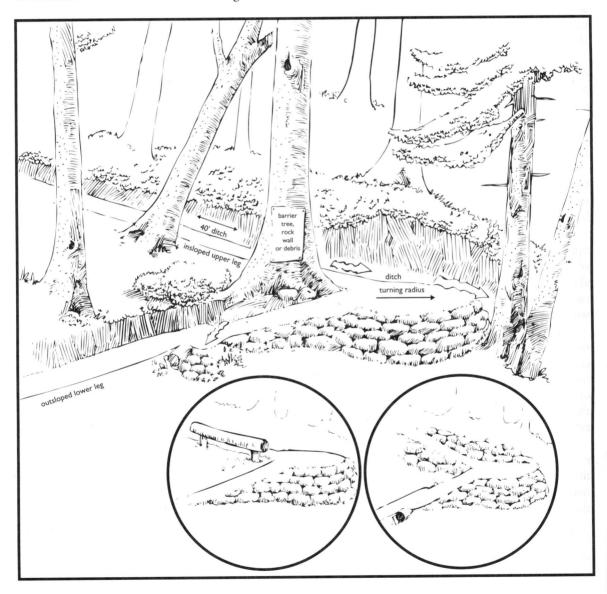

Whenever possible, the switchback should wrap around a tree, rock outcropping, or some other natural feature that will stabilize the location of the turn and discourage travelers from cutting across the switchback. Where natural barriers do not exist, it may be necessary to create one by installing a few boulders between the switchback legs or building a barrier of rock or timber. Stands of yucca, devil's club, raspberry bushes, and other confrontational flora also serve well in keeping people on the trail.

A construction crew will generally find the location of a switchback marked with survey stakes to indicate the lines of the upper and lower legs of the trail, and the point at which those two pathways intersect. Some surveyors will also outline the turning platform with stakes, but in most cases that job will fall to the crew leader.

The size of the turning platform will vary according to the users expected on the trail. For hiker-only trails, a 3-foot radius is common. Horses require a turning radius of 6 feet or more. Switchbacks on bicycle routes vary from 3 to 6 feet, depending upon the difficulty level of the ride. Cyclists may swing wide or skid to negotiate a switchback turn, causing the breakdown of the outer edge of a turning platform. Rock or log barriers installed near the edge of the platform may slow riders and guide them nearer the center of the turn.

Pin flags are invaluable in laying out a switchback. By outlining the circumference of the turning platform with pin flags at 1-foot intervals, you will be able to visualize the task at hand, and can make wise location decisions from the beginning.

Switchback layout can be confused by the fact that while the tread of the upper leg of the trail will be created by digging down into the earth, a portion of the turning platform and the ramp of the lower leg of the trail will be built above the surface of the slope. As you are staking out the dimensions of the switchback, imagine the turning platform existing in thin air, to be filled in later with rock or soil behind a retaining wall.

Build the upper leg of the switchback first, using straightforward construction all the way to the stake marking the intersection of the upper leg's outside edge with the inside edge of the lower leg. For a distance of 100 feet from the turn, the tread of the upper leg should be insloped and ditched. Water flowing onto that portion of the trail will drain into the ditch rather than running off the tread and down the slope where it may endanger the lower leg of the switchback.

Build the turning platform next. Some of the platform's diameter may be established by digging into the backslope, but the steeper the hillside, the less that can be gained by excavation. Construct a curved retaining wall to shape the remainder of the turning radius. The surface of the platform will be level with the upper trail tread where it touches the point of intersection.

Complete the structure by extending the retaining wall down along the lower leg, tapering it to form a ramp that will blend into the trail beyond the switchback. At the point where the tapered wall ends, resume regular full-bench tread excavation.

During switchback construction, protect the area between the upper and lower legs. Staying off the area will minimize damage to existing vegetation and prevent soil compaction that could hinder future plant growth.

> Because of the nature of switchback design, the likelihood of accurate tread placement is much greater when you build down through the turn than if you try to go the other way. If the general direction of trail construction has been uphill, stop the upward excavation about 100 feet from a proposed switchback. Move up the stake line 50 feet beyond the turn and build the trail back down to the switchback location. Construct the switchback itself, and then continue downhill construction, fine-tuning the location until you link up with the tread that has already been completed.

Building through Boulder Fields

Trail construction through boulder fields can be very heavy going, but once in place, such a trail is virtually immune to the ravages of weather, erosion, and wear that affect pathways composed of less durable materials.

Careful surveying through boulder fields can simplify the challenge facing a construction crew. Sometimes a thoroughfare presents itself that requires little more than moving a few large rocks and then filling the voids among those that are left with smaller rocks and crushed stone to form a passable tread. In other cases, construction may necessitate the incorporation of rock retaining walls, steps, and other structures to hold crushed stone in place and carry the trail across complicated terrain.

Whatever the situation, work with the shape of the boulder field rather than fighting against it. A large boulder blocking a potential route may, with a minimum of effort, be moved a few feet to fit into an outside retaining wall. A route that won't quite accommodate a trail through the rocks might become very feasible with the inclusion of a couple of steps or a ramp consisting of a retaining wall holding in crushed stone.

Plating the Tread

Crushed rock may be used in locations other than boulder fields to create a dry, durable tread. It is especially useful on trails that receive extremely heavy use, that cross muddy areas where an earthen tread would be difficult to maintain, or where ease of access for a wide range of trail users is of high importance.

Stones used for tread plating should be no larger than 1.5 inches in diameter, laid across the full width of the tread to a depth of at least 3 inches. Where the underlying soil is particularly mucky, a layer of geo-textile fabric placed beneath the rocks may prevent them from sinking into the mud.

Tread can sometimes be plated with rock found near the trail and crushed with a sledgehammer. Gravel may be moved from a trailhead to a work site in wheelbarrows, panniers on mules or pack horses, or even by helicopter.

Signing and Blazing Trails

Trail marking is done for a variety of reasons:

- Identifying the beginning of a route
- Indicating distances to probable destinations
- Reassuring travellers that they are on the correct path
- Drawing attention to points of interest
- Restricting use as a means of resource protection
- Warning of potential hazards
- Marking junctions with roads and other trails
- Pointing out lakes, streams, campsites, and other features noted on maps, area guides, or trailhead signs
- Locating administrative boundaries

Painted blazes work best on bark that is clean and fairly smooth.

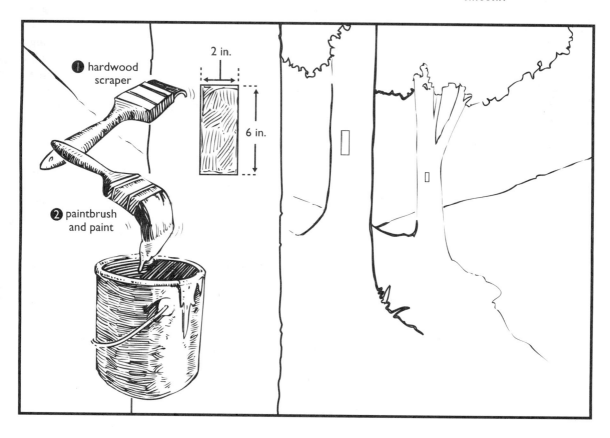

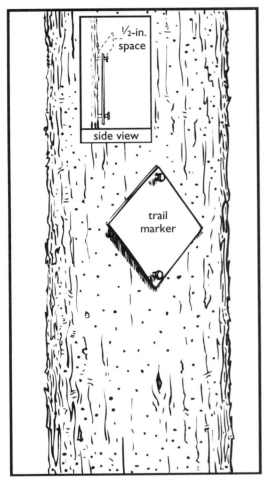

Metal or plastic trail markers can be moved if a route changes or the tree grows.

The broader the variety of user groups expected on a trail, the more intensively a route will probably be marked. Thus, a short barrier-free trail that includes numerous points of interest will usually have more signs than a long wilderness route used only by backpackers and an occasional horseback rider.

The way in which a trail is signed or blazed can have a great impact on the feel of the pathway and the experience of users. As with many other features of backcountry work, the methods of marking trails are heavily influenced by the traditions of the regions they cross. For example, the entire 2,100-mile length of the Appalachian Trail is marked with painted blazes 2 inches wide and 6 inches high. A hiker can conceivably travel all the way from Georgia to Maine with no more navigational help than simply looking from one blaze to the next.

On the other hand, the Pacific Crest Trail makes its 2,600-mile journey from Mexico to Canada with minimal reliance on blazes. There are signs at major intersections, and a tag with the Pacific Crest Trail emblem may appear every few miles. One result of the PCT's sparing use of markers is that hikers must be somewhat skillful with a map and compass to be certain they are going the right way.

An interesting case in point is the experience at Philmont, a national camp of the Boy Scouts of America. For several decades, the camp's 300-mile trail network in New Mexico's Sangre de Cristo Mountains was heavily marked with location and mileage information routed into wooden signs placed at almost every point where backpackers might become confused. In recent years, though, Philmont has removed signs at all but the most important trailheads and junctions. The camp has realized a savings in sign maintenance and replacement costs, and Scouts in the backcountry have come to rely more on their route-finding abilities.

Due to the maze of trails crisscrossing some regions, and the complexity of the terrain through which those trails pass, painted blazes are common in Eastern states. Historically, each trail club had a distinctively colored blaze with which to mark the routes they built and maintained. The Dartmouth Outing Club, for example, used three bands of paint—orange, black, orange—to mark their trails in western New Hampshire and Vermont. Vermont's Long Trail was the first major route to use white blazes, followed by the Appalachian Trail, which also used blue blazes to indicate side trails.

In the Rockies and other Western mountain ranges, foresters of the 1800s and much of the 1900s chopped blazes into trees. Early Forest Service manuals describe the proper blaze as being a cut about 2 inches square centered above a second cut that was 2 inches wide and 6 inches high. In recent decades, chopping blazes into trees has been abandoned in favor of trail signs or metal or plastic route emblems attached to posts. When emblems must be placed on trees, it is best to use aluminum nails to avoid rust, and to drive the heads no closer than an inch from the bark. As the tree grows, the nails can be pulled and the emblem reset without undue damage either to the tree or to the sign.

Determining whether and how to mark trails is freighted with as many factors as most other backcountry work decisions. In general, minimalist marking is probably the best approach, leaving to trail users those navigational decisions they will be capable of making on their own. Any blazing should be done in such a way that it can be reversed if the route changes or user patterns demand a different kind of trail marking. Painted blazes can be obliterated by covering them with bark-colored paint, and stone cairns can be dismantled. Metal and plastic emblems can be removed with little harm to the trees.

Trail Drainage

A SAYING AMONG TRAIL MAINTENANCE CREWS is that the three greatest enemies of a trail are water, water, and water. Where water can run down a trail, it may gully out the tread and eventually destroy the pathway. If water stands in puddles, travelers will try to go around it, breaking down vegetation and creating bootleg trails paralleling the main route. Trails cut into hillsides sometimes open seeps that saturate the tread. Springs or creeks may change course over time and send water onto the route. A flat section of trail may fall victim to pools of rainwater or snowmelt.

One of the chief challenges facing backcountry workers is devising ways to prevent water from damaging trails. Ideally, pathways built along hillsides will have an outsloped tread that allows water to flow off the pathway before it can do any damage. However, where an outslope cannot be maintained, where the volume of water coming onto a trail overwhelms the ability of the outslope to shed it, where pools of water form, or where trail users exacerbate the effects of erosion, drainage structures may be needed to insure a long life for the trail.

Your first temptation when you find water on a trail may be to start digging ditches and installing water bars. Before you touch a shovel, though, figure out the overall causes of the problem. Look uphill. Follow streamlets up the slope far enough to see how they are interconnected and to locate their sources. Walk up a creek 50 yards or more to understand the shape and effects of the channel. Look for vegetation that thrives in moist soil. Where a saturated backslope oozes water onto the trail, probe the earth with a stick until you have defined the extent of the seep. If possible, explore the trail and its surroundings during a rainstorm; there is no better way to decipher drainage patterns than when there is a whole lot of drainage going on.

With a knowledge of where the water is coming from and how it is reaching and affecting the trail, you can devise an effective means of dealing with it. There are two clear options—moving the water away from the trail, or moving the trail away from the water.

Grade Dips and Drain Dips

In the new construction of a sidehill trail, *grade dips* can be surveyed into the route so that a descending pathway occasionally reverses grade, gently rises to create a foot of elevation gain called *freeboard*, then resumes its descent. Water flowing down the trail will be diverted from the tread because it cannot climb over the freeboard. Known in the East as Coweeta dips, grade dips are permanent and usually maintenance-free. They often take advantage of natural features, descending into and then climbing out of slight folds in the terrain. Grade dips are ideal for trails frequented by bicycle riders or wheelchairs because they provide for barrier-free drainage.

A grade dip is especially important when a route crosses the bed of a stream or some other terrain feature that could carry water in a storm. Shape the trail so that it descends into the drainage and then climbs back out. That will prevent water in the drainage from flowing onto the tread. (For more on designing grade dips, see Chapter 8, "Trail Survey and Design.")

Dips can also be dug into existing tread. U.S. Forest Service specifications refer to these as *drain dips* to differentiate them from the *grade dips* surveyed into new trail construction. Drain dips can most effectively be installed in trails with a prevailing grade of no more than 12 percent. The dip must be large enough to divert water from the trail and to withstand the impact of travelers' feet, hooves, and wheels. Outslope the dip to direct water toward the spill point, and protect the spillway with rocks.

Water Bars

Where grade dips have not been surveyed into the original trail design and drain dips are inappropriate, water bars can be used to solve a wide range of drainage problems. They can be placed in a trail to improve upon existing drainage patterns, and to divert snowmelt, rain, and seepage from the tread. Water bars are almost always placed in switchbacks and in climbing turns to prevent water flowing down the upper leg of a trail from continuing onto the lower leg.

A water bar is made up of three parts:
- A log or rock bar that rises no more than a couple of inches above the tread
- 5 feet or more of tread called an *apron* that is shaped to direct water off the trail
- An outlet ditch

Angled across the trail, the bar stabilizes the apron and serves as the barrier of last resort to redirect water that has not been turned from the tread by outsloping. The factors determining the angle of a water bar in relation to the tread are the grade of the trail and the velocity of the water that will approach the barrier. On gentle

Wooden Water Bar, bird's-eye view

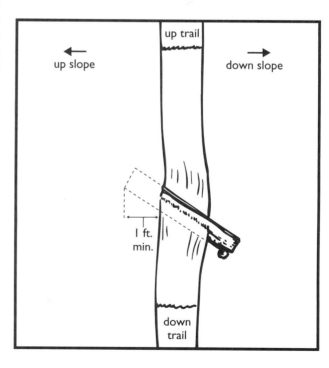

up trail

← up slope

down slope →

1 ft. min.

down trail

trails, a bar set at a 20- to 30-degree angle may be enough. On steeper routes where the speed of the water may wash out barriers embedded at shallow angles, bars may need to be set at angles of 45 degrees or more.

The smaller the angle, the less material will be required to build the barrier and the easier it will be for travelers to step across. Water slowed by bars without much of an angle may drop silt against the barrier, while bars set at sharper angles may be self-cleaning because the water moves past them quickly enough to carry silt off the trail.

In determining where to place a water bar, select a site where travelers will be discouraged from going around the ends of the bar. A tree or boulder can be a good barrier. If no natural barriers present themselves, embed a few large rocks near one or both ends of the water bar to direct traffic toward the center of the trail.

Once the bar has been installed, sculpt the tread for 5 feet or more leading down to the bar in such a way that water will gradually turn off of the pathway, exiting the trail a foot or more before hitting the bar itself. Test the effectiveness of this funnel-shaped apron by rolling an orange toward the water bar; the track of the orange will indicate the route that water will take.

Complete the water bar by digging an outlet ditch from the low point of the apron far enough to assure that water will be carried away from the trail. Steep sideslopes may not require ditches at all, while a water bar ditch on a moderate hillside may extend several yards or more. Cut each ditch wider than the blade of a shovel to facilitate easy maintenance in years to come. On steeper slopes, stones placed below the end of the ditch will dissipate the force of exiting water and help protect the downslope from erosion.

Soil removed during the construction or maintenance of a water bar can be shoveled against the down-trail side of the bar to reinforce it and to lessen the height of the step over the structure. Some trail builders also advocate packing soil against the upper side of a water bar barrier to restore the curving outslope of the tread, especially when erosion has begun to undercut the bar.

BUILDING WATER BARS WITH ROCK

Because of its durability, rock is the material of choice for building water bars. As with all rock construction, use large, well-shaped stones. Dig a trench across the tread at the appropriate angle, extending it 12 inches into the backslope. Make

Rock Water Bar, bird's-eye view

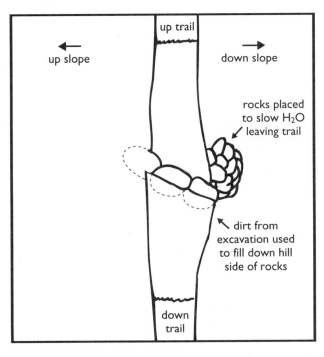

up trail

← up slope

→ down slope

rocks placed to slow H$_2$O leaving trail

dirt from excavation used to fill down hill side of rocks

down trail

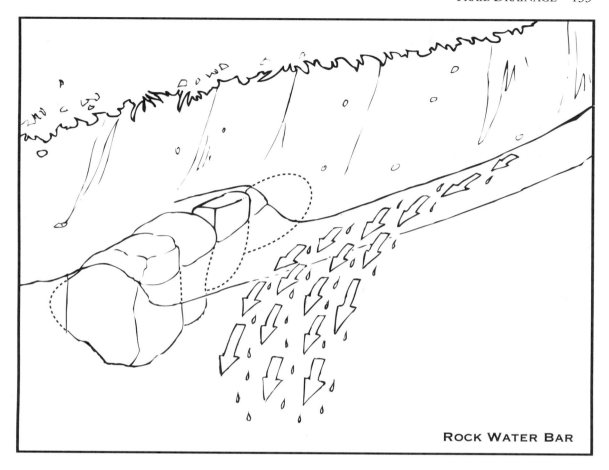

ROCK WATER BAR

the trench deep enough to accommodate most of the height of the rocks, then set them in the trench to form a water bar that rises no more than 1 to 2 inches above the level of the tread. Place each rock so that its length and mass are embedded low in the trail in such a way that people stepping on them will drive them deeper into the tread rather than kicking them loose. The contact points between the rocks must be secure, and the sides of the rocks facing up the trail must be matched and fitted tightly together to prevent water from washing through the barrier. Test the rocks by dancing on them. If they wiggle, try again.

Large, thin rocks and stone slabs can sometimes be tipped up on edge and embedded vertically to form a water bar. Prop the rocks in place so that they fit together tightly to stop water, or overlap them like shingles from the inside of the tread to the outside to allow water to flow from one to the next and off the trail. Pack smaller stones into the spaces between the sides of the ditch and the rocks, pounding the stones with a hammer to wedge the water bar rocks into place.

The rocks embedded in a rock water bar are the barrier of last resort. The slope of the trail itself should shed most of the water.

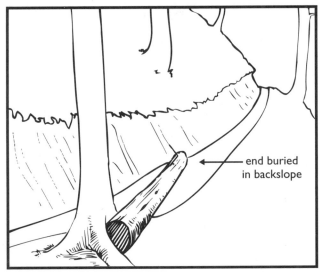

Above: *A log used as a water bar can be butted against a tree or large rock.*
Below: *A water bar log embedded in a trench can sometimes be further secured with wooden stakes.*

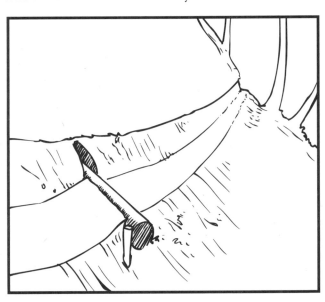

BUILDING WATER BARS WITH WOOD

A timber water bar should be built with a sound, peeled log of the most rot-resistant species available. It should be a minimum of 8 inches in diameter, and long enough to be angled from the outside edge of the trail to a point 12 inches deep in the backslope.

Dig a trench across the tread and 1 foot or more into the backslope. Lay the log in the trench. The log should lie at a depth so that only a couple of inches extend above the tread. Crews sometimes score the top of a water bar log with a saw and then flatten it with an adz to provide a more secure step for travelers.

In some parts of the country, crews building water bars embed the end of the log with the greater diameter in the hillside in the belief that burying the extra bulk will help prevent the log from sliding out of position. Crews elsewhere advocate orienting the end with the larger diameter toward the outside edge of the tread where the additional size can be used to turn the water flowing against the bar.

Abutting one or both ends of the log against trailside trees or boulders will help make it more permanent. However, a subject of regional debate is whether to drive wooden stakes on either side of the downslope end of the water bar. Many trail maintainers are convinced that stakes add enough stability to the water bar that they are worth the time and bother. Some crews in rocky regions pin the ends of their water bars to the ground with lengths of steel reinforcement bar driven into holes drilled through the logs. Others, also working from their own observations, don't believe stakes make much difference.

As with many points of trail work, deciding whether to stake water bars or which end of a log should go uphill is a matter of specific conditions, local precedent, and loyalty to the traditional methods used by one's crew.

BUILDING WHEEL-FRIENDLY WATER BARS

Many agencies are designating certain backcountry trails for use by bicycle riders. Most

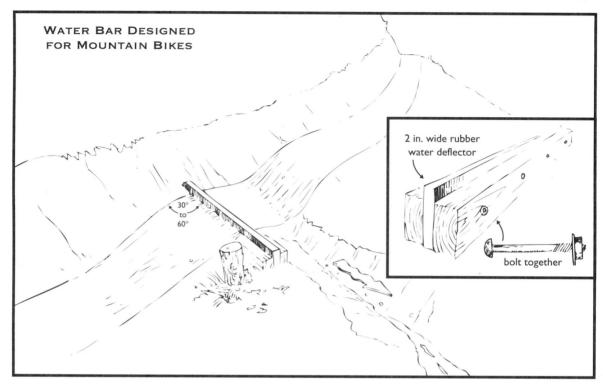

WATER BAR DESIGNED
FOR MOUNTAIN BIKES

30°
to
60°

2 in. wide rubber
water deflector

bolt together

mountain bikers seem immune to the jolt of pedalling over traditional water bars, but the water bars themselves take a tremendous beating from the direct impact of the wheels.

The U.S. Forest Service has designed a water deflector for trails that will receive heavy bicycle use. Two 2-inch x 10-inch pieces of treated lumber, cut to water bar length, are bolted together with a stiff strip of ½-inch x 13-inch rubber conveyor belt inserted between them. The boards are buried in a water bar trench at a depth that allows several inches of the rubber to extend above the tread. The rubber will divert water as effectively as a rock or log water bar, but will flex under the weight of a bicycle wheel.

Bicycle water bars require frequent monitoring to insure that the boards remain buried and do not become a hazard to cyclists.

The rubber barrier of a wheel-friendly water bar will flex as a bicycle passes over it.

A check step or check dam should be securely embedded in the earth.

Check Dams and Check Steps

Check dams slow the flow of water in gullies in order to prevent further erosion and to allow silt to build up behind the structures. Check steps serve the same purpose in rutted-out trails. They are effective tools

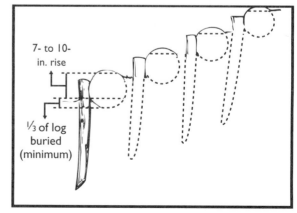

7- to 10-
in. rise

⅓ of log
buried
(minimum)

*Check steps can slow
erosion in rutted trails.*

for salvaging badly eroded tread and for restoring closed trails and damaged slopes, but are not suitable on routes used by livestock or wheeled vehicles.

Construct check dams and steps from peeled logs or sizeable rocks, extending the ends of each dam or step well into the sides of the ditch so that water cannot sneak around them. Filling behind the rock or logs with small stones or mineral soil will allow the structures to be used as steps. On closed trails or in gullies that are not traveled, the space behind the rock or logs can be left empty to provide room for silt to accumulate, or it can be filled with fertile soil and planted with native vegetation.

Over time, wooden check dams will decompose and melt into the landscape. After they have served their purpose, check dams made of rock can sometimes be removed and the rocks scattered to give the area a more natural appearance.

Open Drains

On hiker-only trails, a shallow trench can sometimes be cut through the tread to channel water across a trail. An open drain of this type may be especially effective for dealing with a constant water source such as a spring. However, an open trench should never be used on trails frequented by horses or pack stock that could be injured by stumbling into it. Excavated trenches tend to collapse under the impact of hikers' boots. The walls and floor of the drain can be reinforced with carefully placed rocks, the faces matched to provide an even walking surface.

Filling an open drain with gravel turns it into a *French drain* that may provide safer footing for travelers and prevent the sides of the ditch from breaking down. French drains are effective where the water is clear, such as a spring or seep, and the rock filling the ditch is not too small. If silt clogs the spaces in the gravel, it will block the flow of water and render a French drain useless.

Culverts

Culverts are drainage structures designed to conduct water beneath a trail. Their great advantage over ditches and water bars is that the tread extends across

The end of a culvert pipe buried in a trail can be shielded from view with a facing of rock.

PIPE CULVERT, CUTAWAY VIEW

PIPE CULVERT, SIDE VIEW

culverts without interruption. They have relatively little visual impact on a trail, and are not likely to be kicked out of place by hikers or horses.

PLASTIC AND METAL CULVERTS

The easiest culverts to build feature a plastic or metal pipe. Dig a ditch across the tread sufficiently large to accommodate a piece of culvert pipe. The culvert should be buried deeply enough to allow at least a foot of soil to shield it from damage, especially by the hooves of horses. Cut the pipe so that it is about the width of the tread, then build a rock facing around each end to hide the pipe and prevent it from being washed loose.

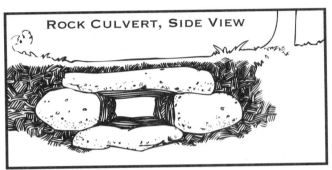

Plastic culvert is often preferable to metal because it is lighter to transport into the backcountry and can be cut to length with a hacksaw or a sharp knife. The drab color of most plastic culvert pipe will not catch a hiker's eye. When using aluminum pipe, many crews paint each end black, both inside and out, to camouflage it.

Where large, well-shaped rocks are available, a rock culvert is a durable, aesthetic drainage solution.

A rock culvert must be built with care so that each stone fits tightly against the others.

ROCK CULVERTS

Begin the construction of a rock culvert by laying large, flat stones in a trench to form the culvert floor, then install large, well-matched stones along either side of the trench. Place them so that the sides of the culvert will be at least a few inches wider than the width of a shovel blade, enabling maintainers to scoop silt and debris out of the structure. Complete the culvert by spanning the side rocks with large, flat stones placed securely enough to withstand the footsteps of trail users. If possible, cover the top rocks with an earthen tread to conceal and protect the culvert.

WOODEN CULVERTS

Culverts can sometimes be constructed from logs harvested and peeled near a project site. Since the wood will be in contact with water and soil, the life span of the structure may not be great. Monitor wooden culverts regularly, and repair or replace them before they become a danger to livestock or travelers.

Dig a trench deep enough to place base logs below water level, then build on top of them, securing the sill logs with spikes. The logs forming the platform for the tread should be split and spiked to the sills. Larger

logs on either side of the platform will hold in place the soil that forms a tread over the platform.

For culverts built of milled lumber, select materials hefty enough to do the job right. Line each side of the ditch with planks no smaller than 4 inches x 12 inches, and place planks of similar dimensions across the top. Lay an earthen tread over the culvert and, if possible, build rock facings to shield the open ends and to hold fill material on top of the structure.

Ease the work of future trail maintainers by building culverts wider than the width of a shovel.

CULVERT SETTLING BASINS

Water flowing toward a culvert is often laden with silt. If the water slows as it goes under the trail, the silt may settle out and eventually clog the culvert. One solution to that problem is to dig a *settling basin* at the mouth of the culvert. The basin should be at least a foot deeper than the floor of the culvert, and can

A wooden culvert may feature logs spanning the drain. The logs will be covered with stone and earth to form a continuous trail tread over the culvert.

be lined with rocks. Before flowing into the culvert, water should stand long enough in the basin to drop its silt. Trail maintainers will find it much easier to scoop silt out of an open basin than to remove it from inside an obstructed culvert.

As with all drainage structures, it may be wise to use rocks to plate the slope beneath the exit of the culvert. The rocks will dissipate the force of water discharging from the culvert and prevent downslope erosion.

Bogs and Mudholes

In flat terrain, water collecting on a trail may form pools. Likewise, bogs can impede traffic during certain seasons of the year. Construction and maintenance crews can approach these wet areas with a series of increasingly involved steps:

1. Drain the area. Ditching toward a slight slope of the landscape may be enough to persuade water to flow away from the trail.
2. Move the trail. Rather than fighting through wet ground, crews may simply relocate the route to a higher, drier location.
3. Install stepping stones.
4. Build a turnpike.
5. Construct puncheon.

Stepping Stones

Where there is foot traffic but no use of livestock or bicycles, stepping stones may provide dry footing through wet terrain. Schedule this work with a eye to the calendar and the weather. Deciding where to place stepping stones is best done during the wettest time of the year; installing stepping stones is easiest to do when the trail is dry.

Trail crews of the Adirondack Mountain Club and Appalachian Mountain Club embed stepping stones by using the same principle that allows a ball of ice cream to fit snugly into a cone. Choose a large rock of 100 pounds or

A stepping stone won't wobble if it is set in place like a ball of ice cream in a cone.

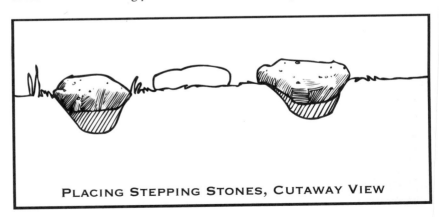

PLACING STEPPING STONES, CUTAWAY VIEW

more for each stepping stone, one with a flat face that will assure good footing. Dig a cone-shaped hole with a rim about the size and shape of the rock's circumference.

Flip the rock into the hole. If the cone is properly sized, the rock will drop until the edges seal tightly against the soil, leaving the walking surface of the stone several inches above the surrounding earth. There may be an air pocket beneath the rock, but the tapered walls of the cone will prevent the stone from sinking too far.

Stepping stones or fords are simple, low-maintenance ways for trails to cross shallow streams.

Turnpikes

Turnpikes lift trail tread above saturated soil. They are often combined with ditches, culverts, and other drainage structures to relieve a trail of water from seeps and streams. Building a turnpike is labor- and material-intensive, and it may be easier to reroute a trail to drier ground than to construct a turnpike. If there are no alternative pathway locations, though, turnpikes made of rocks or logs can carry a trail across problematic terrain.

BUILDING TURNPIKES WITH ROCK

Dig a foundation trench on either side of the trail, keeping the inside edges of the trench 36 inches apart for hiker trails, or 48 inches for horse trails. The depth of the trenches should measure about two-thirds the height of the rocks they will hold.

Lay a row of rocks in each trench to form a one-tier wall. Match the rocks to form a fairly flat top surface. Fit every rock tightly against the stone beside it, and embed each rock solidly in the earth. Fill the spaces around the rocks with smaller stones, packing them tightly to wedge every rock in place. While the fit is not as critical in a turnpike as it is in a retaining wall, water bar, or set of steps,

Rocks set tightly together form the sides of a rock turnpike.

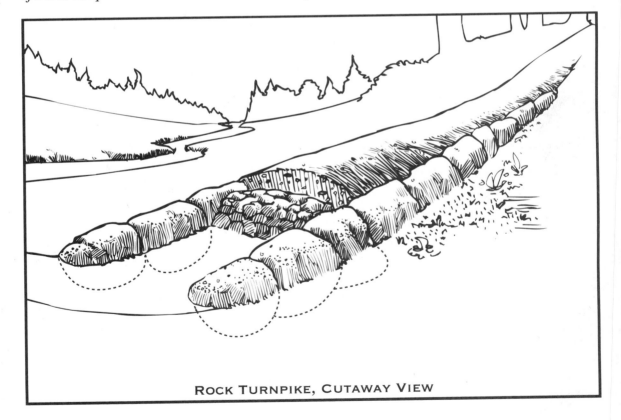

ROCK TURNPIKE, CUTAWAY VIEW

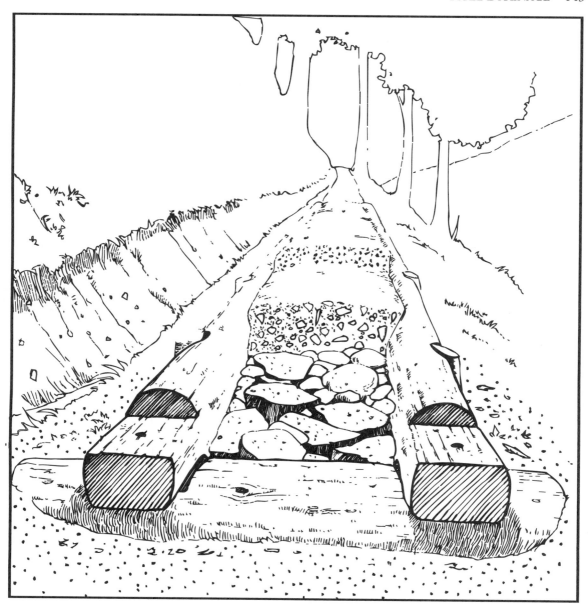

do not be satisfied with the placement of a rock until it remains motionless when you dance on top of it.

After the parallel rows of rocks are in place, fill the area between them with layers of small stones or crushed rock and, where it is readily available, a top layer of soil. The stones will allow moisture to flow through the turnpike while the dirt, crowned up in the center, forms a tread that will shed rain. Turnpikes sometimes have ditches along one or both sides to facilitate drainage. The

Log turnpike, cutaway view. The structure is filled with rock and gravel, and the gravel is often topped with soil to form an inviting tread.

earth excavated from the ditches may be appropriate for use as fill material in the turnpike.

Muddy ground may suck up crushed stone almost as fast as you can dump it into a turnpike. Some crews have had good success lining the bottom of their turnpikes with *geo-textile cloth,* a durable fabric designed specifically for use in outdoor construction projects. Secure the cloth to the ground with horseshoe-shaped pins made of heavy wire to prevent the geo-textile from sliding out of position. Stone and earth placed on top of the cloth will not sink into the ooze.

BUILDING TURNPIKES WITH LOGS

Peeled logs used for a turnpike must have a minimum diameter of 10 inches at the smaller end. If the structure will include culvert pipe to allow cross-trail drainage, install the pipe first. Secure the logs on either side of the tread by partially embedding them in the soil, driving large wooden stakes into the ground against the outside faces of the logs, or both. The distance between the logs will vary depending on local specifications, but is generally 3 feet for hiking trails and 4 feet for trails used by horses and pack animals. Fill between the logs with crushed stone and mineral soil, just as you would for a turnpike built with rock.

Logs laid end to end for a long turnpike can simply be butted against one another or joined together with lap joints. In particularly boggy locations, consider placing sills under the turnpike logs; the turnpike will be higher than if there were no sills, and stringers spiked to sills will be less likely to roll out of position.

Puncheon

Building puncheon is but a small remove from constructing bridges over wet ground. (For more on puncheon, stringers, and sills, see Chapter 15, "Bridge Construction.")

Corduroy

Corduroy was once a common construction method for carrying roads and trails across wet ground. A stretch of corduroy consisted of logs 4 to 6 inches in diameter laid side by side to form the travel surface. The logs were sometimes staked in place or nailed to timbers placed beneath them. Corduroy is still used with success by Eastern states crews to harden ski routes, in the Pacific Northwest as a makeshift way of getting hikers over a bog until a more permanent solution can be found, and in some wetland regions of Alaska to allow access through otherwise impassable terrain.

The problems with corduroy are many. If the wood does not remain wet all the time, it can quickly rot. Rather than solving a drainage difficulty, corduroy may simply compound it by obstructing the flow of water with a mass of wood. Corduroy is dangerous for horses, and should be removed from trails they are likely to use.

Stream Fords

Fords should not be built in streams where the water is swift or its depth exceeds 3 feet during the normal season of use. The safety of travelers, not the ease of construction or cost of a project, should be the primary factor for choosing between a ford or a bridge.

That said, given the choice of crossing a stream with a bridge or a ford, build the ford. It will be simple and quick to construct and maintain, and has virtually no visual impact on an area.

To build a ford, select a location where the stream is shallow. Remove large rocks and level the stream bottom to make a smooth crossing for foot or horse traffic. The trail approaches should descend toward the ford in such a way that water from the stream will not flow onto the tread.

In fast-moving streams, the ford can often be improved by pulling large rocks into a line across the stream parallel with the trail and just below the downstream edge of the crossing. Sand and gravel deposited by the stream above the barrier will result in a smooth, level, underwater tread. The same result may be achieved in streams with slow currents by placing a large log across the lower edge of the ford and securing it in place with rocks.

In fording deeply, a heavy stone in the hands, above water, will strengthen your position.

Howard Henderson
PRACTICAL HINTS ON CAMPING (CHICAGO: JANSEN, MCCLURG AND CO., 1882), P. 43.

CHAPTER 11

Trail Maintenance

THE ARTISTRY OF BACKCOUNTRY MAINTENANCE involves problem-solving of the highest order. Where trails have been neglected for a long time, or in places where avalanches, floods, fires, switchback cutters, or other natural and unnatural acts have caused havoc, even the most experienced backcountry workers can find challenge and satisfaction in restoring tread to a safe, usable condition. Likewise, basic maintenance can be broken down into steps that are manageable by people of almost any skill and energy level, from gradeschoolers to senior citizens.

In the long run, regular repair of a trail is cost-effective. A modest program each year can keep a trail in good shape, while failing to care for it will eventually lead either to much heavier and more expensive maintenance, or to the closure and loss of the trail. Crews going into the field must take advantage of the opportunity to care for trails by working as efficiently as possible since another crew may not return to the area for some time.

Trail Maintenance Survey

Information is power. The more that land managers know about a pathway and the entire trail network of an area, the more effectively they can decide where and how to deploy the labor resources available to them. Chapter 8, "Trail Survey and Design," includes guidelines for conducting maintenance surveys that can be used to document the general condition of each section of a trail and to catalog the stations where specific maintenance tasks should be performed.

Crew leaders visiting an area to examine a project before the work begins will, ideally, be given the results of a maintenance survey and the assurance that stakes and flagging have been used to mark work points along the trail. By walking the route with the survey log in hand, especially in the company of a land-management representative, work-group leaders can readily see what is expected of them and their crew.

Of course, the ideal seldom happens in real life. Crew leaders are much more likely to have a land manager point out a trail on a map and leave it to them to determine what should be done to bring the route up to acceptable standards. Even so, try to persuade the land manager to walk the trail with you and, if possible, conduct a thorough maintenance survey to pinpoint specific maintenance tasks before the crew arrives.

Nature is at work when man sleeps. By lack of use or want of proper care, an ordinary path in a section of country not much frequented, becomes extinct in a few years, and a camp a mass of ruins.

"COUNCILLOR OF IMPROVEMENTS REPORT," *APPALACHIA* (JULY 1880), P. 166.

All trails should be repaired every year.

TRAIL CONSTRUCTION ON THE NATIONAL FORESTS, (U.S. FOREST SERVICE, 1915), P. 60.

Typical Maintenance Problems, Causes, and Solutions

BRUSHING TRAIL CORRIDORS

Beating back the biomass is a never-ending task to keep many trails open. The goal of brushing is to restore the clearances specified for the travel corridor. For hiking trails, that usually means clearing 2 to 3 feet on each side of the center of the trail and about 8 feet overhead. Pack and saddle stock require a clearance of 4 feet to each side of the centerline and 10 feet overhead. Some crews decide how extensively to brush by asking themselves if they could walk a segment of a hiking trail or ride a horse path after a rainstorm without becoming soaked by wet foliage.

With that in mind, common sense should guide your decisions about what to remove and what to leave. It is a balance of cutting back the vegetation that truly impacts the trail corridor now (or will in the future), while leaving plants that by their size have gained tenure in their locations. A large tree within the boundaries of the trail corridor should probably not be cut down if travelers can get past it without difficulty or if a slight alteration in the tread location will create sufficient clearance. On the other hand, crews should not be so timid about using their loppers and saws that they fail to create a passable corridor. Cutting back small trees today, for example, may relieve a future maintainer from having to contend with them when they are full-grown and creating a real obstruction.

Brushing a trail during maintenance embraces the same principles as does clearing a corridor in preparation for the construction of a new route. Grass and other succulent plants can be cut back with a weed whip. Use loppers to nip bushes and saplings. Saw tree branches close to the trunk, first undercutting each branch so that it will not strip the bark as it falls. Reach branches overhead with a pole saw, and cut them near the trunk. Protect travelers from tripping by cutting stumps flush with the earth.

At obvious viewpoints along a route, removing a few branches, clearing away brush, and perhaps felling a snag or a small tree may open up views that will enhance the experience of trail users. In many cases, improving a vista so that it can be enjoyed from the trail will subtly encourage travelers not to leave the pathway in search of a better view.

Keep an eye out for *hazard trees*—snags that are leaning toward the trail and that may fall across the tread. Since dead trees are often home to many forest animals, crews should remove them only if they present an immediate danger to travelers, or if maintenance is so infrequent that trees that do fall will cause considerable problems for trail users until a crew returns. Dead trees standing outside a trail corridor may also be outside the scope of

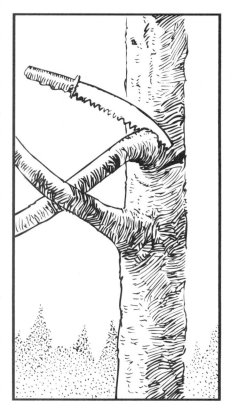

Saw branches flush with the trunk to avoid leaving **hat racks.**

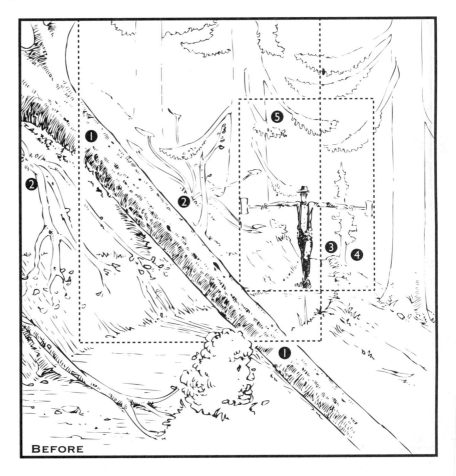

BEFORE

general maintenance. Consult with land managers before removing them.

Pathway maintenance at high altitudes, especially in alpine tundra, presents special challenges for trail workers. Alpine vegetation grows much more slowly than vegetation in the valleys below. Plants in harsh environments are also dependent upon one another for shelter from the wind, stability of the soil, and other factors that insure their survival. Removing one plant may have long-term effects on the health of neighboring greenery. Dislodging rocks can leave fragile soil susceptible to erosion by wind and water. The bottom line is to be extremely conservative and prudent in maintaining trails near or above timberline.

Brushing and User Psychology. Deciding what to cut and what to leave is best done when maintainers take into account the psychology of trail users. Hikers and horses tend to travel on the outside portion of the tread, keeping a

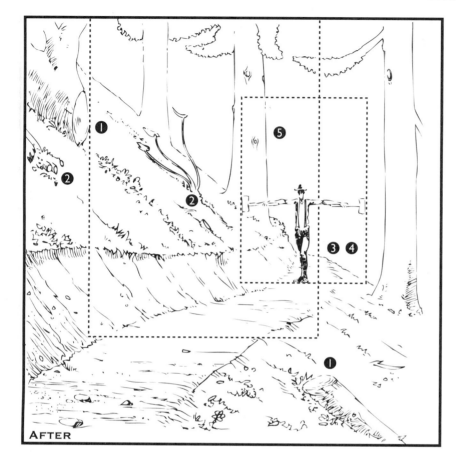

AFTER

*Restoring a trail corri-
dor (dotted lines) may
involve sawing logs (1),
cutting brush and sap-
lings level with the
ground (2 and 4), and
removing tree branches
(5). Crews may also
remove any earthen
berm from the edge of
the tread (3).*

cushion of distance between themselves and the backslope. Bicyclists also drift toward the outer edge of a trail so that they will not scrape a pedal against the backslope. Some crews combat that behavior by cutting brush only on the uphill side of a trail. Travelers attempting to maintain their sense of space may shy away from the brushier lower side of the trail and stay more to the center of the tread.

User behavior may also lead a crew to leave vegetation untouched. For example, cutting brush too far back from the trail can open up a corridor that may tempt trail users to travel side-by-side, thus widening the compacted tread, while a less aggressive approach to brushing can encourage single-file travel. A large log lying across the tread near the beginning of a trail closed to bicycle and motorcycle riders can be an effective deterrent to inappropriate use. Hikers can step over the log or through a notch cut into it, while riders may be less inclined to make the effort to get past.

CLEANING WATER BARS, CULVERTS, AND OTHER DRAINAGE STRUCTURES

A trail may already have a number of water bars, culverts, and other drainage structures built into it. Light maintenance of those structures includes clearing them of silt and organic debris. More ambitious efforts may also involve repairing or replacing the structures themselves, or installing new drainage structures in trail sections that warrant their use.

WATER BARS

- Reset loose water bar rocks and replace water bar logs showing signs of decay.
- With a shovel, McLeod, or fire rake, reshape the tread to form a funnel-like apron approaching the bar so that water will again run off the pathway before hitting the bar itself. Do not undermine the bar by sculpting the apron too deeply. Pile loosened soil against the down-trail side of the water bar to ease the slope of the tread as it descends away from the bar, or pack the earth against the uphill side of the bar to restore the apron and to shield the bar from erosion.
- Remove any debris from the ditch through which water exits the trail.

Maintain drainage structures by removing silt and debris from ditches and culverts.

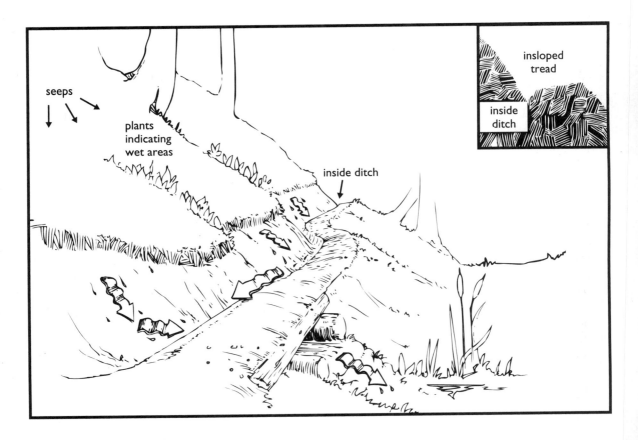

Some crews refer to this as *daylighting* a water bar—that is, clearing the drainage route so that water coming off the tread has an open run to daylight. Clear any ditches that are above the trail, too.

CULVERTS

- Run a shovel through culverts to remove silt and debris. If a culvert is too narrow to accommodate a shovel blade, use the handle.
- Clear debris from ditches and settling basins leading to and from culverts. Silt can be used to fill ruts in trail tread.
- Repair or replace culverts that are in poor condition.

BRIDGES, TURNPIKES, AND PUNCHEON

Load-bearing structures made of wood must be inspected regularly for signs of decay. Evidence of rot may require the dismantling and reconstruction of a bridge or puncheon to keep it in safe, passable condition. The soundness of logs in turnpikes is not as critical, since they do not bear the weight of trail users.

Accurately assessing the condition of a bridge or puncheon should be done by land-management professionals versed in applicable safety standards. To get a general sense of whether a timber is suffering significant rot, try sticking the blade of a pocketknife into it. If the blade goes in easily, the wood has probably lost much of its original strength.

- Remove all organic material and soil from wooden surfaces. Accumulations of moss, pine needles, and debris on bridge and puncheon decking and at the ends of stringers can hold moisture that may decay the wood.
- Planks used for decking of puncheon or bridges are usually the first components to become worn. Crews can sometimes extend the lives of planks by turning them over and nailing them back in place.
- Inspect wooden structures for nails or spikes that have become exposed. Drive them flush with the wood or remove them so that they will not trip hikers or injure horses or mules that step on them.
- Reshape the approaches to bridges and puncheon, crowning the tread and smoothing the transition from the trail to the span.

ROCK STRUCTURES

Rock walls, steps, water bars, and other stone structures that have been properly built should require little maintenance. Even so, freezing and thawing, abuse by trail users, the growth of vegetation, and the effects of gravity can sometimes weaken rock constructions.

- Test rock structures by dancing on them. Every rock should stay firmly in place.
- Inspect walls for any indications that rocks are working loose. A wall can sometimes be stiffened by chinking smaller stones between large rocks.
- Rock structures that have become loose and wobbly should be dismantled and rebuilt. The same stones can almost always be used for the reconstruction, often in the same order.

DITCHED-OUT TRAIL BEFORE REPAIRS

An ever-widening braid of beaten-down trails is a common problem in meadows and alpine tundra.

- Examine the bottom tier of a wall and be sure it is still firmly embedded in solid soil or tightly fitted against rock. Where soil has eroded away, you may be able to prevent further undermining of a foundation tier by piling heavy stones against it.
- Restore the level of the fill material behind walls and inside cribbed steps.

DITCHED-OUT TRAILS IN OPEN TERRAIN

A trail that crosses a meadow, alpine tundra, or other open land can become a lacework of pathways worn down to varying depths. The underlying difficulty is that the original trail was in the wrong place. A route across open country is highly visible. Without obstacles such as rocks, underbrush, or trees bordering the trail, there is little to encourage travelers to stay on the tread. As the tread becomes worn down enough to make footing uncomfortable, hikers and horseback riders will begin beating secondary pathways into the ground next to the original route.

- Whenever possible, relocate the pathway to the edge of the open area and back into the trees. Trail users will still have occasional views of open

DITCHED-OUT TRAIL AFTER REPAIRS

country, but the route will be placed where people will be more inclined to stay on the tread and where drainage can be accomplished more successfully.

- If a trail cannot be moved, trenched-out tread may be restored to a usable state by filling it with mineral soil or crushed rock. Crown the filled trail, making it slightly higher than the surrounding ground to encourage water to run off to either side. Use restoration techniques to close and heal abandoned segments of tread alongside the chosen route.
- Unless a repaired trail is the most inviting way to go, travelers will continue to walk alongside it and create more bootleg paths. Scattering rocks or logs as though they had appeared naturally alongside the tread can encourage trail users to stay on the main route.

Close off unwanted trails and make the remaining tread the most inviting route for travelers.

TRENCHED-OUT TRAILS ON HILLSIDES

Trenched tread is a common problem on steep trails, especially those that come straight down a slope and leave nowhere for water to flow except along the tread itself.

Begin maintenance of a trenched trail by dealing with the cause of the erosion by slowing or diverting water from the route. There are several ways this can be done:

- Use water bars, ditches, and culverts to channel water beyond the tread.
- Where trails are too steep for drainage structures or where a trail goes straight down the fall line of a slope, install steps that will harden the tread and act as check dams to slow the velocity of water.
- Reroute the trail at a reasonable grade, then close the original location and use restoration techniques to help it heal and blend back into the landscape.

SLOUGH AND BERM ON HILLSIDE TRAILS

On trails traversing hillsides, *slough* is the name given to soil, rock, and silt that have accumulated on the inside of the tread, narrowing the walkway. *Berm* is debris that has built up on the outside of the tread, forming a barrier that prevents water from sheeting quickly off the trail. Both slough and berm can become overgrown with vegetation. Their removal is among the most customary and important tasks facing maintenance crews.

- Loosen compacted slough and berm with a mattock or Pulaski adz, then remove the soil with a shovel or McLeod. You may be able to place the soil behind retaining walls or use it to fill holes eroded in the tread. If not, scatter the earth some distance from the trail. Do not use loose soil to widen the tread, since it will almost never hold.
- Reshape the tread to restore a slight outslope that will allow water to drain immediately away from the trail rather than running down it.

SWITCHBACK MAINTENANCE

Switchbacks usually require maintenance more frequently than straight sections of trail. The outslope and inslope of a switchback and the shape of the turning platform are all critical to the structure's effectiveness and durability. Hikers cutting across switchbacks can trample vegetation and loosen rocks and soil, creating steep shortcuts that are prone to extreme erosion.

- Remove slough and berm to restore the original size to the switchback's legs and turning platform.
- Regrade the outslope of the lower trail leg and the inslope of the upper leg. Insure drainage by cleaning any debris from the inside edge of the upper leg and the ditch along the inside of the turning platform.
- Close off shortcuts in such a way that erosion will be stopped and hikers encouraged to stay on the trail. Shortcuts can be blocked with brush, rocks, or check dams, by transplanting thorny plants such as yucca, or by a combination of these methods.
- Where traffic is heavy or the hillside lacks the natural screening of underbrush to discourage switchback cutters, you may need to construct a rock wall or a log barrier along the top leg of the switchback.

BOGGY TRAIL

A section of tread that is very muddy or that holds standing water from storms or seeps can be a messy hassle for travelers and maintainers. Trail users will try to avoid getting wet feet by detouring around the mucky area, enlarging the problem by beating down vegetation and soil. Trails that are boggy in the spring-time may dry out by late summer. A good plan is to conduct a maintenance survey when the trail is very wet, mark with wooden stakes the locations of maintenance tasks to be accomplished, then return to perform the work when the trail is dry.

- As with all drainage situations, the first step in developing a solution for boggy trail is finding the source of the water. Explore the area around the trail for springs or seeps. If possible, visit the trail during different times of the year to monitor the seasonal wetness and dryness of the tread.
- Determine a way to channel water away from the trail with the use of ditches or drainage structures. Where standing water cannot be per-suaded to move on, consider elevating the tread above the mud with a turnpike or puncheon. Stepping stones may be appropriate on hiker-only trails. In most cases, draining a trail is easier than lifting the tread above wet ground.
- If a long section of tread is plagued by sloppy conditions, rerouting the trail to a drier location may be the best solution.
- Basic human kindness holds that crews working extensively in mud should be outfitted with rubber boots.

(For more on turnpikes, see Chapter 10, "Trail Drainage." For more on pun-cheon, see Chapter 15, "Bridge Construction.")

CHAPTER 12

Building with Rock

Something there is that
doesn't love a wall,
That sends the frozen-
ground-swell under it,
And spills the upper boul
ders in the sun;
And makes gaps even two
can pass abreast."
Robert Frost
"MENDING WALL," *NORTH
OF BOSTON* (NEW YORK:
HOLT, 1914).

Rocks for rustic
construction come
in three sizes: double
hernia, single hernia,
and too small.
Anonymous

ALL HUMAN CREATIONS EVENTUALLY MELT BACK into the land-scape, but the most enduring reminders of earlier generations are built of rock. Few wooden structures survive the centuries, especially if they are exposed to the elements. Ceramics, pottery, and items of metal may, if buried, travel gently down the continuum of time, but the pyramids, temples, statues, aqueducts, great walls, and other monumental stone edifices of humankind thrust themselves through the ages in full view.

If you have a selection of materials for rustic construction, rock is almost always preferable. The reason is simple; rock won't rot. Build it well, and a rock structure will be around long after you are gone—long after your entire civilization, too, if history is any indicator.

Rock has a multitude of uses in backcountry construction, from stepping stones and retaining walls to water bars, culverts, bridge foundations, turnpikes, and steps. Building with stone requires a particular kind of patience and spatial awareness that appeals to some people and frustrates others as they struggle to make round rocks (and triangular, flat, and other weirdly shaped rocks) fit into holes that are seldom square. It is not unlike putting together a jigsaw puzzle without the guidance of a picture to suggest where the pieces should go, assuming you can find the pieces in the first place.

In the 1920s, project engineer Samuel Lancaster toured Italy to study mountain road construction before beginning work on a highway along the Oregon side of the Columbia River Gorge. Near Naples he saw magnificent rock work. "There—that's the stuff we want, exactly!" he said. "Who built it? We'll hire him to duplicate it out there in the gorge. Has he got a reputation?"

"He's quite well known," replied the Italian engineer accompanying Lancaster, "but . . . "

"It doesn't matter. He's hired. Who is he?"

"That is the difficulty," said the Italian. "The builder, he is no longer here. His name was Julius Caesar."

Robert Ormond Case and Victoria Case
LAST MOUNTAINS: THE STORY OF THE CASCADES (GARDEN CITY, NEW YORK:
DOUBLEDAY, DORAN, INC., 1945), P. 73.

Choosing Good Rocks

Good rocks for building have well-defined edges and fairly flat sides. Big is better than small, and angular is better than round. Best of all are large, rectangular, keystone-shaped rocks with smooth faces.

Of course, the idea of good rocks is relative to what you can find and transport to the construction site. If there are plenty of large blocks of granite close to a project, conduct yourself with proper humility, for you are in rock heaven. If the only stones you can find are small and irregularly formed, the same construction guidelines will hold true, but the challenge of applying those guidelines will be greatly increased.

Whether you plan to harvest rocks from talus slopes, streambeds, or forest floors, consider the environmental impact. Stones stabilizing hillsides or stream banks are often better left where they are. Some rocks cannot be moved without tearing up fragile plant communities. Moving others could have a negative effect upon the visual aesthetics of an area.

All signs of disturbance should be erased from places where rocks have been taken. Holes should be refilled, particularly along trails that will be used by horses, and vegetation restored.

Shaping Rocks

Some rocks can be shaped to suit the demands of a project, and some rocks cannot. In general, hard igneous or metamorphic rock such as granite, gneiss, and basalt will fracture cleanly along fissures. Shale, sandstone, limestone, and other soft, sedimentary rocks are more likely to break apart in layers or to disintegrate into rubble. The best way to discover how rocks at a project site will respond to being shaped is to try breaking a few and seeing what happens.

Most shaping of rocks involves tapping off corners, removing nubs, and making other small adjustments to improve the fit of one rock against another. A geologist's hammer or a single-jack hammer is a good tool for this, sometimes aided by a cold chisel or a wide masonry chisel. Wear goggles whenever you swing a hammer against a rock or chisel.

Splitting large rocks into manageable blocks for construction or for removal from a trail tread can sometimes be done by drilling holes in line with an intended break and inserting sets of wedges and feathers. Driving the wedges with a hammer should crack the rock.

In the same way that the chain saw replaced the crosscut saw in the backcountry as the timber-cutting tool of choice, gasoline-powered rock drills have all but made drilling by hand obsolete. Gasoline drills can complete in ten or fifteen minutes a series of holes that would take all afternoon to drill manually.

However, just as crosscut saws have some advantages over chain saws, hand drilling can, in certain practical and aesthetic ways, justify the time it consumes.

Barrier Rock proved to be a very difficult piece of work. The rock laid in floors, tapering to a feather edge on the overhanging side, and when a tread was blasted out these floors would slide off. This was repeated several times before a tread was obtained that would hold, and a short pitch exceeding 20 per cent had to be used.

John M. Hughes, Foreman
MUIR TRAIL CONSTRUCTION CREW, 1917

Power drills are expensive and require trained personnel to use and maintain. The weight of a gasoline drill outfitted with bits, fuel, oil, and wedges and feathers can easily approach 150 pounds. By comparison, a couple of drill rods, a hammer, and wedges and feathers can be carried by one person in a day pack. While the labor may be very slow and tedious, the technique of hand drilling is easy to learn, and in practice is safe, quiet, and perhaps even contemplative.

But the strongest point in favor of hand drilling is that the 1964 Wilderness Act virtually prohibits the use of motorized equipment in designated wilderness. That leaves many wilderness trail crews with the choice of drilling by hand or not drilling at all.

HAND-DRILLING

The drill traditionally used for hand-drilling operations was a steel rod featuring a beveled bit shaped somewhat like a chisel or, more commonly, a star. Modern drill rods have a carbide insert in the bit. Drill rods are made in varying lengths, depending upon the depths of the holes to be made. When wedges and feathers are to be used to break apart rocks, one drill of 12 to 18 inches will usually be enough.

In many mining operations and in much trail and road construction as late as the mid-twentieth century, rock drilling was often done by teams of two. One person held and turned the rod while the other drove it with the full swing of a long-handled hammer. In fact, the names *double jack* for that large hammer, and *single jack* for a smaller one can be traced to hand-drilling done either by two workers or by one. The difficulty and inherent risks of double jacking make it an unsuitable option for most modern trail crews.

Squatting a day in the
    sun,
one hand turning the
    steel drill,
one, swinging the four
    pound singlejack ham-
    mer
        down.
three inches an hour
granite bullhump boulder
    square in the trail.
        Gary Snyder
    "FIRE IN THE HOLE," *THE
    BACK COUNTRY* (NEW
DIRECTIONS PAPERBOOK
    249, 1968), P. 12.

How It Used to Be

The man holding the drill should keep his hat-brim pulled well down over his eyes, should keep his face turned downward, and should never watch the drill-head. Blows from the double jack may cause this to sliver or splinter, and fragments of steel are often thrown off as if shot from a gun.

Jay L. B. Taylor

HANDBOOK FOR RANGERS & WOODSMEN (NEW YORK: JOHN WILEY & SONS, INC., 1917), P. 73.

Begin a hand drilling operation by studying the rock and deciding where to place the holes. Drilling them in line with cracks or seams will take advantage of weaknesses in the rock and increase the possibility of successfully breaking it.

Sometimes a few blows with a pick will chip the start of a hole, making it easier at first for the drill to bite into the stone. That done, seat yourself comfortably near the hole site. Goggles and leather gloves are mandatory protective gear for anyone involved in hand drilling.

Place the drill bit against the rock and strike the butt end of the rod with a single jack hammer. Rotate the drill an eighth of a turn after each hammer blow so that the bit can cut through fresh stone. (Drill rods often have eight faces. Rotate the rod one face after each hit with the hammer.)

Remove rock dust from the hole with a long, slender tool known as a *spoon* so that the dust does not impede the action of the drill. If you don't have a spoon, you can use a hardwood stick, beaten into splinters at one end, to swab out the dust. Pour water into deeper holes to flush out rock particles. Wrap a rag around the rod where it enters the hole to prevent the water from splashing as you hammer the drill. Pull out the rod now and then and rap it against the rock to knock loose any muck from the bottom of the hole.

Hand-drilling prepares holes for the sets of wedges and feathers used to split a rock.

WEDGES AND FEATHERS

After the holes are bored into a rock, use *wedges and feathers* to break it apart. Feathers are metal guides inserted in pairs into drilled holes. Slide a wedge between each pair of feathers, then use a hammer to pound the wedges down, alternating blows among the wedges to drive them simultaneously. If the rock does not break, tap the wedges and feathers back and forth to loosen and remove them, or drill another hole and increase the pressure on the rock with an additional set of feathers and another wedge.

When building with rock that has been drilled and split, hide the signs of your handiwork by turning the drilled faces toward the interior of the structure.

(For a detailed discussion of drilling, see *Hand Drilling and Breaking Rock for Wilderness Trail Maintenance* by Dale Mrkich and Jerry Oltman, published in 1984 by the U.S. Forest Service and made available through the USFS Technology and Development Center in Missoula, Montana.)

Moving Rocks

A rock lying flat on the ground is very unlikely to fall on your toes. Skidding a large rock is safer than rolling it, since there is more surface in contact with the ground, and thus less of a chance of dropping it or losing control of its motion. Rock bars are almost essential for moving rocks of medium and large sizes. Use the bars to pry rocks up out of the earth and then to guide them toward their destination. When crew members slide three or four bars from different directions under a large rock, they can apply leverage to the stone and virtually "float" it to a new location with a rowing motion at the end of each bar.

> Skidding rocks is better than rolling them. Rolling is better than lifting. Lifting sucks.
>
> HIGH SIERRA TRAIL BUILDER DOLLIE CHAPMAN'S THEORY OF ROCK DELIVERY

> ### Flesh and Rock Bars Don't Mix
> A wise rule for protecting your fingers is this—if a bar is touching a rock, keep your hands away.

The mechanical advantage of block and tackle may allow a trail crew to drag large rocks with ease. Several workers can walk alongside a stone as it is being dragged, using rock bars to leverage its leading edge over rocks, logs, and other obstacles. Two or three rock bars can also be used as rails by placing them side-by-side in the path of a rock and then sliding the stone onto and along the bars. As the rock clears the bars, reposition them in front.

When moving rocks in steep terrain, skid them in a controlled manner rather than kicking them loose and letting them roll down the hillside. Rocks so seldom get to wander about on their own that a rolling stone will eagerly develop a travel itinerary that is nothing like the trajectory you had hoped it would follow. Tumbling rocks can knock down small trees, gouge the bark off larger ones, and wipe out trail structures. They almost never stop where you want them to, often bounding so far beyond the project site that they cannot be retrieved. On the other hand, if you do lose control of a rock on a hillside, let it go; attempting to tackle a bounding stone is an act of futility that will almost certainly cause your first-aid kit to be depleted of tape and gauze.

On level ground, rolling a rock is a better way to move it than lifting it, since at least some of the rock will always be touching the earth. Tipping a rock up onto an edge does mean, of course, that it will eventually come back down. Pull the rock toward you, keeping it between you and the ground until you can look underneath and see if you've uncovered any critters made cranky by so sudden a change in their surroundings. Stand to the side of a rock as you roll it, keeping your feet and fingers clear.

Rock Moving Safety

Whenever a rock is being moved downhill toward a pathway, crews should take steps to protect trail users and themselves in the event that the rock gets loose and hurtles down the slope. The safest course is to close the trail and clear the work site until the rock has reached its destination.

The technique of last resort for moving rocks is to lift them off the ground. Be sure to keep your back straight and to lift with the strong muscles of your legs. Work in teams of two or more to distribute the weight. Before beginning, settle on a few clear signals to guide one another in lifting the rock together and safely putting it back down.

Rocks can also be moved in wheelbarrows, horse-drawn stone boats, and motorized toters, slung beneath tensioned cables, or hoisted in nets by helicopters. To load a large rock into a wheelbarrow, tip the barrow on its side next to the rock. Scoot the rock partway into the wheelbarrow, then lift the barrow and rock together until the wheelbarrow is upright, taking care to keep your fingers clear.

(For details on transporting rock with cable, blocks, and tackle, see Chapter 17, "Rigging.")

In addition to moving large rocks, crews may need to transport quantities of small stones for use as fill material behind retaining walls and in turnpikes and cribbed staircases. Individuals can gather the rocks in buckets and haul them to the project, though a more social technique is to line up workers an arm's length apart and then pass the rocks from one person to the next. The line can swing in an arc to bring it close to fresh supplies of stones. If the rocks are further away, the crew can pass them up the line to a central gathering point, then extend the line from that point toward the project and pass the rocks the rest of the way to the work site.

Regardless of how you move a stone, be exceedingly cautious. Rocks seem possessed of a strong streak of acrophobia. Once airborne, they will do everything they can to get back down, and they are not very particular about how they do it or who might be in the way.

Rock Walls

Retaining walls are among the greatest problem-solvers of trail construction and maintenance. Walls can carry a trail across rugged terrain, around switchbacks, past washouts, and over tree roots or stone outcroppings.

Rock walls are durable, aesthetically pleasing solutions to many trail construction and maintenance problems.

Most rock walls in rustic settings are *drywalls,* meaning they are built without mortar. An obvious advantage of drywall construction is that crews won't have to pack cement and water to the site. But without mortar, gravity becomes the only glue that holds together the pieces of rustic rock walls. Each stage of drywall construction—from selecting large rocks to placing each one with care—enhances the effectiveness of gravity and increases the sturdiness of the wall.

Keys to Rock Wall Construction

- Inslope the foundation.
- Use the largest rocks available.
- Build in tiers whenever possible.
- Work from the low end of the foundation toward the high end.
- Butt the beginning of the wall against a boulder, a rock outcropping, or other anchor.
- Match the faces of the rocks.
- Establish contact points between each pair of rocks.
- Place wedges only in the inside face of a wall, not the outside face.
- Rocks in each tier should "break the joints" between the rocks in the tier immediately below.
- Fill behind the rising wall with small stones or crushed rock, and pack rock into all the voids in the back of the wall.
- Lay a final tier of capstones of a size that will not be easily dislodged.

STARTING WITH A SOLID FOUNDATION

Prepare a foundation for a rock wall by digging down until you reach firm, undisturbed earth, then clear a shelf a bit wider than the average width of the rocks you will be using. Tilt the footing slightly inward so the wall will lean into the hillside. Save the soil for use as fill material or to plate the tread of the trail.

LAYING THE FIRST TIER

Lay the first rock at the lower end of the foundation. Since it will act as a buttress for the entire wall, use one of the largest rocks you have. Turn it so its two flattest surfaces are on top and facing out. If possible, anchor the rock by abutting it against a stone outcropping or boulder.

Test the placement of the first rock by standing on it and dancing about. The rock should remain motionless beneath your frisky feet. A rock that is not quite solid can be stabilized by wedging small stones behind it. Fill material added later will bury the wedges and lock them in place. Do not rely on wedges in the face of a wall where they may be loosened by freezing and thawing or dislodged by people climbing on the rocks.

It is sometimes tempting to pound on wedge stones with a hammer, but that much force can drive a wedge too far and lift a rock out of position. Instead, push wedges into place by hand, or tap them lightly with another stone until they are secure.

Place the second rock tightly alongside the first so there is at least one point of solid contact between them. Contact points closer to the outside face of the wall are better than those further back. Keep the top surface of the row of rocks as level as possible; that will make it easier to lay the second tier on top of the first. Check the flatness of a tier by placing a rock bar across the stones.

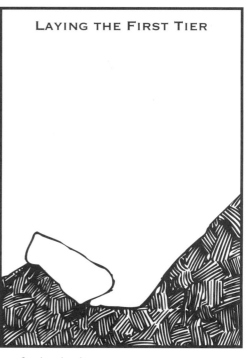

LAYING THE FIRST TIER

Form the first tier of a rock wall by laying large stones on an insloped foundation.

Testing Each Rock

Trial and error are critical to building with rock. You must be willing to turn a rock different ways and to try out a number of different rocks until you find the one that has just the right size and shape to fill a space in the wall.

Always test the stability of each rock by standing on it and performing a little rock dance. If there are good contact points between it and its neighbors, the rock should not move beneath your weight. If it wobbles, keep adjusting it or pull it out and try other rocks until you find one that does fit well.

ROCK WALL, CUTAWAY VIEW

Even after you have set a rock, think of it as being on probation until you have placed the next two or three stones in the tier. Circumstances sometimes make it necessary to lift out several rocks to reconstruct a portion of the wall. A rock is really assured its place only when the wall is complete.

You may need to excavate beneath some of the first-tier rocks to give them a snug fit in the foundation and the proper amount of inward lean. Rocks that are too tall for the tier can be embedded deeper to bring them down to size. A garden trowel is handy for shaping the foundation to accommodate each rock in the first tier, a process not unlike setting very large wisdom teeth into a gum line. By working from the lower end of the foundation to the higher, gravity will pull each against the adjoining rock.

If the foundation is level and there are no natural buttresses at either end, it is sometimes possible to start a wall in the middle and build it in both directions, thus opening up room for more people to work on the structure. However, it is almost impossible to begin at each end and build toward the middle, since the last rock placed in the tier will have to be exactly the right width and height to fit into the gap formed in the center.

When the first tier is done, fill behind it with small stones, dirt, or crushed rock, plugging all the voids. Leaving the level of the fill material a little lower than the front of the wall will make it easier for you to place the next tier of rocks and to maintain the inward lean of the structure.

Fill Material

Some trail builders argue that fill material should consist of nothing but stone so that rainwater and snowmelt can drain through. Others believe that soil mixed into the fill makes the structure impermeable to water, thus protecting it from damage by freezing. In fact, walls built long ago show no signs of being adversely affected by the kind of fill behind them. Build with what you have on hand, leaning toward stone or soil with a low content of organic matter.

PLACING THE UPPER TIERS

Lay the second tier of rocks on top of the foundation row, working, as always, from the lower end toward the higher. Fit the rocks in place with the same care and attention to contact points you used for the foundation tier. Each rock in the second tier must make contact with the rocks underneath it as well as with those on either side. A rock that teeters can sometimes be tilted forward until its lower edge makes contact with the tier below. Stones pushed beneath the rock from behind may stabilize it with the contact points in place.

Do not put dirt and gravel between tiers of rocks. While they may lessen the difficulty of laying the tiers, dirt and gravel will quickly wash out of a wall, leaving it weakened. On the other hand, tight rock-to-rock contact makes the wall a solid unit capable of standing up to the demands placed upon it.

BREAKING THE JOINTS

Consider how masons building a brick wall lay each brick so that it spans the gap between the two bricks below it. *Breaking the joints* in this way stiffens the structure by tying the bricks together. If they were stacked directly on top of one another, the bricks would form independent, side-by-side pillars instead of a wall, each pillar prone to teetering forward and collapsing.

Place each wall rock so that it breaks the joints by overlapping the gap between the rocks in the tier below. Rocks are not as symmetrical as bricks, and so you may need to try several before a stone of the proper shape and size presents itself.

HEADERS

Laying a stone with its longest axis in line with the length of a tier results in the most wall for the rock. However, it is a good idea now and then to turn a long rock into the wall so that its mass extends deep into the structure. Called *headers,* these rocks can greatly increase the internal strength of the wall.

CAPSTONES

Save some large rocks for the top tier. The weight of these *capstones* will help hold all the tiers in place, and their size will lessen the possibility that they will be kicked loose by livestock or hikers. Since no tiers will be built on top of them, capstones need to be flat only on the bottom where they will rest on the wall. Keep that in mind when you run across humpbacked rocks and other large stones that may be too asymmetric to fit easily into the middle tiers.

Fill in behind the capstones with crushed rock. If soil is available, perhaps saved from excavation of the foundation, spread 4 to 6 inches over the top of the fill rock to create an inviting tread surface for hikers and pack animals. Use enough fill to raise the trail tread slightly higher than the top tier of the wall. Outslope the tread toward the edge of the wall so that the structure will shed water.

Rock Stairs

Where trails are especially steep, stairways made of rock can play a critical role in stabilizing hillsides, keeping tread in place, slowing the flow of water, and making travel more comfortable for hikers and horseback riders. Most rock stairs

A rock staircase takes time to build correctly, but will require little maintenance over the decades.

are solid rock staircases, cribbed stone steps, or a blend of the two styles. Whatever the design, always begin working at the bottom of a structure and build toward the top.

SOLID ROCK STAIRCASES

On gentle slopes, a series of rocks placed as ascending stepping stones can provide secure footing for hikers. Set each one in the soil as you would a stepping stone.

Steps on steeper slopes may be close enough together that each one rests on the step below, forming a solid rock staircase. Firmly embed the first step, then place the front edge of the next step on the back of the first. The front, lower

ROCK STAIRCASE CUTAWAY

corners of the upper rock should make contact with the surface of the one below it in a way that prevents the upper step from wobbling. If necessary, use smaller stones to wedge behind the step rock to hold it in position; succeeding steps will protect the wedges from dislodgment. Do not place wedge rocks under the front edge of a step. Weathering and foot traffic will almost certainly loosen exposed wedges and weaken the staircase.

The lower front edge of each step in a solid rock staircase rests directly on the back of the step below it.

Since rock steps must withstand the impact of hikers' boots, stones used in solid staircase construction should be large—200 pounds or more. Two or three rocks can be fitted side-by-side to form a single step, but take care to match the faces to form a level walking surface. There must be good points of contact between each rock and the step on which it rests, and between the rock and any alongside it. Rock steps that wiggle when you stand on them will not last very long. Try different rocks in those spots until you find ones that fit tightly.

(For information on placing stepping stones, see Chapter 10, "Trail Drainage.")

CRIBBED STONE STEPS

In areas where stones are not big enough or properly shaped to build a solid rock stairway, cribbed steps may offer a solution for lifting a trail up a hillside. Use the largest available rocks to box in the sides and front of each step, then fill the enclosed space, or *crib,* with crushed rock.

Wide, thin rocks can be set on edge to form the sides of a crib. Embed them as you would for a water bar by tipping most of their mass into a foundation ditch and then jamming stones between the rock and the wall of the ditch. Build the cribs for several steps before filling them with small stones; once a step is filled, your options for making adjustments to it are limited.

STEPS FOR HORSES AND MULES

Livestock do not like steps. Whenever possible, trails for pack strings and horse-back riders should be designed without any steps. Where steps cannot be avoided, several criteria should guide their construction:

- Each step on an equestrian trail must be at least 48 inches long, and preferably 60 inches. An animal will have the security of standing with all four feet on the longer step, or with its feet on adjoining steps.

- The fill behind cribbed steps must be crushed rock or some other durable material that cannot be kicked loose or eroded by the hooves of livestock.

- Visual barriers should be placed alongside the steps to persuade animals to stay on the tread rather than walking around the sides of steps and landings. Known as *scree,* rocks placed along the steps in a seemingly haphazard pattern can make the stairway the easiest and most attractive route to follow.

Cribbed stone steps can be built where rocks are not flat enough or large enough for solid staircases.

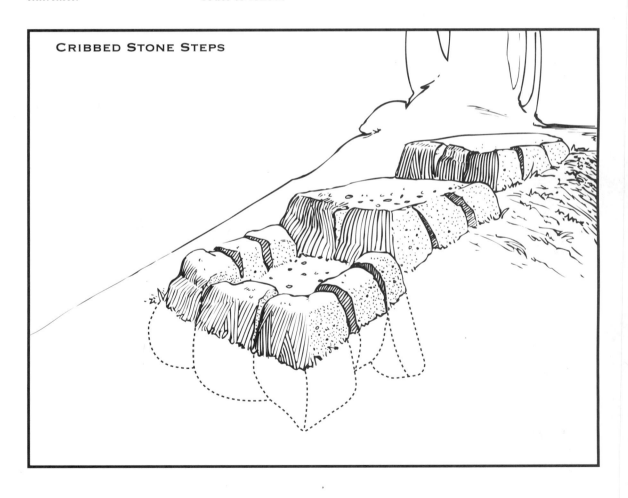

CRIBBED STONE STEPS

CHAPTER 13

Felling and Bucking

THE TRADITIONS OF FELLING TREES are as ancient as mankind's use of forests. Likewise, the methods used to bring down a tree and to cut it up, or *buck* it, once it is on the ground have been thousands of years in the making. Backcountry work crews with a mastery of felling and bucking can harvest trees for use in bridges, turnpikes, retaining walls, and other structures, and can clear away trees that have fallen into trail corridors.

The key, of course, is safety. If you are not accomplished at felling and bucking, do it only under the supervision of qualified instructors or agency professionals who can teach you proper techniques and safety considerations. There is no substitute for experience when learning to fell trees, and no shortcut to learning from those who know what they are doing.

As with any rustic work, if you ever have doubts about your ability to undertake a timber task safely, don't do it. Back off and figure out a new approach so that the job can be done without danger. Even the best sawyers will refuse to fell a tree if they feel the conditions are hazardous. Share any concerns you may have with agency personnel or land resource managers during the planning stages of a project. If necessary, they can almost always arrange to have cutting done by qualified fallers.

This chapter provides only a brief overview of felling and bucking methods. While it is a compilation of techniques found by professional trail workers to be safe and useful in the field, it should not be considered definitive. Improperly done, timber operations can be very dangerous. Sawyers must always use common sense. Each cutting situation is different and will require fresh attention to the hazards involved.

Furthermore, anyone felling trees on public lands must adhere to all regulations of the appropriate land-management agency. These may include completing an agency-approved certification course.

Felling Trees

A crew planning to harvest a tree for the construction of a bridge, water bars, or other trail structures should be guided by the following considerations:

- The base of the tree should be out of sight of the trail so that the stump will not be noticeable.

Experienced woodsmen can fell trees with great precision. Felling small timber of the East is a relatively simple operation. In the dense stands of the Pacific Coast forest where trees attain heights of more than 200 feet and diameters of 3 to 10 feet or more, the problem is greatly intensified. Felling trees in the southern pineries and in the ponderosa pine stands of the West is relatively simple because of the open character of the forest, the paucity of trees per acre, the short and open crowns of individual trees, and the generally favorable topography.

Nelson C. Brown
LOGGING: THE PRINCIPLES AND METHODS OF HARVESTING TIMBER IN THE UNITED STATES AND CANADA (NEW YORK: JOHN WILEY AND SONS, INC., 1949), P. 115.

- A tree uphill from the work site will be much easier to move to the project than a tree below the trail.
- Measure the height and diameter of the tree to be sure it satisfies project specifications.
- When a number of trees are needed, do not harvest them all from the same area.

TREE FELLING SAFETY

Begin the felling process by sizing up the tree and its surroundings to determine how the tree is likely to fall and how you can most effectively reduce any risks.

- What are the weather conditions? Gusts of wind can blow a tree backwards off a stump. Precipitation can blur your vision, make it difficult for you to hold onto your saw, and cause your escape routes to become slippery. If the weather is not favorable, do your felling another day.
- Which way does the tree lean? A tree can be most easily felled in the direction it is already going. While advanced felling techniques may coax a tree to drop elsewhere, overcoming natural lean is no sure thing.
- Are there more limbs or larger limbs on one side of the tree than the other? Their weight may affect the fall of the tree.
- What species is the tree? Sawyers with local experience can tell you how the characteristics of different kinds of trees affect the ways they should be felled.
- Is the tree dead or weakened by internal rot? Are there dead branches or loose bark that could break loose while you are sawing? These *widow makers* have not come by their nickname by chance. Their presence may cause you to reconsider your choice of tree or, if you go ahead with the felling, to station a lookout to keep an eye overhead and warn of changing situations.
- What will the tree land upon? Beware of uneven ground or rocks in the fall zone. They can cause cracks or breaks in the wood when the tree hits them. In steep country, the fallen tree may slide or roll downhill.
- Does the tree have an awkward shape? A *schoolmarm,* for example, is the traditional name (albeit politically incorrect) given to an evergreen with two distinct tops forking out of the main trunk. A schoolmarm with a high fork can be felled in the same way as an ordinary tree as long as you are aware that the double top may affect the direction of the fall. If the fork is no more than a few feet off the ground, it is usually better to fell each top separately.
- What is the condition and location of nearby timber? Is there room for the tree you want to fell to drop cleanly to the ground, or is it likely to become hung up against other trees? Are there nearby snags or dead branches that could break loose as your tree comes down?

CLEARING ESCAPE ROUTES

Plan at least two escape routes you can use to get away from the tree as it falls. Select your routes so that you will have someplace to go regardless of which way the tree comes down. Clear underbrush from around the base of the tree and from the escape routes.

VISUALIZING THE FALL

Do not begin cutting until you have in mind a clear picture of the sequence of events you want to put into motion:

- Decide what you want the tree to do.
- Figure out the steps you must take in order for the tree to fall as you wish.
- Consider all the things you *don't* want the tree to do, and determine everything you can do to prevent the tree from falling the wrong way.
- Walk along each of your escape routes, thinking through which you will use under various circumstances.

POSTING A LOOKOUT

Clear the area of everyone not involved in the felling, and post a lookout who will keep an eye on the tree and alert you to any situations you should know about while you are doing the cutting. Tell the lookout what your plan is, what you expect will happen, and where you intend to run to make your escape. That will not only inform the lookout, it will also require you to explain your intentions to another human being who may be able to point out any flaws in your plan.

- Lookouts must understand the plan for felling the tree.
- They must stand well clear of the tree and have their own routes of escape to get away from the falling tree or its branches.
- They must position themselves where they have a good view of the entire tree.
- They must have a clearly understood method of communicating with the sawyer.

If you are felling the tree with a crosscut saw, the lookout can communicate with you by yelling. The roar of a chain saw, however, makes verbal communication almost impossible. A lookout who is stationed in your line of sight can throw a handful of pebbles at you as a warning of danger.

UNDERCUTTING, BACKCUTTING, AND LEAVING HINGE WOOD

The following steps assume the tree you want to fell is sound and that it has no lean, or is leaning slightly in the direction of the intended fall.

- Make the *undercut* on the side of the trunk facing the direction you want the tree to drop. It should extend about a third of the way through the

I could tell you stories about falling and bucking that are so scary it took me an hour to build up my evacuation plan.

Steve Wennstrom

tree. If you are using a chain saw, the wedge-shaped chunk will usually fall out on its own. When using a crosscut saw, you may find it easiest to make only the horizontal cut with the saw, then chop out the wedge of wood with an axe.

The horizontal portion of the undercut should be level, regardless of any lean in the tree. The second cut of the undercut must meet the first at a clean angle. If one cut is deeper than the other, it can result in a hazardous situation called a *Dutchman* that may cause the tree to splinter or fall in an unexpected direction.

■ When the undercut has been completed, make the *backcut* on the opposite side of the tree. The backcut should be one or two inches above the horizontal face of the undercut and, like the undercut, should also be level. While making the backcut, do not saw all the way through to the undercut; always leave a section of *hinge wood* between the undercut and the backcut. If the undercut has been properly made, the tree will begin to fall while the saw is completing the backcut. The hinge wood will aim and control the fall as the tree comes down.

USING WEDGES

In larger timber, wedges help ensure the safety of the sawyer and may influence the direction of the fall. They should be used in any situation where the direction of lean is unclear, where the lean is in any direction other than the desired line of fall, or where the behavior of the tree during the falling sequence cannot be clearly predicted. Start the wedges in a backcut as soon as the kerf is deep enough to receive them without them hitting the chain or crosscut saw.

If the saw nears the hinge wood and the tree has not yet begun to fall, you can sometimes leverage it over with wedges. Withdraw the saw (if necessary, remove one handle of a crosscut so that the saw can be pulled from the backcut without disturbing any wedges already in place), then drive wedges into the backcut until they force the tree to go over.

Vibrations caused as you drive wedges may knock loose a limb or chunk of bark from high in the tree. Keep your eyes directed skyward, and remind your lookout to warn you of anything that falls.

THE FALL

Watch the top of the tree. When it starts to move (not just to quiver), pull out your saw, shut it off if it is a chain saw, yell, "Timber down the hill!" or whatever direction the tree appears to be falling, and make your escape. Before felling with a two-person crosscut saw, decide whether you or your partner will lay down the saw or carry it away from the tree. If a falling tree traps either a chain saw or crosscut in the kerf, leave it and go—your safety is far more valuable than any tool.

Make your escape by moving quickly behind and off to one side of the dropping tree, then turn and watch to be sure the tree is falling away from you. Trees tend to come down slowly at first, so you should have time to reach safety in the seconds that the tree is beginning to drop. Watch for breaking limbs that may sail toward you from the falling tree or from any trees it strikes. When the tree hits the ground, limbs may be snapped off and thrown in the air, though these usually present little hazard to the sawyer. More dangerous is the possibility that the butt of a falling tree will jump off the stump or kick up into the air.

FELLING SNAGS

Use the same techniques for cutting down snags as for felling sound green timber, but with these additional considerations:

- Snags are more likely than green trees to drop limbs or bark on a sawyer's head.
- One side of a snag infected with rot may be weaker than the other, causing it to twist as it falls. Indications of internal rot include sawdust piles from carpenter ants, termites, or bark beetles, and water oozing out of knots. Pound on a snag with your fist and you may hear a sodden thump indicating the possibility of wet, rotten interior wood, or an empty boom from a hollow tree.
- The roots of a snag may have decayed so much that the stump will pop out of the ground as the snag falls.

SWING FELLING

The direction a tree naturally leans is not always the direction in which you want it to fall. An advanced felling technique called *swing felling* can sometimes put a tree on the

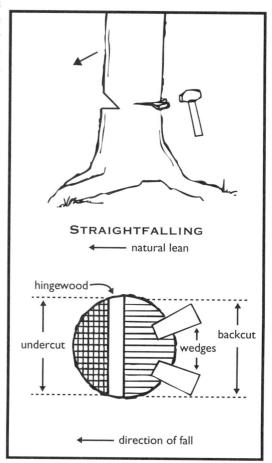

STRAIGHTFALLING

← natural lean

hingewood

undercut

backcut

wedges

← direction of fall

ground someplace other than where it wants to go. Swing felling can be hazardous, and should be done only by trained, experienced fallers.

A normal undercut is made on the side of the tree facing the target point of the fall. The backcut is sawed in such a way that the hinge wood between the cuts is thicker in the direction of intended fall. As wedges driven behind the thinner portion of the hinge push the tree over, the irregular shape of the hinge wood causes the falling tree to twist on the stump, arcing the tree sideways.

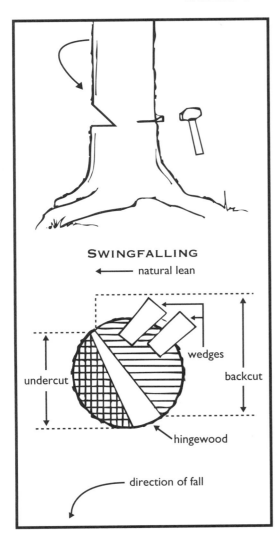

SWINGFALLING

direction of fall

Dangerous Situations

BACK FALLS

If you pay attention to the lean of a tree and then make the undercut and backcut correctly, the tree will usually fall in the direction you expect. However if you misjudge the lean, if the undercut is not deep enough, if the backcut is made too low, if you fail to place wedges behind your saw, or if the wind kicks up, the weight of the tree may settle onto the backcut, or the tree may even fall over backwards.

Any time a tree you are cutting begins to lean the wrong direction, get away from it. Assess the situation from a safe distance and decide what to do next. If the saw becomes pinched in the kerf of the backcut, you will probably need to use another saw or an axe to deepen the undercut until the tree goes on over.

BARBER CHAIRS

Barber chairs are among the most dangerous situations in felling. The name comes from the fact that the stump can be left in the shape of a high-backed chair, but *barber chair* could also refer to the close shave it may cause.

Barber chairs are often triggered by Dutchmans or by making the backcut below the undercut. They can occur during almost any stage of the cutting process. The undercut may be nearing completion or the backcut just started when splits explode up the trunk. The tree will splinter as it falls, often throwing off slivers of wood. The trunk may bound off to one side of the stump with great force, or kick backward.

Be on guard for barber chairs every time you cut into a tree, especially if there are signs of rot or a moderate to severe lean. If you hear wood splintering in the tree before it should fall, make your escape immediately and reassess the situation. Never attempt to fell a tree that is swaying in the wind.

BARBER CHAIR

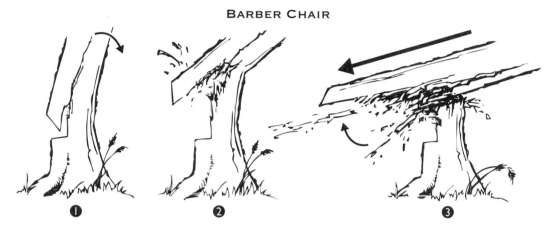

❶   ❷   ❸

HUNG TREES

A falling tree that becomes tangled with neighboring trees will cause all sorts of headaches. If the butt of the tree is still resting on the stump, the timber may have a tendency to roll, increasing the hazard. The safest way to bring down a hung tree is to throw a choker around it, rig up block and tackle, and then from a safe distance pull the butt off the stump and along the ground until the crown falls free.

Limbing and Barking a Tree

When using an axe to cut branches from a downed tree, stand on one side of the trunk and cut on the other, chopping into the undersides of the branches. Your shins will be shielded from the axe blade by the tree itself.

Bark can trap moisture against wood fibers and provide a haven for insects, so it is usually best to remove the bark before using a log in a timber structure. You may have luck stripping bark with an axe, a sharp shovel, a peeling spud, or a drawknife, depending on the species of tree and whether it is green. Scatter branches and bark over a wide area beyond sight of the trail, laying them flat on the ground to hasten decomposition.

Saw Operations in Downed Timber

A common trail maintenance task in many parts of the country is clearing away trees that have fallen across the tread. Whether done with a chain saw or a cross-cut, three basic rules should guide your behavior:

- With very few exceptions, never stand underneath or on the downhill side of a fallen tree.
- Always clear at least two escape routes for yourself.
- Before you pick up your saw, study the timber and its surroundings to determine how the forces of tension and compression are acting upon it.

LIMBING

Stand on the opposite side while limbing a tree.

Springers, Tension, and Compression

Any time you cut a downed tree or log, tension and compression within the wood can make it move. To understand tension and compression, lay a pencil across two books spaced a foot apart. Press down on the center of the pencil with enough force to bend it. The pressure of your finger is causing a great deal of strain in the pencil's wood fibers. Those on top of the pencil are being squeezed together; that's *compression*. Those on the underside of the pencil are being pulled apart; that's *tension*.

The terms *tension* and *compression* are common in the logging industry and among Western states' trail crews. More common among Eastern trail workers is the word *springer*, a descriptive term referring to a log, loaded with tension or compression, that may spring dramatically when pressures in the log are altered by a saw.

The species of tree can make a difference in how it will respond to shifting tension and compression. A brittle pine will break faster and sharper than a limber fir, for example. Decaying timber can be highly unpredictable, breaking sooner and with more twist than a solid tree. Look for external signs of rot and notice any change in the color or texture of chips being removed by the saw; they can be a warning of internal decomposition of a log.

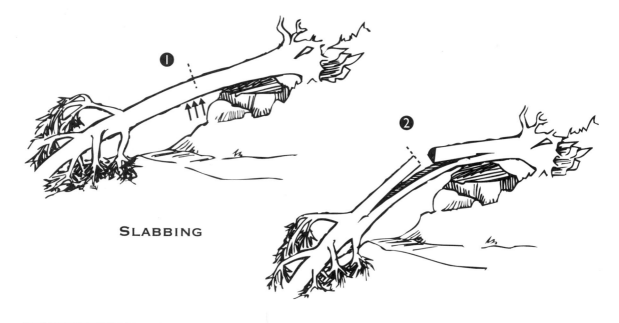

SLABBING

Slabbing

Slabbing occurs when the weight of the free end of a timber creates enough tension in the wood fibers that they split off from the unfinished cut—a sort of horizontal cousin of the barber chair. Splits caused by slabbing may travel many feet along a log. Slabbing may be minimized by undercutting a log before completing the cut from the top.

Types of Cuts

Techniques of cutting logs will provide sawyers with options they can apply to almost any tension/compression situation. All of the cuts described below can be performed with a chain saw; topcutting and undercutting can also be accomplished with a crosscut saw.

In selecting the saw to use, remember that events tend to unfold gradually when you are using a crosscut. There is often time, upon hearing the first cracking of wood fibers, to insert another wedge, redirect a cut, or adjust your position in relation to the log. Chain saws cut so fast that sawyers must be extremely alert to anticipate and counter shifts in the position of the timber. On the other hand, releasing the tension or compression in a timber is sometimes best accomplished by cutting the wood quickly, something almost impossible to achieve with a crosscut.

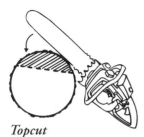

Topcut

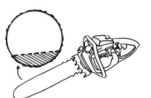

Undercut

Sidecut

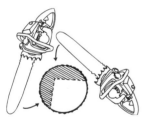

Overcut

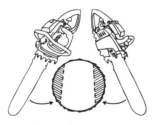

Side Notching

TOPCUT

The topcut is a straight cut into the top of the log. If carried completely through the log, it may cause the lower edge of the cut to splinter, or can result in the underside of the log splitting and slabbing.

When a crosscut saw is used, it is almost always followed into the kerf of a topcut with wedges to hold the kerf open. A chunk of wood or large piece of bark laid under the log will shield the teeth from the soil when the saw breaks through the log.

UNDERCUT

The reverse of a topcut, the undercut is made by bringing the saw blade up from beneath the log. An undercut completed before using a topcut to saw through a log will prevent splintering and slabbing, and lessen the chance of trapping the saw in the kerf.

When using a chain saw, be sure there is plenty of clearance between the log and the ground, and guard against the saw kicking back. Efficient undercutting with a crosscut saw can be accomplished by resting the back of the saw on a vintage underbucker or on the handle of an axe driven horizontally into the log. (For more on underbucking, see Chapter 6, "Crosscuts and Chain Saws.")

SIDECUT

The sidecut is used to relieve tension in a timber, or as a step in bucking a log that is too big to be sawed with a simple undercut/overcut sequence. Make the sidecut in the same way as a topcut, only on the side of the log. On very large timber, the sawyer may need to stand atop the log to make this cut.

OVERCUT

Logs with a diameter greater than the length of a chain saw bar can be sawed with an overcut—a combination topcut and sidecut.

SIDE NOTCHING

These cuts can be made in the same way as a sidecut, or with the tip of the chain saw bar. The notches will reduce compression and tension, and prevent the log from splintering or slabbing when sawed with an undercut/overcut sequence.

BORING

Boring is a handy method for undercutting large timber with a chain saw, though the hazard of the saw kicking back out of the cut is high. Start boring with the underside of the tip against the wood and the bar slightly raised. As the tip digs into the log, lift the saw until the bar is horizontal.

ANGLE CUT

Sawing at an angle may reduce tension in a log and direct the fall of the log sections so that the ends do not wedge together.

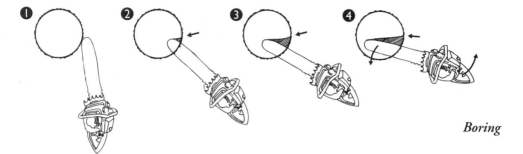

Boring

Approaches to Bucking

The following illustrations show common occurrences of tension and compression sawyers are likely to encounter while bucking timber, and a *general* cutting approach to handle each one. Every log will have a quirk or two all its own, and if more than one log is involved, a crew must assess the effect that cutting one log will have on the others.

BUTT RISE

As a saw cuts through a blown-down tree with a top bow, the weight of the roots may pull the stump upright. Stumps as high as twenty feet can be lifted this way. If you suspect butt rise will occur, undercut the log first, then topcut through it.

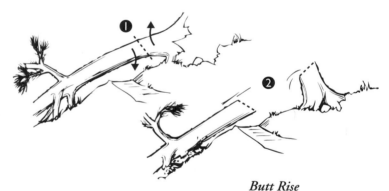

Butt Rise

BUTT TWIST

The butt of an uprooted tree may have a tendency to roll to one side or the other. Undercut the log, then notch it on the side toward which the butt will roll. Complete the job by topcutting the log while standing on the side opposite the notch.

BUTT DROP

If an uprooted tree lies with its crown downhill of the roots, cutting the trunk may cause the butt to drop or flip over toward the sawyer. Topcut or overcut the log until the kerf begins to close, then undercut. Side notches may be lifesavers in this situation. *Use extreme caution.*

BRANCHES AND SAPLINGS

Take into consideration the tensions placed on downed timber by branches and saplings that are bent under the fallen trunk. The best precaution is to limb a fallen tree before cutting it.

view from above

tension
(expansion)
here

compression
here

INTERLACING

INTERLACING

A timber interlaced with others, as when a snag falls among three or four standing trees, may have a variety of tensions and compressions acting upon it. Sawing it can involve several types of cuts to relieve upward and downward pressures, and may include felling one or more of the trees tangled with the timber.

SPLINTERED TRUNK

A tree will sometimes twist and splinter when it falls, but not break apart. The result can be a mass of splinters and blades of wood under a complex array of tensions and compressions. Carefully cut through each splinter until you reach solid wood (if there is any).

Sawing Out a Windfall

While the information above deals with single logs, windfalls that must be cleared from a trail may contain many trees tangled like jackstraws, each a potential springer. A cut made in one log may cause the movement of other trees in the windfall, and even of nearby standing timber.

STEPS IN PREPARING TO CUT WINDFALL

- Take plenty of time to study a windfall before you begin sawing. Estimate how far and in what direction the timbers will move when cut, and where you are going to put the pieces when you are through with them.
- Select and clear your escape routes.
- Cut off and remove all the limbs that may be causing tension or are within the area where you intend to make your log cuts. Cut any bent saplings.
- Determine whether there is a *key log* in the windfall, a log that, when cut, will set the rest of the trees in motion.
- As you saw, be on guard for timbers to move in unexpected ways.

Bucking and Felling Safety

Know your limits. Do not take unnecessary risks. If you decide to walk away from a situation because of its hazards or your lack of experience, you are exercising one of the most sought-after qualifications of a crew leader—sound judgment.

Transporting Logs

With log carriers, teams of workers can lift and move logs of modest size. Two tools useful for rolling logs and leveraging them into position are the cant hook and the peavy.

If you have no log carriers but are blessed with an abundance of people, zigzag a rope beneath a log that's not too large and, using the bends in the rope as handholds on either side, form a net in which the log will ride. The rope setup can also be used to provide additional lifting power on timbers being toted with log carriers. Placing skid poles or roller logs beneath large logs will make them easier to drag with block and tackle. (For more on cant hooks, peavies, and log carriers, see Chapter 5, "Tools.")

CHAPTER 14

Building with Timber

WOOD HAS TREMENDOUS VERSATILITY as a rustic building material. Trees harvested near project sites can be transformed into structures as simple as water bars and as complex as bridges. Wood can be shaped with great precision. It is aromatic, pleasing to the touch, and a delight to the eye. Structures made of wood blend aesthetically with natural surroundings.

The techniques used by modern trail crews to shape timber are essentially the same methods practiced for hundreds of years by foresters, shipwrights, and pioneers. Saws, chisels, axes, and other tools of timber work harken back to the early days of the American frontier. Crews today involved with traditional timber construction are keeping alive a wealth of skills that can be extremely useful in the building and maintenance of backcountry trails.

The allure of working with wood does, however, carry with it a caution. Wooden structures require regular repair and eventual replacement. If not maintained, they can become hazardous to users. Backcountry timber construction should be avoided if there are more durable alternatives.

The design of wooden turnpikes, cribbed steps, and culverts may be left up to crew leaders. However, resource managers will usually take responsibility for planning bridges and other major load-bearing structures that must conform with agency standards. Managers may also be required to prepare environmental impact statements before approving construction of larger timber structures.

Of course it is still true that the expert in Woodcraft takes every advantage that his skill in the use of knife, ax, saw, and compass may give to him. . . . The laying of a trail . . . becomes not only a pleasure in itself, but an inducement to plan a better way of life, to construct worth-while things, or to weave a better product in the loom of our being.

Earle Amos Brooks
A HANDBOOK OF THE OUT-DOORS (NEW YORK: GEORGE H. DORAN COMPANY, 1925), P. 98.

Selecting Wood

Material for a wooden structure may come from standing trees, downed logs showing no signs of decay, or dimensional lumber that has been treated with chemicals to slow deterioration caused by exposure to the elements. Telephone poles and railroad ties are sometimes incorporated into backcountry work, but should be avoided if those timbers contain creosote or other toxins that can leech into the soil.

The selection of wood species for use in timber construction depends upon local availability, tradition, and lore, particularly where trail workers will choose and harvest trees themselves. During the planning stages of a project, crew leaders should seek guidance from agency personnel to determine the most appropriate wood for their projects.

If you want something to last forever, build with rock.
If you want it to last ten years longer, use locust.
TRADITIONAL, SOUTHEAST-ERN UNITED STATES

Possibilities vary greatly depending on the region of the country. In much of Vermont, for example, hemlock is the tree of choice for construction material, but hemlock is scarce, and so spruce and beech find their way into bridges and puncheon. Maple is another good building wood, but some crews tend to shy away from felling it because it is also the Vermont state tree. In the Northwest, spruce, hemlock, and Douglas fir are sought after by backcountry construction crews, though cedar may be the wood they prize most highly for its durability, strength, and the pleasure with which it can be worked. In the Greater Yellowstone Ecosystem, on the other hand, crews rely almost entirely upon lodgepole pine because that section of the Rocky Mountain region offers little else in the way of material.

Preservative-treated Wood

Species of trees vary in their susceptibility to decay. Some that are used in backcountry construction are naturally resistant to rot, while other varieties may not survive long unless they are sheltered from the elements, painted to seal out moisture, or treated with preservatives.

Wood decay is caused primarily by fungi that cannot survive without air, food, and moisture. Remove one leg of that triad, and fungi cannot become established. Wood preservatives act by making toxic the food supplies of fungi.

Some preservatives such as creosote are painted onto the wood, or timbers are soaked in large containers of the chemicals. More effective is pressure treating to drive preservatives deep into the wood. Pressure-treated lumber can often be recognized by a symmetrical pattern of perforation marks.

Lumber treated with preservatives presents trail crews with a dilemma. Preservatives can increase by many years the useful life of wood used in bridge construction, cribbing, sign posts, safety railings, and other structures. However, what is poisonous to a fungus may also be harmful to the environment and to trail workers.

An alternative to introducing preservative-treated material into the backcountry is to select wood such as cedar, locust, cypress, and redwood that is naturally resistant to rot. These species can last as long as treated lumber, but without the danger of side effects.

The major types of wood preservatives are these:

CREOSOTE

Without creosote to protect railroad ties from decay, the network of rail lines built throughout America in the 1800s and early 1900s would have been almost impossible to maintain. A derivative of coal, creosote effectively counters decay, but can bleed out of the wood and contaminate soil and water. Contact with creosote or its vapors can also be harmful to humans, wildlife, and vegetation. Today, creosote is almost never used on lumber intended for backcountry use, though trail crews may encounter it when reusing railroad ties to build steps or retaining walls, or when transforming old telephone poles into bridge stringers. Use of creosote is prohibited by most land-management agencies.

PETROLEUM-BORNE PRESERVATIVES

These preservatives consist of chemicals mixed with oil, natural gas, or other carriers that are then pressure-injected into the wood. Pentachlorophenol, also known as *PCP* or *penta,* is the most common of these chemicals. It is extremely poisonous, and wood treated with it should not be used in picnic tables, benches, handrails, or other structures where penta may come in contact with food or human skin. Like creosote, use of penta is no longer allowed by most land-management agencies.

WATERBORNE PRESERVATIVES

Chemicals in solution with water can also be pressure-injected into lumber. When the water evaporates, the fungicidal agents are left in the wood fibers. These agents include forms of inorganic arsenic, chromium, and copper. While less messy than other forms of preservatives, they should not be used around sources of food or drinking water.

Precautions for Handling Preservative-treated Wood

The Environmental Protection Agency requires that a consumer information sheet be distributed at the point of purchase to buyers of wood that has been pressure-treated with preservatives. Among the precautions cited by the EPA are these:

- Do not use treated wood where the preservative may become a component of food or animal feed, such as structures for storing silage.
- Do not use treated wood for cutting-boards or countertops.
- Treated wood should not be used where it may come into direct or indirect contact with public drinking water, except for uses involving incidental contact such as docks and bridges.
- Do not burn treated wood in open fires, stoves, fireplaces, or residential boilers because toxic chemicals may be produced as part of the smoke and ashes. Instead, dispose of treated wood by ordinary trash collection or burial.
- Avoid frequent or prolonged inhalation of sawdust from treated wood. When sawing and machining treated wood, wear a dust mask and perform these operations outdoors to avoid indoor accumulations of airborne sawdust.
- When using power saws and machinery, wear goggles to protect your eyes from flying particles.
- Thoroughly wash exposed skin after you have worked with treated wood, especially before eating, drinking, or using tobacco products.
- If preservatives or sawdust accumulate on clothes, launder before reuse. Wash work clothes separately from other clothing.

Tools and Equipment for Timber Work

Tools for timber work can be divided into two groups—those that a crew will probably need in order to make saddle notches, lap joints, and to construct most straightforward backcountry structures; and those that should be added if the work will involve advanced joinery such as splines, dovetail notches, mortises, and tenons.

TOOLS FOR BASIC TIMBER WORK
- Tape measure
- Level
- Single jack hammer
- Adz
- Axe
- Marking pen
- Chalk line
- Dividers
- Chisels (¾-inch and 1½-inch)
- Mallet (30-ounce)
- Draw knife
- Crosscut saw
- Sharpening files, stone, oil

ADDITIONAL TOOLS FOR ADVANCED TIMBER WORK
- T-bevel (the small size with a 3-inch blade is best)
- Combination square
- Backsaw
- Auger (¾-inch or 1-inch diameter bit)
- Peeling spud
- Slicks (2-inch and 3½-inch)
- Calipers
- Double jack hammer

SAFETY EQUIPMENT
- Shin guards (for use while adzing)
- Toe guards (for use while adzing)
- Sheaths for all edged tools

Joinery

The heart of rustic timber construction is *joinery,* the art of joining together pieces of wood with notches rather than nails, screws, or bolts. Over the centuries, builders have perfected many kinds of notches. Two of the most versatile for trail crews are the *saddle notch* and the *lap joint.* Mastery of laying out, or *scribing,* and then cutting saddle notches and lap joints will give a backcountry crew expertise for addressing most timber construction needs.

SADDLE NOTCH

The saddle notch is a simple, effective notch for joining two logs set at an angle to each other—the corners of log cabins and trail shelters, for example, or the headers and logs in retaining walls.

The following instructions explain how to scribe and cut saddle notches to fit together a long bridge support beam called a *stringer* and the stout foundation logs, or *sills,* upon which it rests. The same technique can be used whenever saddle notches are needed.

1. Position the stringer on the sills and secure it with log dogs or prop it in place with wedges of scrap wood.

    The depth of the notches cut into a log will determine how high it will sit atop the sills. A notch in a load-bearing member such as a bridge stringer should not exceed a quarter of the log's diameter, since deeper notching can compromise the strength of the stringer. Logs that do not bear a load, such as those in a retaining wall, can be notched more deeply.

    Establish the depth of a notch by laying a level across the stringer and above the center of the sill. True the level and use it as a point of reference for measuring. If, for example, you want the notched log to rise 3 inches above the sill, measure straight down 3 inches from the level and mark the log; that point will be the apex of the curve of the notch.

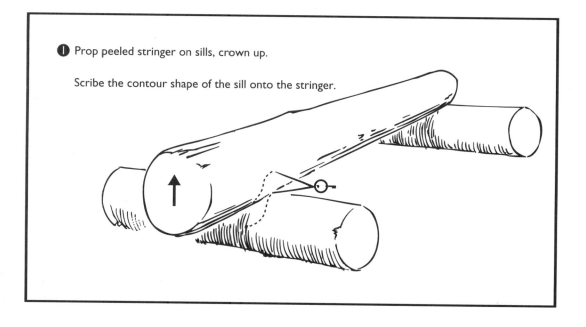

❶ Prop peeled stringer on sills, crown up.

Scribe the contour shape of the sill onto the stringer.

2. Set the *scribing dividers* for the distance from the apex mark down to the top of the sill log. Use the dividers to scribe the setting somewhere on top of the stringer in the same manner that you would scribe a short arc with a geometry compass. That will give you a reference mark so you can reset the dividers if they fall out of alignment.

Hold the points of the dividers perpendicular to the ground. Some dividers are equipped with a small level to help you keep them properly

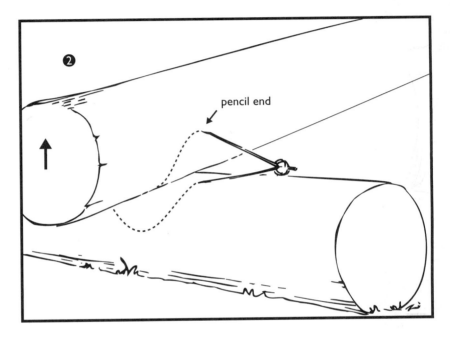

oriented, though in most cases you'll need to estimate the plumb line with your eye.

NOTE: If you are scribing with a permanent pencil, you must first moisten the wood with water from a spray bottle or a wet rag. Some dividers have no pencil, relying instead upon a sharp point to make a scratch line in the wood.

As you trace the shape of the sill with one point of the dividers, let the other point scribe an outline of that shape onto the stringer. Adjust your position so that you can move the dividers by pulling them rather than pushing. Keep two hands on the dividers to hold them steady, and move with your body, always keeping the points in a vertical plane.

If the other end of the stringer will be notched to fit on a second sill, repeat the steps outlined above to scribe that notch. Do not allow the stringer or the sills to move until both notches have been scribed. Depending on

❸ Invert stringer and cut into notch wood every few inches.

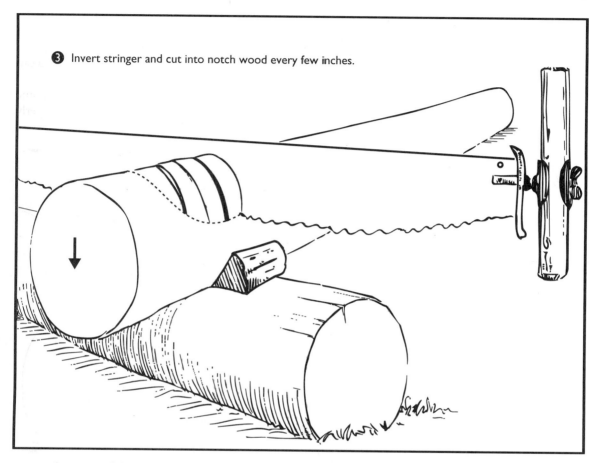

the taper of the log, the second notch may not be the same depth as the first. By increasing or decreasing the width of the dividers, and thus changing the depth of the notch, you can adjust the way the stringer lies on the sills.

3. Turn the stringer over so that the outline of the notch faces up, and secure it with log dogs or wedges of wood.

   With a small chisel or a sharp knife, score the wood just inside the scribed line. That will protect the wood from splintering and leave the notch with a clean edge.

   Use a crosscut, bow saw, or backsaw to make parallel cuts across the waste wood at intervals two finger-widths apart. Saw down to, but not through, the scribed line.

4. Chop the waste wood out of the notch with an axe, taking care not to come too close to the edges, then do the finish work with a chisel or gouge and mallet. The completed notch should be slightly concave in

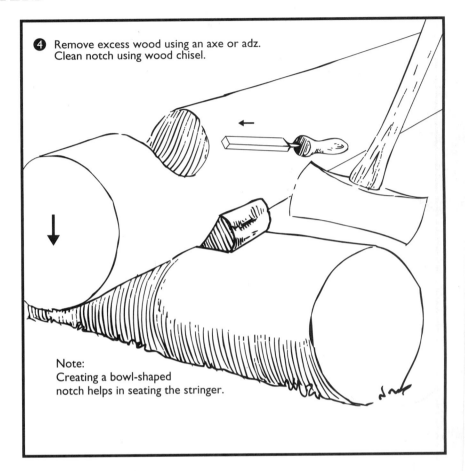

4 Remove excess wood using an axe or adz.
Clean notch using wood chisel.

Note:
Creating a bowl-shaped
notch helps in seating the stringer.

shape—cupped so that only the rim of the notch will touch the sill. If the notch is not scooped out, the center may ride on the sill and prevent the notch edges from sealing against it. Test the shape of the notch by laying a straightedge across it.

5. Turn the stringer and fit the notch in place. Because the notch is cut into the underside of the log, the open grain of the wood will be shielded from rainwater and snowmelt.

If you are building a bridge with more than one stringer, follow the same steps to scribe notches on subsequent stringers. After the first stringer has been notched and set in place, position the second stringer next to it and use the dividers and the level to measure the difference in their height at the point directly over a sill. That difference is the divider setting to use as you scribe and cut the notch in that end of the second stringer. If the stringers have different diameters, the notches in the thicker logs may be deeper than those in the smaller timbers.

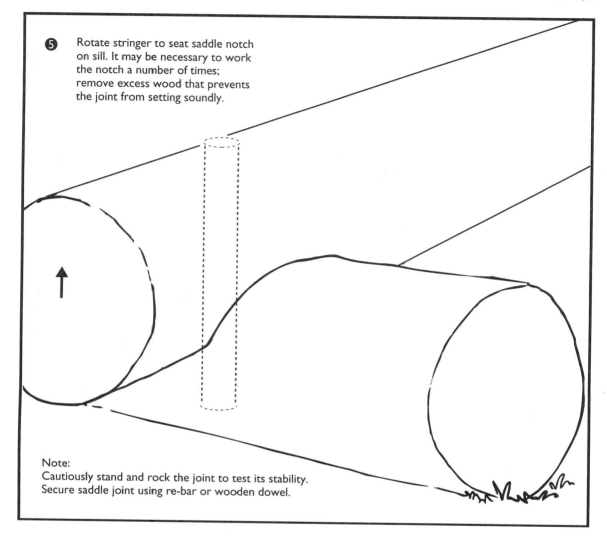

⑤ Rotate stringer to seat saddle notch on sill. It may be necessary to work the notch a number of times; remove excess wood that prevents the joint from setting soundly.

Note:
Cautiously stand and rock the joint to test its stability. Secure saddle joint using re-bar or wooden dowel.

LAP JOINT

Use the lap joint to join two logs lengthwise. The following steps explain how to scribe and cut a lap joint:

1. Use a level to draw horizontal diameter lines across the end of each log.
2. Extend the horizontal lines along the sides of the logs for a distance equal to the length of the lap joint—usually about the same measurement as the log's diameter.
3. With a saw, score the waste wood down to the side lines, then remove it with a saw or an adz. Remember that the notch on one log will face upwards while the notch on the opposing log will face down.

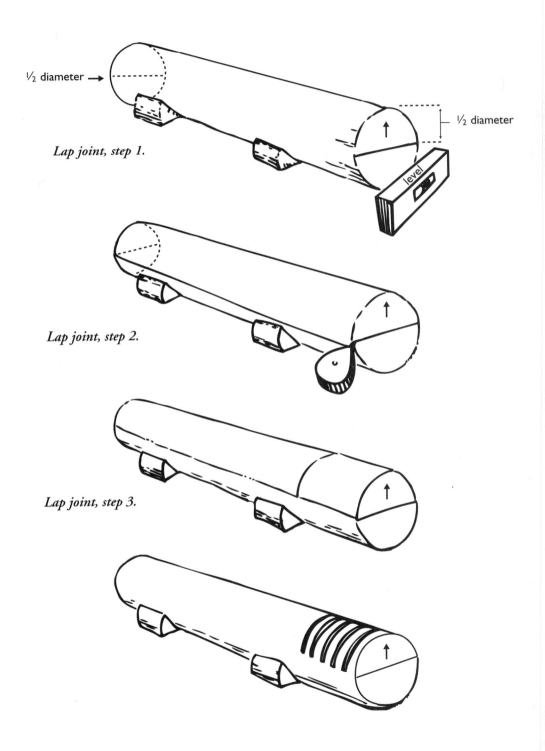

½ diameter →

½ diameter

level

Lap joint, step 1.

Lap joint, step 2.

Lap joint, step 3.

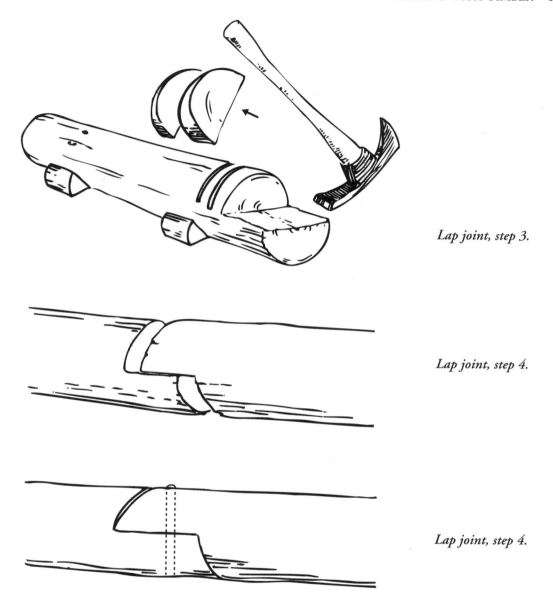

Lap joint, step 3.

Lap joint, step 4.

Lap joint, step 4.

4. Fit the logs together. If the diameter of one log is larger than that of the
   other, use a drawknife to smooth out the difference. If the lap joint cut
   into one log is longer than that in the other, creating a gap between the
   logs, adjust the longer one by cutting off a portion equal in length to the
   size of the gap.

Splitting Logs

Splitting a log in half will produce two rough timbers for use in puncheon or bridge construction. You will need splitting wedges, an axe, and a sledgehammer or maul.

1. Start with a log that has a fairly straight grain; a spiraling grain can sometimes be discerned by the appearance of the bark. Examine the end grain of the log for cracks that can be exploited, and look over the length of the log for knots to avoid. Draw an index line on the end of the log to show the best plane for splitting.
2. Hammer steel wedges into the end of the log, spacing the wedges along the index line and driving each wedge just deep enough to hold it in place.
3. Drive the wedges home, alternating hammer blows among them to drive them evenly.
4. As the log begins to split, drive another wedge into the split from the top of the log. When the wedges fall out, move them along the split and drive them again. Fashioned on-site with an axe, wooden wedges called *gluts* may prove useful in holding open a split.

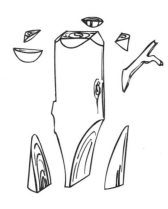

If the split begins to wander off course, drive several wedges in the intended line beyond the point of deviation. If the second line runs true, you can join it to the errant split by chopping through the wood fibers with an axe.

Splitting a very large log can be made easier by using a chain saw to cut a kerf the length of the intended split line. Finish splitting the log with wedges driven into the kerf.

A set-up called an *Alaska saw mill* can be used to cut planks from a log with a chain saw. Rails mounted along either side of the log will guide the saw the length of the log to yield cleanly shaped timbers.

Adzing

Adzing smooths the face of a rough-hewn timber, either to make an even walking surface or to allow one timber to fit tightly against another. The work is best done with an adz, though crews without access to that tool can use the finely honed adz blade of a Pulaski.

A log that has been split in half is ready to be adzed, while a round log should first be *canted*—marked with a chalk line, then scored with a saw and the waste wood chopped away.

(For more on marking a log, see "Canting Stringers" in Chapter 15, "Bridge Construction.")

Adzing is often done by standing on the timber itself. Using both hands, swing the adz with short, controlled strokes. Some timber experts use the adz to chop across the grain, while others prefer to wield it in line with the grain.

Gluts can be used along with wedges to split logs into useable timbers.

Since the blade is swung toward the legs, workers are advised to strap on metal or plastic toe protectors. They may also want to use shin guards such as those worn by baseball catchers.

Timber Structures

RETAINING WALLS

Log retaining walls, also known as *cribbing,* have many uses, including shoring up stream banks, serving as foundations for scenic overlooks, acting as bridge abutments, and holding trail tread in place against steep hillsides.

A log crib can be built with the same saddle notch construction used for the corners of log cabins. The difference is that the side logs, known as *headers* or *deadmen,* have most of their length buried at alternating angles in a hillside. Enough of each of these headers extends from the earth to support the notched cross-logs. The method of scribing and cutting saddle notches on angled logs is the same as for logs that are square with one another.

Gravity will hold together well-built cribbing. To provide more stability, the   *Log Retaining Wall*

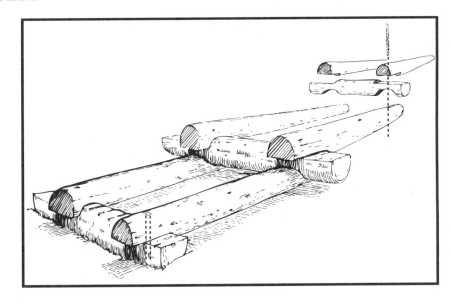

Right: *Cribbed steps made of timber can be filled with gravel or mineral soil to form the tread.*

Below: *Retaining wall logs set into the hillside are called* headers *or* deadmen.

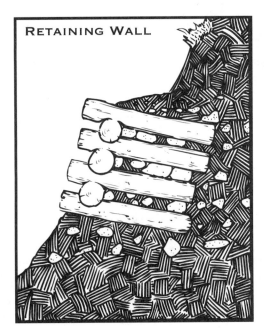

RETAINING WALL

logs can be pinned to each other as they are being laid in place by drilling pilot holes into the notches and then driving spikes or lengths of steel reinforcement bar through them. Pack rocks and dirt behind the log crib to support a stream bank or to form a foundation for a trail tread or overlook.

If the long logs of a retaining wall are to rest tightly against one another, set the scribing dividers at half the diameter of each header. Sometimes, though, the dividers are set at a third or a quarter of the header diameter, resulting in shallower notches that will leave a gap of several inches between each pair of logs. These gaps can be packed from behind with rocks that, along with the logs, will hold the fill dirt and stone in place. The advantage of this method is that it requires fewer logs to build a crib.

CHAPTER 15

Bridge Construction

THE CASCADE RANGE OF THE PACIFIC NORTHWEST comes by its name honestly, for the rugged backcountry is cut through by thousands of streams thundering down the mountains toward the sea. Dwarfed by the size of old-growth trees, hikers find rustic timber bridges carrying trails across streams that are anything but serene. Spanning the most remarkable gorges and torrents, those bridges did not come about by chance.

In the misty past of the Northwest, trail crews would ascend into the Cascades with their axes, crosscut saws, and pack horses loaded with enough provisions to get them through a long run of trail work. When they came to a stream crossing in need of a bridge, they felled cedar, hemlock, and Douglas fir, then used hand tools to fashion bridge abutments, stringers, decking, and rails. With block and tackle they moved the stringers over the stream, then notched together the pieces of the bridge. When the work was done, they loaded up their gear and traveled deeper into the forest.

It is a splendid vision, this notion of trail workers able to construct bridges using only simple tools and the materials that can be found in the backcountry. It also represents a set of skills that can be mastered by crews today, and that will serve them well wherever they are using timber to build rustic structures.

Craftsmanship, science, the art of design, human aspiration, social utility and striving after beauty, as expressed by the builders of bridges, are here fused into one. . . .

William E. Wickenden
"INTRODUCTION," IN
BRIDGES IN HISTORY AND LEGEND BY WILBUR J. WATSON AND SARA RUTH WATSON (CLEVELAND: J. H. JANSEN, 1937), P. VII.

Bridge Location Considerations

The thought that goes into planning a bridge is every bit as important as the effort invested in its construction. One of the most important is its location.

- The span must be above seasonal high water. Sticks, leaves, mud, and other debris washed up on stream banks can give an indication of annual high water marks, as can rocks scored by ice. Judge the size of snags that may float downstream during flood stage, and estimate how far above high water the bottom of the bridge should be. Achieving that elevation may require raising the span by placing it on high banks, on elevated abutments, or on a combination of both.
- Stable banks. Bedrock makes the best bridge foundation. Earthen banks may need abutments constructed of rock or timber. Avoid locating on or just below a bend in a stream where bank erosion can be more pronounced.

direction of river flow

face wall

45° 35°

rock fill

bank | tie logs

Log Bridge Abutment

Location is a key to the durability and ease of construction of a bridge.

- Banks close together. The narrower the crossing, the shorter the bridge. Shorter bridges require less material and often less labor, and they are not as susceptible to the structural stresses caused by the weight of hikers, stock animals, or snow loads.
- Sunny location. Snow and rainwater will disappear more quickly from a bridge in the sun than one that is shaded.
- Acceptable approach trails. In order to cross it, travelers must be able to reach a bridge. The trails approaching either side of a span should provide easy access and still fit aesthetically into the landscape.
- Environmental impact. A construction project as ambitious as a bridge can have major consequences upon its immediate surroundings. Trees may be felled, timber moved to the site, and footings excavated. Vegetation near the bridge will be trampled and waste wood may pile up around the structure. Crews can be creative in limiting their impact—hanging a tarp beneath the bridge to catch chips, bark, and sawdust, for example. Scheduling the construction of a bridge must also allow for enough time to clean up the area and restore its appearance.

Stringers and Sills

A log or a timber beam crossing a span is called a *stringer*. A *single stringer* bridge, then, is a bridge built on one stringer; a *three stringer* bridge distributes the weight of trail users among three logs or beams. Stringers are often made of trees felled near the bridge site, especially if the location is remote. Milled lumber can also be used, either as solid timbers or as boards laminated together to form stringers of sufficient size. Some bridge designers sheath a steel I-beam with wood to approximate the appearance of a timber stringer while incorporating the strength and durability of the steel.

Logs and timbers used as stringers are seldom absolutely straight. Stringers should be installed in bridges with any bow, or *crown,* facing up. That gives the stringer the shape of a shallow arch, increasing the strength of the bridge.

Stringers are notched or otherwise shaped at each end to fit onto *sills*—short

Nearly every bridge will have one or more **stringers** *resting upon* **sills.** *The bridge in this illustration also features railing posts set in dovetail notches.*

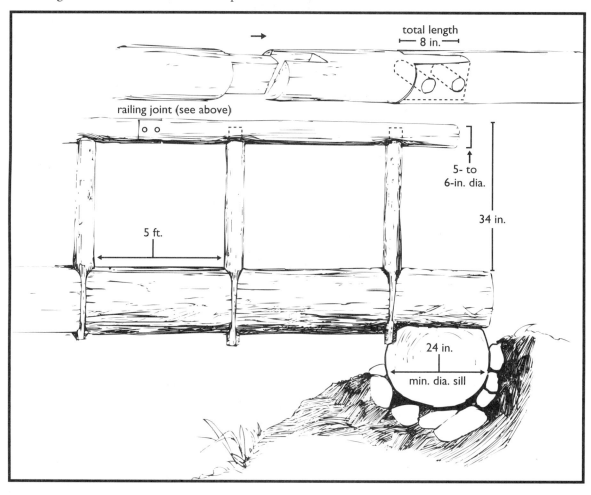

logs or timbers set on the ground perpendicular to the stringer or built into bridge abutments. Sills are used to support almost every rustic bridge, from the most modest to the most complex, even when a bridge is built on bedrock. The sills can be leveled so that the bridge will lie square with the world. They are also expendable. If a sill rots due to contact with moist soil, maintenance crews can jack up the end of the bridge and place a new sill beneath it. Without sills, the ends of the stringers themselves will be more prone to decay, and stringers cannot be replaced without rebuilding the entire bridge.

The simplest wooden sills are short logs of the same or greater diameter than the stringers. They should be about twice as long as the width of the bridge. Railroad ties and pressure-treated milled lumber are sometimes used as sills, but with the attendant problems of creosote or fungicidal agents leaching into the soil and water. (For more on using treated lumber, see Chapter 14, "Building with Timber.")

Sills resting on soil will rot more quickly than those that are shielded from the earth. One solution is to dig a shallow trench where a sill will be placed, then fill it with crushed stone and set the sill on that. Laying a sill on bedrock may involve shaping the underside of the log so that it will fit over irregularities in the rock. An axe, bow saw, chisel, and adz may all come in handy.

Unless the bridge is quite small or the fit quite good, sills resting on bedrock should also be fastened to the rock. Begin by drilling several ¾-inch holes through the sill, then use a rock drill to bore matching holes a few inches into the bedrock. Pack mortar or epoxy into the holes in the rock and position lengths of steel reinforcement bar in them. After the adhesive has set, fit the sill holes over the re-bar and drive the sill into place.

If the foundation of the bridge includes abutments made of timber or rock cribbing, the sills can be built into the abutments. Better yet, place the sills in beds of crushed stone laid behind the top tier of the abutments so that replacing the sills will not require reconstructing the abutments themselves.

Leveling the sills for a small bridge is best done by temporarily installing them and using a bubble level to guide your final adjustments. Position the stringer or stringers on top of them, then check to see that each stringer is level. If not, adjust the height of one or both sills until the stringers and sills are properly aligned.

The difficulty of handling heavy stringers makes it imperative to level the sills before the stringers for large or long bridges are moved onto them. The easiest way is to sight from one sill location to the other with a clinometer or hand level. The initial measurements can be done while standing on one sill and shooting a grade at your eye level on a person standing on the sill on the opposite side of the span. Once the sills are tentatively installed, place the clinometer directly atop a sill and, lying behind it, sight across to the other sill. For the bridge to be level, you should get a reading of zero percent regardless of where on top of the near sill you place the clinometer or where on top of the far one you take your readings. (For more on using clinometers, see Chapter 7, "Measuring Distances, Grades, and Heights.")

POSITIONING THE STRINGERS

After the sills are positioned, you can move a log stringer into place, then scribe it and cut notches that will fit over the sills. Saddle notches are often used for short bridges, while modified lap joints allow the stringers of long bridges to be more easily moved laterally to align them with the sills and with each other. (For more on scribing and cutting notches, see Chapter 14, "Building with Timber.")

To determine whether a pair of stringers resting on sills in front of you are square with one another, measure diagonally from the near end of the stringer on your left to the far end of the stringer on your right. Measure the remaining diagonal, from the near end of the stringer on your right to the far end of the stringer on your left. If the stringers are square with one another, the two diagonal measurements will be the same.

The open grain at the ends of the stringers tends to absorb moisture, accelerating decay of the wood. Boards called *mud sills* or *stringer end caps* nailed to the ends of the stringers will help seal out water and prolong the life of a bridge.

Modified Lap Joints for Bridge Stringers

A modified lap joint is often used to fit a bridge stringer onto a sill. Unlike the saddle notch, the lap joint will allow the stringer to be adjusted horizontally on the sill to square it with the overall bridge design. Flattening, or *canting*, the top of the sill results in a level surface that eliminates the effects of any crowning. Canting the sills also removes the sapwood; a stringer lying on heartwood is less susceptible to decay. Sometimes the canted surface of the sill will be slightly sloped to facilitate drainage of rainwater and snowmelt.

The modified lap joint in the underside of a load-bearing stringer should be cut no more than a quarter the diameter of the log; cutting it deeper may compromise the stringer's structural strength. Instead of leaving the notch with a right-angled cut that could lead to splitting, exit the notch at a 45-degree angle. Sometimes called a *dap*, the modified lap joint will be stronger in standing up to loads put upon it from above.

Bridge Designs

From simple foot logs to suspension spans, the variety of backcountry bridge designs is limited only to the materials at hand and the ingenuity of the builders.

A lap joint may be used when joining two rail sections

bull rail

deck

stringer (clears ground)

sill   sill

Linear Section

bull rail

deck

stringer (hewn flat on top)

sill

Cross Section

PUNCHEON

PUNCHEON

To the trail crews of Vermont's Green Mountain Club, *puncheon* refers to two flattened logs nailed side by side on sills to form an elevated walking surface. The Appalachian Mountain Club and Appalachian Trail Conference call that construction a *topped log bridge, split log bridge,* or *bog bridge.* In the West, *puncheon* is more likely to involve stringers, sills, and decking.

Whatever it is called, simple decked bridgework using milled lumber or native logs as stringers can lift a trail route above wet areas that are neither feasible to drain nor readily passable with a turnpike. When premium material is used (old-growth red cedar or redwood, for example), the puncheon may have a useful life of 30 years or more. Puncheon constructed of less water-resistant, untreated material may last less than a decade.

Puncheon for a horse trail consists of a deck 48 inches in width with a minimum thickness of 4 inches, laid on stringers with a minimum diameter of 10 inches. The deck of a hiker trail may be narrower, while that intended for use by cross-country skiers will be wider. The stringers are notched and pinned to sills placed at intervals of 6 to 8 feet. The wetter the ground, the longer the sills will need to be in order to prevent the puncheon from sinking. Sills are placed directly on top of the soil, or dug in just enough to level them with each other.

Planks for puncheon decking are usually made of milled lumber that has

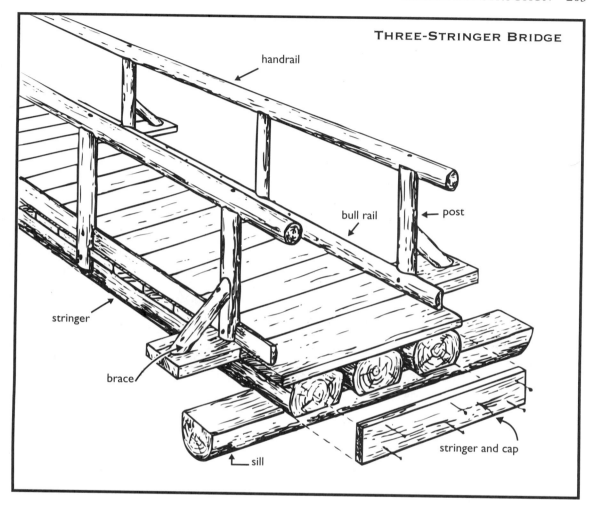

THREE-STRINGER BRIDGE

handrail

bull rail

post

stringer

brace

stringer and cap

sill

been transported to the project site. Leave a small space between each pair of planks to allow for drainage and any swelling of the wood. Hold a nail as a temporary spacer between planks to establish the correct separation while you spike them to the stringers.

In the Cascades, Sierra, the Ozarks, and Alaska, crews sometimes use a froe to split planks out of rounds of cedar. California crews may also split redwood. The planks' resistance to rot can be increased by removing any sapwood before installing them in a bridge or puncheon.

STRINGER BRIDGES

A standard design of bridges found throughout the National Forests and National Parks has much in common with decked puncheon. The stringers that provide the primary structural strength of these spans can be as great as 50 feet or more. Two-stringer bridges are usually sufficient for hiker use, while bridges intended for livestock or cross-country skiers will have three or more stringers.

Livestock bridges also feature a *bull rail* on each side of the decking to prevent the hooves of a horse or mule from going over the edge of the bridge if the animal slips. Wooden spacers that lift the bull rails an inch or two off the bridge decking allow for better drainage. Depending on user requirements, stringer bridges can be equipped with railings stabilized by longer planks of decking called *outriggers*.

The components for the decking and railings for bridges of this sort are often cut in an agency workshop, then transported in pieces to the backcountry site for final assembly. Sometimes the stringers are also fabricated from milled lumber and hauled or flown by helicopter to a bridge location, though it is more common to fell trees near the bridge and convert them into stringers.

Standard Dimensions of Puncheon and Bridge Decking

TRAIL TYPE	DECK WIDTH	DECK THICKNESS	BULL RAIL
Hiker	36 inches	3 inches	optional
X-C Skier	60-inch minimum	3 inches	no
Horse	48-inch minimum	4 inches	yes

Nails—For 3-inch decking, use #50 to #60 galvanized nails.
For 4-inch decking, use 3/8-inch x 8-inch galvanized spikes.

Having built a lot of various types of bridges, I'll argue strongly that an experienced crew can build a Gadbury bridge in one-half to one-third the time it takes for a stringer bridge.

Mike Shields
NATIONAL PARK SERVICE

GADBURY BRIDGE

Not every bridge needs to have decking on it. The simplest alternative is a log with its top adzed flat to form a walking surface.

The Gadbury bridge, developed in the early days of the U.S. Forest Service, is traditionally made with a log split in half. One log half is turned end for end to equalize the width of the bridge, and the two halves are spiked to sills. When using larger timbers, bridge builders must often shape, or *cant,* the inside faces of the halves so that they will fit together tightly. To reduce the tendency to bounce, longer Gadbury bridges may also have *splines* driven into dovetail notches cut across the log halves.

A variation on the Gadbury bridge is made of logs that are canted rather than split. The canting squares the logs so that they will fit against one another. They can then be secured to the sills with wooden pegs. If handrails are required, they, too, can be installed using notches rather than bolts, screws, or other hardware.

Building a bridge that relies completely on joinery is the height of the backcountry timber worker's craft. However, opportunities to build these bridges are few. Resource managers accustomed to approving bridges that have

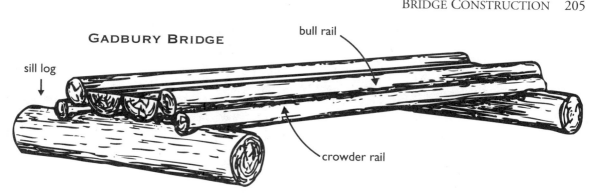

GADBURY BRIDGE

sill log

bull rail

crowder rail

decking, spikes, and bolts may be uncomfortable with the Gadbury design or its variations. Crews that have not built such a bridge may be intimidated by the techniques involved.

Their reluctance is unfortunate. Properly constructed, the Gadbury bridge should satisfy the structural demands placed upon it. In appearance, a joinery bridge fits into natural environments as well as other wooden bridges, and will be as durable. Most importantly, trail workers who have mastered the craft of constructing a bridge by using canting and joinery will have the confidence to handle almost any timber project that comes their way.

A Step-by-Step Guide to Joinery Bench and Bridge Construction

The best way to learn to do something is by doing it. The SCA Work Skills Program has developed a bench as a teaching device that allows backcountry workers to practice basic and advanced timber skills. The bench is a miniature version of a joinery bridge, requiring the same measurements, cuts, and notches needed to build a bridge, but completed on a scale that is easy to manage and requires little in the way of materials. As an added bonus, builders will end up with a handsome bench where they can sit at the end of the day and admire their handiwork. (For a listing of tools required for joinery work, see Chapter 14, "Building with Timber.")

1. Select the timber and peel off the bark. For a bench of average size, you'll need the following materials. The diameter measurements may vary depending upon the type of wood available and desired dimensions of the bench:
   - 2 sills—12 to 14 inches in diameter, about 5 feet long
   - 2 or 3 stringers—6 to 8 inches in diameter, about 5 feet long
   - 1 rail—minimum 5 inches in diameter, the same length as the stringers
   - 2 rail posts—same diameter as the rail, each about 3 feet long
   - 1 spline blank—3 feet × 5 inches

Building a joinery bench allows timber workers to practice the joinery skills used to construct backcountry bridges without nails, spikes, or other metal hardware.

- 15 wooden wedges such as those used for rehandling axes
- 6 wooden dowels, each 18 inches long and the same diameter as the auger bit (usually ¾ inch or 1 inch)

    If ready-made dowels are not available, they can be hewn on site from 1-inch × 1-inch × 18-inch blanks of hardwood or cedar.

2. Cut sills to length. For a bench, they should be wide enough so that a few inches will project in front of the stringers, and extend 18 to 24 inches behind them to balance the bench when sitters lean back. (For a bridge, the length of each sill should be twice the width of the intended tread.)

3. Cut the stringers to the desired bench length. The cuts should be square with the logs.

4. Cant the stringers. *Canting* a log is a means of producing a flat surface. Logs can be canted to form walking surfaces for bridges, or to fit two logs lengthwise against one another. The steps below illustrate how to

cant the inside faces of two bridge stringers to be fitted against one another. If there is a third stringer in the center, it should be canted on the two faces that will be flush against the canted faces of the left and right stringers.

a. The stringers should be straight. If there is a slight bow, orient the stringers with their crowns up to prevent the crowns from creating an awkward fit between the stringers.

b. Using a level as a straight edge, scribe a vertical *diameter reference line* through the center of the end of each stringer. Clearly mark which end of the line is UP.

c. Lay the stringers side by side, alternating butt ends to compensate for any taper. Write location information on each stringer, indicating which will go on the left side and which on the right, and also which end of each stringer goes which way.

d. Roll the stringers 90 degrees, checking with a level to make sure the *diameter reference line* at the end of each stringer is exactly horizontal.

e. Use the level to locate and scribe a *cant line* on each end of each stringer—a horizontal line marking off the portion of the log to be removed.

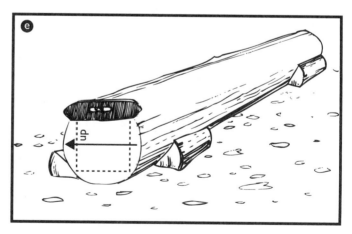

f. Stretch a chalk line between the cant lines on the ends of a stringer and snap the line. The chalk line must be pulled out on the same plane as the intended flat surface of the log. (Marking a long log may be more accurately achieved by turning the log so the chalk line is pulled vertically. That will eliminate any sag in the chalk line.)

Repeat the process to connect the opposite ends of the cant lines. When you are done, the chalk lines and the cant lines will

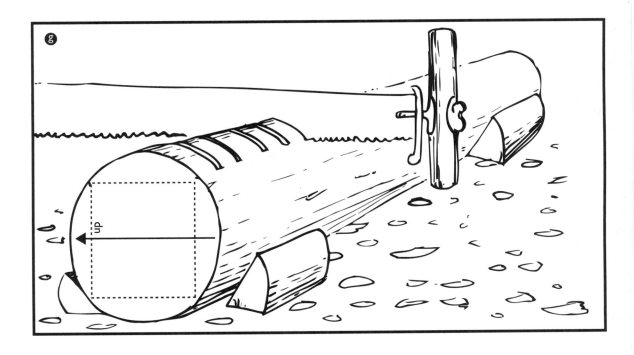

form a long rectangle outlining the waste wood to be removed from the stringer in order to create a flat, canted face that will fit flush against the canted surface of its neighboring stringer.

g. Turn the stringer upright and use a saw to score the wood at 3 to 4-inch intervals down to, but not through, the chalk lines. The closer together you cut the score lines, the easier it will be to re- move waste wood. If there are knots in the wood above the lines, put saw cuts through them to facilitate easier removal.

h. Cut away the waste wood with an axe, adz, or chisel. Start at the ends of the stringer where the wood will be easiest to chop out, and work toward the center. A slick can be used to finish smooth- ing the face.

    When all the stringers have been canted, position them against each other and check the fit. Make any final adjustments with an adz or slick.

5. Next, prepare the sills. For a bench, turn the sills so any crown is up. For a bridge, where the earth can support an embedded sill, the crown can be turned down so that the bow of the sill will discourage the stringers from rolling off. However, in neither structure should the crowns of the sills be laid to the side since the weight of the stringers will tend to ro- tate unbalanced sills out of position.

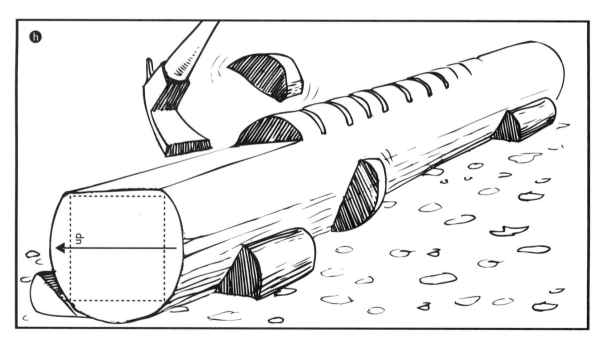

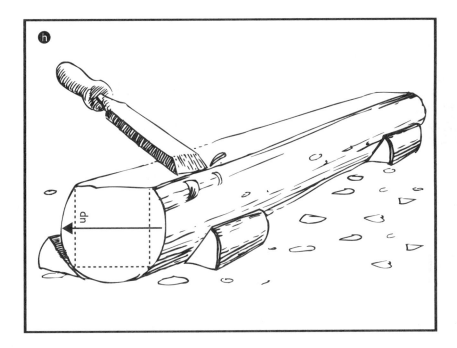

6. Scribe and cut saddle notches or lap joints to fit the stringers onto sills. (For guidelines on notching, see Chapter 14, "Building with Timber.")

7. After all the stringers have been notched and placed on the sills, bind the stringers together with load binders or some other tensioning system. Arrange the binders so that they do not cover the center of the bench stringers—the eventual location of the spline that will hold the stringers together when the tightening system is removed. (Bridge stringers are usually secured with two or more splines, uniformly spaced along the length of the structure. An even number of splines insures that there will not be one in the center of the bridge where the greatest stringer strength is required.)

The stringers of a structure as small as a bench can be held together temporarily by wrapping a rope loosely around them and tying the ends with a square knot. Place a stout stick under the rope and bind the stringers by twisting the rope with the stick as you would a tourniquet. Tie off the stick to maintain the tension in the rope.

The logs of a large bridge can be bound by wrapping ¼-inch wire rope around them tightly, clamping the rope with cable clips, then driving wedges under the rope to create enough tension.

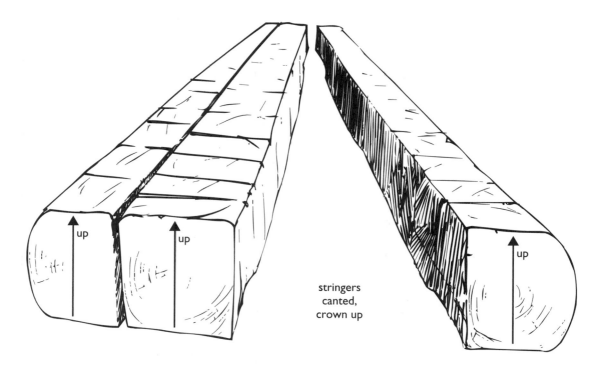

stringers
canted,
crown up

8. Flatten the surface of the stringers. Determine the plane of the bench seat (or bridge walkway) by estimating the least amount of wood that must be removed in order to achieve a flat surface. The *depth* of the stringers will determine the strength of the structure far more than their *width,* so reduce the diameter as little as possible by removing a minimum of wood.

    Next, use a level to mark the surface plane on the ends of the stringers. In the same manner as was done in preparation to cant the logs, snap chalk lines along the length of the outside stringers, and connect the plane lines to outline the wood to be removed. Score the waste wood down to the chalk lines with a saw, then chop away the extra material. For the time being, leave untouched that portion of waste wood beneath the rope, straps, or chains binding the stringers together. It will be easy to remove that wood when the binders are taken off at the end of construction.

9. Cant the spline. The piece of wood from which you will shape the spline should be a foot or two longer than the width of the bench or bridge.

Canted logs will fit tightly together.

The extra length of the spline blank will allow your partner to stabilize the wood while you are shaping it.

Using a level, draw a straight line across the end of the blank on a plane with the desired bottom face of the spline. Use a chalk line to extend that line along each side of the blank for a distance a little longer than the width of the bench's seating surface. Score the waste wood down to the chalk lines with a saw, then hew away the excess wood.

Canting the 4-inch width of the spline at this time in the construction process will assure you that you will have a spline large enough to fill a dovetail notch with a floor 4 inches wide. If the canted surface of your spline is smaller, either start again with a new spline blank or adjust the dimensions of the dovetail notch accordingly.

Splines fitted into dovetail notches will stiffen a bench or bridge and help hold the stringers in place.

10. Lay out the dovetail notch to receive the spline.

a. Mark a center line perpendicular to the stringers across the bench surface. Extend the line down both the back and front of the bench. Scribe a mark at each end of the line at a point 2 inches down from the top of the stringers.

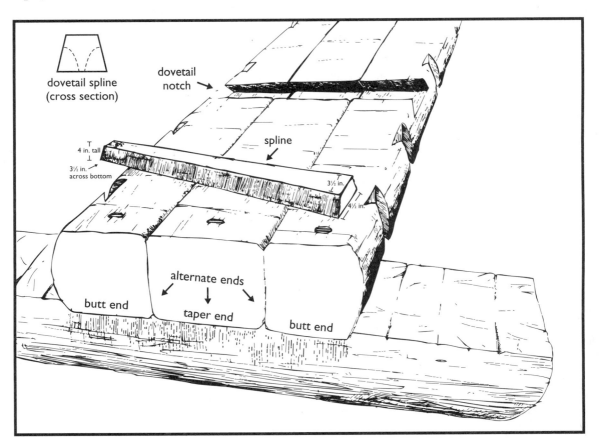

dovetail spline (cross section)

dovetail notch

spline

4 in. tall

3½ in. across bottom

3½ in.

4½ in.

alternate ends

taper end

butt end

butt end

b. On the back side of the bench, extend a horizontal line 2 inches on either side of the back mark. (As referenced from the front of the bench, the ends of the horizontal lines are *Back Left* and *Back Right*.)

c. On the front of the bench, scribe a horizontal line 1½ inches on either side of the front mark. (The ends of the front horizontal line are *Front Left* and *Front Right*.)

d. Mark the center point of the line on top of the stringers. Extend a perpendicular line ¾ inch on either side of the center line. (As seen from the front of the bench, the ends of the perpendicular line are *Center Left* and *Center Right*.)

e. Using a flexible straight edge (the edge of a foam sleeping pad, for example, or a piece of cardboard or plastic), draw a curved line that connects Back Left, Center Left, and Front Left. Draw a second curved line connecting Back Right, Center Right, and Front Right. The curved lines indicate the left and right sides of the dovetail notch. The horizontal lines scribed 2 inches below the surface of the bench indicate the floor of the notch.

11. Cut the dovetail notch. It may be helpful to have three people involved in cutting this notch—one on each end of a crosscut saw and one straddling the bench to sight the line and, with a careful hand on the back of the saw, to guide the teeth into the wood at the proper angle.

a. Cut along the left and right angles of the notch, keeping the saw just inside the lines.

b. Make a third cut down the center of the notch, again stopping just before the saw touches any lines.

c. Use chisels and slicks to remove the waste wood from the notch. Flatten the floor of the notch and smooth the sides, taking care not to chew up the wood fibers in the notch.

12. Shape the spline. (If you have not already canted one face of the spline, return to step #9 and do so now.)

a. Measure the length of the dovetail notch from the front to the back of the bench. Transfer that length to the spline, scribing a *spline-length mark* onto the canted face of the spline to indicate how much of the blank must be shaped in order to fill the notch in the stringers.

b. Mark a centerline on the end of the spline blank and extend it down the center of the canted face.

c. Measure the width of the floor of the notch at its narrower end, and transfer that width to the end of the canted face of the spline blank.

d. Measure the width of the floor of the notch at its wider end, and transfer that width onto the flattened blank at the spline-length mark. Snap a chalk line to connect the lines so that you transfer

The dovetailed end of a railing post is shaped in the same manner as a spline.

onto the spline blank the shape of the notch floor. Extend the lines several inches beyond the spline-length mark.

e. Using a sliding T-bevel, transfer the angles of the narrow end of the notch to the end of the spline blank, tracing along the edges of the tool to scribe the angles onto the wood.

f. Set the sliding T-bevel to match the angle in the wide end of the notch. At the spline-length mark, use a saw to cut a kerf that approximates the angle set on the T-bevel. As you saw, keep checking the kerf by fitting the T-bevel into it until you have matched the angle at the end of the spline blank. Repeat on the other side of the spline blank.

g. Extend chalk lines from the spline-blank end to the kerfs of the T-bevel angles cut at the spline-length mark, thus completing the transfer to the spline blank of the entire shape of the dovetail notch.

h. Score and cut away the waste wood down to the chalk lines along each side of the spline.

i. Test fit the spline, making adjustments until the spline slides all the way into the notch. Drive the spline in place with a maul and cut off the excess length of the spline blank.

13. Make railing posts. Railing posts for a bench or bridge are shaped and fitted into tapered dovetail notches in the same way that splines and notches are laid out and cut.

a. Starting at the butt end, cant one face of the post in a manner similar to that used to cant the face of a spline (see step #9, above).

b. Using the width of the post's canted face as a reference, scribe the outline for a tapered dovetail notch on the back of the rear bench stringer, then cut the notch. The method is similar to that used for scribing and cutting a dovetail notch to receive a spline. (See steps #10 and #11, above.)

c. Shape the post spline. (See step #12, above.)

d. Install the posts. Determine how high you want the rail to be. Add at least 1 inch to accommodate a tenon, then cut the posts even with each other.

14. Shape the railing. The hidden mortise and tenon joint used to join the railing to the posts is aesthetically appealing. More importantly, the open grain of the wood in the juncture of the railing and posts is sealed against the elements.

a. Scribe and cut the tenon. The thickness of the tenon is dependent upon the diameter of the auger bit with which you will shape the mortise—a 1-inch bit, and thus a tenon 1 inch wide, is ideal.

b. Cut the railing the same length as the stringers. Lay the railing on top of the tenons, positioning the crown of the railing up. Trace the shape of the tenons onto the underside of the railing.

c. Bore most of the waste wood out of the mortise with an auger, taking care to cut only slightly deeper than the height of the tenon. Finish shaping the mortise with a chisel.

d. Use a backsaw to cut a kerf parallel with the stringers into each tenon. Start a wooden wedge into each kerf, then ease the mortises over the tenons. Drive the railing down onto the posts with a maul, alternating blows between the posts to set the railing evenly. As the railing descends over the tenons, it will force the wedges deeper into the kerfs and cause the tenons to expand against the sides of the mortises.

15. Peg the stringers to the sills. Use an auger to drill holes through the stringers and on into the sills beneath them.

Cut a kerf several inches into each end of a dowel. Trim a wooden wedge to make it slightly narrower than the diameter of the dowel, and insert into the kerf at the end of the dowel to be driven into the hole. Drive each dowel home with a mallet. The wedge will be forced further into the kerf when the dowel nears the bottom of the hole, locking the dowel in the stringer. Cut the top of the dowel flush with the stringer surface, then drive a wooden wedge into the remaining kerf to finish tightening the dowel in place.

A mortise and tenon joint fits a railing onto a railing post.

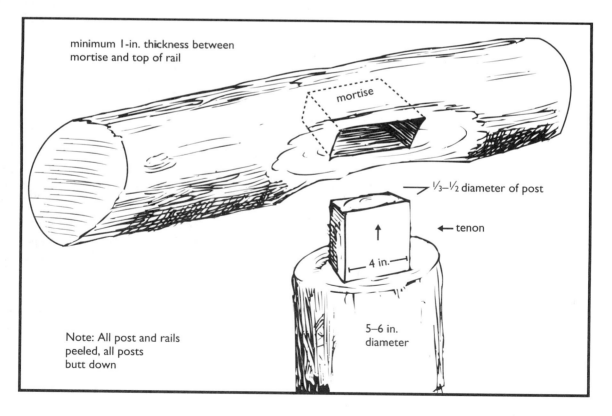

minimum 1-in. thickness between mortise and top of rail

mortise

1/3–1/2 diameter of post

← tenon

4 in.

5–6 in. diameter

Note: All post and rails peeled, all posts butt down

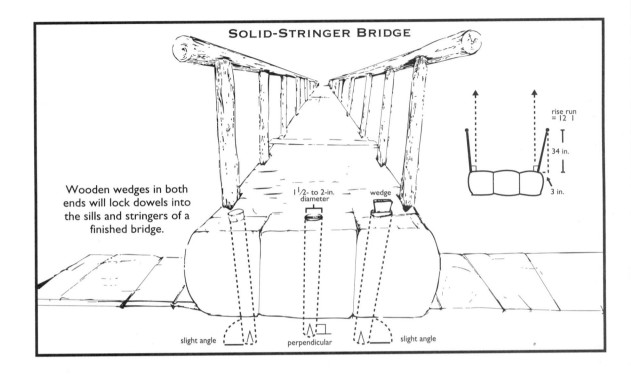

SOLID-STRINGER BRIDGE

rise run
= 12 1

34 in.

3 in.

Wooden wedges in both
ends will lock dowels into
the sills and stringers of a
finished bridge.

1 1/2- to 2-in.
diameter

wedge

slight angle   perpendicular   slight angle

Making Dowels

Dowels can be made on-site from blanks of wood 1 inch x 1 inch x 18 inches. A drawknife and a sharp pocketknife are the tools of choice for rounding the corners. Set a pair of calipers to the width of the auger bit, and use that measurement to test the dowel diameter. Unless the entire dowel is smoothed to the dimension of the bit, it cannot be driven through the stringer and into the sill.

Shaping dowels can be very time-consuming. Once you have made a couple and gotten the hang of it, you will probably be quite enthused about stopping by a hardware store and throwing a few ready-made dowels into your pack for the next bench or bridge that you build.

CHAPTER 16

Revegetation and Restoration

THE INTENT OF RESTORATION—repairing damage to the landscape caused by humans—is most admirable. Rather than leaving evidence of ourselves, restoration is a removal of human effects. It is a way for us to make amends for our past misuses of the earth. It is a gentle art, an act of compassion toward the environment for those who believe we can reestablish what we have abused and, in the process, perhaps redefine our relationship with the land that sustains us.

Restoration leads to better habitat for animals, cleaner water, a richer diversity of species, and healthier ecosystems. It is also aesthetically valuable, allowing people visiting parks and forests to enjoy pristine areas rather than finding terrain marred by overuse and abuse. Restoration is not a substitute for taking care of the environment in the first place. But where conservation and prevention of damage have failed, restoration can work wonders.

The art and science of restoration is still in its infancy. The effectiveness of methods being used today may not be fully understood for years. Unlike other backcountry management, where pouring additional resources and people into projects can bring them more quickly to completion, there is little that humans can do to persuade plants to grow faster. Crews must often be satisfied with the knowledge that they have created the conditions that will allow a meadow or a portion of a forest to grow again.

Restoration work can vary from simple steps taken to erase the impact of a temporary trail crew camp to a multi-year effort to revegetate an alpine meadow denuded by trampling. Other candidates for restoration include:

- Fire lines dug or bulldozed while fighting forest blazes
- Hiking trails that are being permanently closed
- Shortcuts across switchbacks
- Bootleg trails
- Tailings of abandoned backcountry mining operations
- Laceworks of secondary trails across meadows
- Inappropriate campsites
- Riparian areas left bare by trampling or overgrazing

Lousy weather at the Ranger Station means good transplanting conditions in the field.

RESTORATIONIST RUSS HANBEY

- Logged-out areas
- Deserted agency facilities

In some cases, agency personnel may determine that backcountry management goals can best be served by *not* attempting restoration. Heavily impacted areas that are no longer subject to erosion—campsites and trails, in particular—will probably suffer little further damage regardless of future use. Encouraging visitors to limit their activities to these beaten-down *sacrifice zones* will spare the unspoiled terrain beyond.

Ecological restoration is often a prolonged, labor-intensive activity. The decision to restore an area is best made by informed land-management personnel. Their planning must be thorough enough to insure that the work is appropriate and will be successful. Restoration planners should also have a realistic understanding of the size, duration, expense, and long-term demands of the undertaking.

The bottom line is that restoration projects require careful planning, a clear grasp of the breadth of the task, and the commitment to achieve the goals despite the long time frame they may involve.

Mapping an area undergoing restoration will reveal the extent and success of changes happening on the ground.

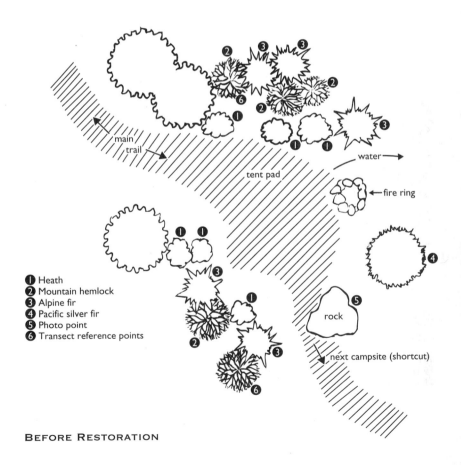

1 Heath
2 Mountain hemlock
3 Alpine fir
4 Pacific silver fir
5 Photo point
6 Transect reference points

BEFORE RESTORATION

Restoration and User Psychology

Restoration is a fruitless undertaking unless the impact that caused the damage in the first place is prevented from recurring. That requires land-management personnel to decide upon reasonable alternatives for resource users. If, for example, backcountry campsites are being revegetated, backpackers need to be directed to more acceptable camping areas. If a trail to a popular lake is to be closed, an alternative route must be made available to visitors who want to reach the lake.

In extreme cases, land managers may decide that the best course is to close an area to certain kinds of use (fencing off riparian areas to prevent livestock from grazing too closely to streams, perhaps), or to prohibit human activity altogether. Crews can install barriers to discourage visitors from encroaching on areas undergoing restoration. Barriers may be as subtle as rocks and logs blended into the landscape, or as overt as *Keep Off* markers and boundary string stretched between wooden stakes. At trailheads and at restoration sites, backcountry visitors often respond favorably to signs that explain the reasons work is being done and the role travelers can play by staying off fragile areas.

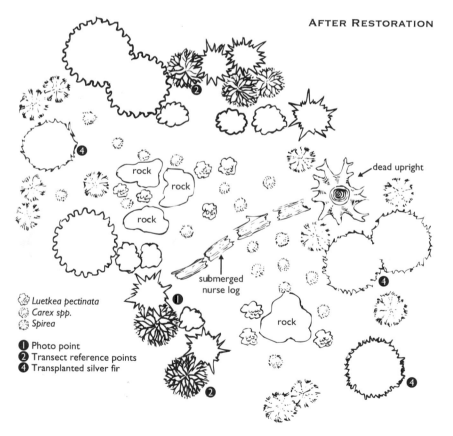

AFTER RESTORATION

Mapping an area undergoing restoration will reveal the extent and success of changes happening on the ground.

Restoration Plan

Seasonal crews are most likely to be involved in only one or two aspects of an overall restoration project—preparing a site for reseeding, for instance, or conducting transplanting operations. An agency must have someone sufficiently invested in the project to oversee it from one stage to the next, often for a period of several years.

A detailed Restoration Plan is one way that agency personnel and crew leaders can plan and implement a long-term environmental repair effort. Drawing up such a plan before the work begins will help land managers to direct most efficiently the people and resources at their disposal, and to gauge their progress and success.

Site Monitoring and Record Keeping

Monitoring a restoration site and keeping a written record will allow project managers to judge the effectiveness of environmental repairs. A well-kept record accompanied by photographs and maps will reveal changes occurring over months and years far better than can the human eye. The record can be used to chart restoration progress and to make changes in work methods, or to study a potential site of restoration work to discover whether degradation is increasing or if the area has stabilized and is recovering on its own. The monitoring method must withstand the test of time. Many parks and forests have developed standard recording methods for their particular situations.

Long-term monitoring is almost always the responsibility of agency personnel or conservation groups working in conjunction with land managers. Crew leaders may be involved in data collection, site mapping, and updating records. That requires a compass, measuring tape, pencils, camera, and a record book with graph paper pages.

A site map will help planners determine what restoration steps will be most productive, and, over time, how vegetation patterns are changing. A map must contain information that allows future users to orient it with the landscape. In most cases, north will be at the top of the page. Take compass bearings on significant landmarks within the site, then draw them on the map, using a grid scale to establish accurate locations.

Next, use transects, pacing, or a tape measure to collect data about existing plant locations and densities, rocks, downed timber, trails, campsites, and other significant features of the site. Transfer this information to the map, again using compass bearings and the grid scale to approximate locations. Include the locations of *photo points*—places from which comparison photographs can be taken over time. Contour lines indicating elevation may also be included if they are relevant to the long-term understanding of the site and its restoration—a steep trail corridor with drainage and stabilization problems, for example.

Maps can be drawn completely by hand, though landscape templates or rubber stamps will speed up the process. Consider using colored pencils to highlight important features on the map, such as newly installed plants. Include clear reference information in the map's margins or on attached pages so that future readers can make sense of each of your markings.

Lessening the Impact of Work Crews

A goal of restorationists is to do their work in such a way that their own actions do not cause further damage to a site. Low-impact work techniques may include:

- Establishing temporary pathways in the most durable areas of collection and restoration sites. Limiting crew movements to those trails will shield other areas from compaction. Use flagging or pin flags to mark trails and to highlight locations of fragile plants.
- Locating lunch spots, tool storage, and other areas of activity away from the restoration work, or in places that can themselves be repaired when you are done.
- Conserving and reusing excavated soil, plants, logs, rocks, duff, and other materials.
- Cleaning up work areas at the end of each stage of a project.

Some restoration crews also wear soft shoes without lugged soles to lessen the chance their footsteps will damage existing vegetation.

Restoration work is a way for people to reverse negative effects of human impact upon the land.

TOOLS AND MATERIALS FOR SITE RESTORATION WORK

Tool	Uses
Scoop shovel	General
Tree spade	Root pruning, transplanting, root division
Plastic bucket	General
Hand trowel	Transplanting, layering
Soil cultivator	Loosening soil, site preparation
Hand pruners	Selective pruning, transplants
Pulaski	Site preparation, landscaping
Mallet	General
McLeod or rake	Mulching, landscaping, loosening soil
Rock bar	Landscaping, site preparation
Soil thermometer	Seedbed monitoring

Supplies	Uses
Rooting hormone	Layering, cuttings
4-mil plastic	Seedbed development, solarization
Liquid fertilizer with vitamin B-1	Transplanting, general application
Transplant shock fluid	Transplanting
Stakes, flagging	Root pruning, layering
Nursery tags	Root pruning, layering
Plastic bags, paper lunch bags	Seed collection
Mulch mat	Mulching, site stabilization
Irrigation equipment	Site maintenance
pH and soil testing kits	Site preparation
Shade cloth	Plant protection, propagation

Site Preparation

The success or failure of restoration work can often be traced to how well the site was prepared.

Begin site preparation by looking for signs of erosion and, if they exist, finding out where the water is coming from and how it can be slowed or diverted. Sites with a gradient of 30 percent or more usually require the installation of erosion devices such as check dams or cribbing. Severely compacted soil, such as that found in worn-out campsites, may be so hardened that water runs off it, carrying soil particles as it goes. (For more on dealing with erosion, see Chapter 10, "Trail Drainage.")

Once erosion has been controlled, install visual barriers to camouflage the area and deter further human use. To that end, rocks, logs, and snags can be especially useful.

ROCKS

Embedding stones in a restoration site can keep people from using a closed trail or campsite. By minimizing the effects of sun, wind, snow, and rain, the placement of rocks may encourage plants to migrate into damaged sites, especially in high alpine regions. Rocks used for restoration work must be large and securely inlaid in the earth so that campers will not be tempted to move them. They should also be a natural part of the surrounding landscape so that they do not look out of place.

LOGS

Decaying logs are a landscape feature in most forests. Large logs firmly set in restoration sites can provide a physical barrier to camping and trampling, and at the same time establish an inviting environment for plants to get a foothold in the site.

SNAGS

A log can sometimes be set upright in the earth as though it were a stump. Such a trick is especially effective for blocking a closed trail or a switchback cut. The fake stump must be embedded securely to ward off the forces of wind, snow, and people.

Loosening compacted soil is often an important step in the restoration of trampled areas.

Borrowing Lightly from the Land

Never unduly disturb one area in order to improve another. In subalpine regions where a borrow site would be very slow to heal, borrowing any amount may be unacceptable. Even in rich areas that will support harvesting seeds, digging up vegetation for transplanting, or borrowing humus, soil, downed timber, rocks, or other matter, do not remove more than a very small amount (10 percent or less) of a given material from any one location. Taking more may compromise or destroy ecological niches.

Soil Preparation

Soil is a dynamic body that, like a living organism, has physical, chemical, and biological properties. Protecting, enhancing, and restoring soil are important aspects of restoration work.

LOOSENING COMPACTED SOIL

Soil that is highly compacted cannot absorb water or air. Roots cannot penetrate into it, and seeds cannot germinate. Loosening the soil with a mattock, pick, or shovel will help water and air penetrate into it and allow plant roots to grow through it. Loosen the soil to a depth of about six inches, but do not turn over the earth; keep the topsoil near the surface where plants can best take advantage of it.

ADDING SOIL

Adding soil to a restoration site may improve the shape of the terrain and enrich the existing soil with additional organic matter. Whenever possible, save organic soil being excavated from work projects such as trail construction, road cuts, or campground development, and incorporate this borrowed soil into restoration sites. The most effective method of applying it is to mix the borrowed soil in with each transplant, or rake it into a seed bed. Transferred soil should be similar in composition to the earth that is already there. Excavated soil can only be stored for six months to a year before it loses biological integrity, so plan to reuse it in the same season it was disturbed.

Additional soil may also allow you to restore the terrain to its original shape. A good example is filling a ditched-out, abandoned trail with fertile earth or with a combination of soil over a layer of rocks. The new soil erases the scar of the trail and provides an environment for vegetation to take root.

If no extra soil is available, consider using other sources of soil-like material to enrich a site undergoing repair. Outside of their burrows, animals such as marmots and badgers often leave *tailings* that are rich in nitrogen and other processed nutrients. Ground squirrels and larger animals leave *castings* that have concentrations of plant nutrients. Collect only well-aged tailings and castings, and mix small amounts into the soil as you are transplanting vegetation. As with all borrowing of natural materials, take no more than a very small amount of the tailings and castings from a given area.

Revegetating Sites

Much of restoration work involves encouraging new vegetation to become established and to flourish. Deciding what plants to use and how to acquire them is a key part of the Restoration Plan. Studying plant communities adjacent to restoration areas can help you understand what plants grow in a certain environment and how they space themselves. Further clues toward plant selection and placement may be found in naturally disturbed sites nearby—avalanche paths, flooded riparian areas, sites of fires, or areas where trees have been toppled by wind. Notice especially the species and the methods by which native plants have returned to those areas, and consider how those processes can be replicated in a restoration site.

Restoring soil nutrients may also influence the selection of plantings. For example, nitrogen is essential for plant survival, but it is easily depleted from the soil. One way to restore nitrogen to a site is by planting native *nitrogen-fixing* vegetation such as lupine and ceanothus.

The most common methods of revegetation are by seeding and by transplanting.

REVEGETATION BY SEEDING

After site preparations have established the right growing conditions (warmth, water, and loose, fertile soil), native seeds can be introduced into a damaged area. The simplest seeding technique is to loosen the soil in a site and then let the seeds from nearby plants drift in and take root. While that sometimes works very well, it is also a method dependent upon variables the restorationist cannot control. There may not be enough nearby seed sources. Those seeds that do reach the site may have low germination and viability rates, especially on bare ground.

More effective is collecting seeds and broadcasting them directly into the restoration site, often done in conjunction with site stabilization, landscaping, and transplanting.

SEED COLLECTION AND STORAGE

Collect seeds from areas similar to those in which they will be planted. Try to match drainage areas, shade or open sunshine, and other environmental conditions. Since they may crowd out native plants, seeds of non-native species should not be sown in wilderness, park, or pristine backcountry areas.

Conduct seed collecting in dry, calm weather. If the seeds are loose, you may be able to collect them with a butterfly net, or place a cloth around the base of a seed-bearing plant and allow gravity to do the rest. Battery-powered vacuums can sometimes be used to strip lightweight seeds from their sources. Cutting an entire stalk and then allowing separation in a storage bag may also be productive.

Place the seeds in paper lunch bags. Label each bag with information pinpointing location, species, and date. As always, limit impact upon a donor site by collecting a very small percentage of available seeds.

The seeds of dry-fruited species must be cleaned before storage or on-site dispersal. Winnow the seed from the chaff by gentle shaking, agitation, blowing, manual separation, or sieving through a strainer. Store seeds in airtight containers placed in a cool, dry area. Label all containers.

Seeds can be stored in this manner until they are sown, ideally at the end of the growing season. That will permit the seeds to follow their natural growing timetable.

Manual seeding does have its drawbacks. It is slower and less visually obvious than transplanting, requires a labor-intensive seed collection system, and limits the restorationist to a narrow range of plant species.

Restoration by Transplanting

Begin lifting *a plant for transplantation by cutting around the dripline.*

Experts familiar with local conditions and plant species can best determine which vegetation is appropriate for transplanting and how to accomplish the work. In general, grasses, sedges, mat-forming plants, and plants with runners have the highest success for transplanting. Woody plants of moderate size that have been root-pruned may also transplant well, though woody plants that are brittle, have long horizontal roots, or are found in dry sites should be left where they are. The same is usually true of plants with long taproots.

TRANSPLANTING NATIVE VEGETATION

Plants can be most successfully transplanted while they are dormant, though transplanting may be accomplished at other times of the year if the plants are not flowering and they can be properly watered and shaded. Vegetation selected for transplanting should be soaked the day before removal, then moved early in the morning or during cool, cloudy weather. Stress on plants is much higher in warm weather or if they are in direct sunlight. Transplant vegetation immediately after digging it up, or practice proper holding-over techniques. (For more on holding over, see below.)

Begin the transplanting process by digging the hole that will receive the plant, then *lift* each plant or plug of tightly grouped vegetation. Hold a scoop shovel or tree spade vertically and insert it deeply around the *drip line*—the outer growth perimeter of the plant or plug. Cut all the way around, severing the lateral roots. Rather than forcing a shovel through heavy roots, cut them with pruners. Circle around the vegetation with the shovel a second time, gently pulling back on the handle and lifting the plant or plug. Reach underneath with pruners to sever any remaining roots, then move the vegetation and attached soil into a bucket or a plastic bag, or onto a tarp. Immediately transplant the plant or plug. *Do not allow the roots to dry out!*

The planting hole should be about a third wider and deeper than the root ball of the transplant. Mix some of the soil taken from the hole with soil from the hole out of which you took the plant, and refill the bottom third of the planting hole. If enough of the original soil is not available, gather duffy ground litter nearby and mix it with the soil in the bottom of the planting hole. Thoroughly moisten the hole with water.

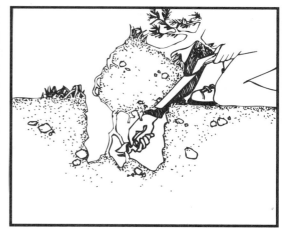

Many restorationists also add a third of a cup of bone meal or blood meal to a transplant hole to enhance root development. They are organic, rich in phosphorus, and have little impact upon the environment other than assuring a strong start for transplanted vegetation.

Center the plant in the hole. If necessary, spread and prune the roots to fit the hole, but do not bend them. Seat the plant so that it is balanced. Fill the space around

Clip remaining roots to free a plant from the earth.

the root wad with a mixture of soil, duffy litter, bone meal, and soil from the plant's original location. Press the soil and plant downward to stabilize it, to collapse large air pockets, and to prevent the plant from being heaved out of the soil by frost. Form a depression around the edge of the plant to catch and hold water.

Soak the new plant twice, the second time with B-1 hormone mixed at a ratio of one to three capfuls with a gallon of water. Like bone meal, B-1 hormone is a transient substance that will help reduce transplant shock and increase the likelihood of plant survival.

Protect the base of the plant with a loose layer of forest litter. This mulch will preserve moisture in the summer and insulate the plant in the winter. However, avoid using pure wood chips or sawdust, as these materials may rob nitrogen from the soil as they decompose.

Any holes from which plants are taken must be filled with soil and obscured with native litter. Mound up the soil to allow for settling.

TRANSPLANTING CONTAINER-GROWN PLANTS

Container-grown plants of native species can be carried from a nursery to a restoration site by helicopter, backpack, or pack stock. Plants grown in a nursery operation should have been *hardened-off*, or pre-adapted to harsher outdoor living conditions, and monitored closely before transplanting in the backcountry.

Plants in containers may dry out rapidly, so monitor them for moisture throughout the transportation and transplanting process. A dry plant is obviously lighter to the feel. Sample plants can also be eased out of their pots and

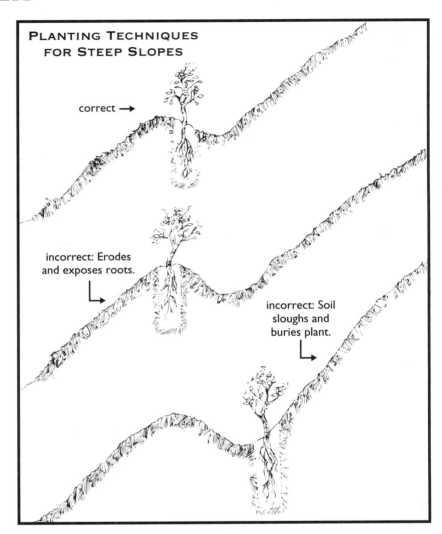

PLANTING TECHNIQUES
FOR STEEP SLOPES

correct →

incorrect: Erodes
and exposes roots.

incorrect: Soil
sloughs and
buries plant.

*Vegetation transplanted
on steep slopes must
be properly placed to
enhance chances of
success.*

inspected for dryness. Packing plants in wet burlap bags or plastic bags with damp moss are two ways to keep plants moist. As plants are moved about, protect them from damage to their stems and branches.

Site preparation and transplanting procedures are essentially the same for container-grown plants as for plants collected in the field. When installing a pot-bound plant, loosen the roots and cut away any that are excessively long.

WHEN TO TRANSPLANT

Transplanting times vary in different parts of the country. In regions with cold winters, transplanting is often done in the autumn just before the dormant season. The days are shorter than in midsummer, and there is less chance of plants drying out. Plants will have a month or two to adapt to their new environment before freezing weather sets in. Come spring, the transplants will be well prepared to begin the new growing cycle.

Unfortunately, the timing of transplanting is often disrupted by factors that have little to do with the needs of vegetation. When autumn rolls around, seasonal work crews may have left the backcountry. Plants taken from construction projects may become available in midsummer when installing them would prove futile.

One solution to increasing the timing options of transplanting is *holding over*.

HOLDING OVER PLANTS

Laying plants in loosened earth and covering them with mulch may keep them viable until they can be transplanted—up to a year in areas with sufficient moisture and shade. Hold over plants even if only a few hours will pass before they can be transplanted, storing them where their root systems will be shielded from sun and wind. Good locations for holding over include the shaded side of decomposing logs, semi-moist forest floors with thick litter layers, and damp terrain near ponds or streams. Plants which can be most successfully held over are small trees and shrubs, perennials, grassy clumps, and some ground covers.

SOURCES OF VEGETATION FOR TRANSPLANTING

In addition to digging up plants near restoration sites, consider the following sources of plants for use in revegetation work:

- Recovery from backcountry construction sites
- On-site propagation
- Layering
- Root division
- Root pruning

PLANT RECOVERY

Collecting plants from the locations of trail work, road building, and campground development allows restorationists to take advantage of plant material that would otherwise be wasted.

Plants recovered from sites near restoration work have several advantages over greenhouse vegetation:

- Salvaged plants tend to be larger and more mature.
- A plant dug up during a construction project can be taken as a unit, including feeder roots and soil mass, thereby increasing the chances of a successful transplant.
- Plants taken from natural settings have not suffered the stress of being root-bound in a pot.

Land managers overseeing trail, road, and campground projects can inform restorationists of work that will be occurring so that transplant crews can remove usable vegetation either before or during the construction. Dig up plants early in the day or in cool, wet weather. Transplant them immediately, or use holding-over methods to preserve them until they can be installed.

ON-SITE PLANT PROPAGATION

Restorationists can sometimes reproduce limited numbers of plants in or near a revegetation site by using layering, root division, or root pruning.

Layering. The goal of layering is to form a new shrub, vine, or tree on a stem that is still attached to a parent plant. As its roots develop, the new plant will receive water and nutrients from the parent plant. Once established, the new plant can be lifted and severed from the parent plant and installed in a restoration site. If left connected to a parent plant that borders a revegetation area, the new plant can help reduce the size of a closed campsite or trail.

Layering *propagates new plant growth on-site.*

Begin the layering process by selecting a healthy lateral branch of a multi-stemmed plant that is displaying new growth. Dig a trench about six inches deep and bend part of the branch into the ditch, leaving 6 to 8 inches of the leafy tip exposed. Remove any leafy material on that portion of the stem in the trench, or slit the bottom of the stem with a knife. Pin the stem down in the trench using a wooden or metal stake such as a piece of coat hanger wire bent in a U-shape. Add some rooting hormone, fill the trench with the richest soil available, and lay mulch around the new plant.

Place a wire pin flag near the plant and write identification information and the date of planting on the flag, or label the plant with a metal nursery tag embossed with the layering date. Remove all metal and flagging when the restoration is complete.

Root Division. Root division is a simple technique for reproducing herbaceous plants and grasses from a limited supply of parent plants. Divided plants can carry with them established roots, soil microbes, plant biomass and potential on-site seeding systems. Multiple-stemmed perennials, grasses, or plants that produce off-sets or runners are good candidates for this procedure. It is not appropriate for plants that are woody, have taproots, or are heavily tuberous.

Dig around and lift a plug of vegetation, or remove a mass of nursery stock from its container, then gently separate it into several parts, teasing apart the roots and stems. Loosely constructed plants can be eased apart by hand much like separating segments of a peeled orange. Tightly compacted root wads may need to be separated using a shovel, hand trowel, or other prying tools. Each division becomes a self-contained plant that can be repotted or installed in the restoration site. Always leave the soil attached to the roots, and don't let the plants dry out.

As with other aspects of transplanting, the timing of root division is critical. Plants that flower early in the season can be separated after flowering or in the autumn. Plants such as tall grasses that bloom late are best divided early in the growing season. Cut back some of the leafy growth or stem in order to reduce moisture loss and to divert energy to root development.

Root Pruning. Root pruning is a way of preparing woody vegetation in non-rocky soil for eventual transplanting by increasing root growth. A year before transplanting, use a spade to cut a circle directly downward and as deeply as possible around the *drip line* of each plant. The blade will sever the lateral roots and encourage new root growth within the drip line of the plant. By the following year, the plant should be in ideal condition for transplanting.

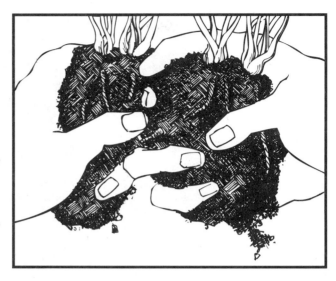

Root Division

Restoration Site Maintenance

Long-term care of a restoration site is often necessary to the success of the revegetation that has been done. Watering and mulching are methods used in all regions of the country.

WATERING

Well-watered plants can resist insects and disease and devote energy toward new growth, not just to survival. Early morning is the best time to water. High humidity, calm air, natural shading, and low sun angles all contribute to the ability of plants to absorb water in the first hours of the day.

Double watering ensures saturation of the root zone by coupling an initial heavy application of water with a lighter watering soon afterward. With healthy plants and good mulch, watering frequency may be as low as twice per week. In exceptionally hot or windy weather, watering may need to be done every other day.

There is no substitute for watering deeply, even if it is done infrequently. Shallow watering will either miss the root system completely or may force new roots to grow upward toward available moisture. Gauge the effectiveness of watering by using a commercially available moisture sensor, by making visual observations of soil around the crown of the plant, or by carefully probing your fingers into the earth to check for cool, moist soil.

Water may be carried in buckets from streams or lakes to a restoration site. Where that is impractical, water storage systems can be set up to catch and store moisture from spring snowmelt or seasonal rainstorms. Forest fire crews of the West have a variety of water collection and storage devices that are adaptable for restoration work. In keeping with backcountry ethics, the systems should be temporary and, if possible, should be camouflaged from view.

MULCHING

Mulching is the application of a covering of native or commercially produced material over a growing or eroded site after the installation of transplants or the creation of a seed bed. Mulch will inhibit erosion, retain moisture, protect plants and seeds, even out surface temperatures, shelter insects and microorganisms, and provide organic matter for building up the soil.

In general, mulching is most useful in assisting plant growth in small sites that experience high soil temperatures over a long growing season. Areas above timberline that have short seed germination seasons do not need the lowered surface temperatures that mulches provide, but mulch may be essential to protect high-elevation restoration sites from erosion and animal predation. Sites that are naturally shaded, cool, and moist are unlikely to benefit from mulching.

The first choice of mulch for any remote site should be leafy material, needles, duff, decomposing logs, or other indigenous materials collected nearby. Bark, sawdust, and wood chips should be used sparingly since material high in

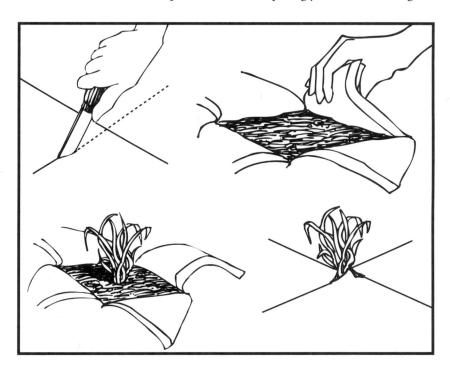

Cut through mulch mat to install transplants in the soil beneath.

raw cellulose can absorb nitrogen from the soil, robbing new plants of a vital nutrient. Use restraint in harvesting mulch, taking only a small amount of the material from any one area.

Spread mulch 2 to 4 inches deep around the bases of plants. The mulch should be loose; blocking air circulation may encourage the growth of fungus or suffocation of the plant.

Native mulches may not be available in amounts adequate for restoration needs. Straw or hay are not used in the backcountry since they may carry with them seeds of non-native plant species. A much better choice for site restoration is commercial mulch mat.

Mulch mat consists of a layer of sterile organic material covered on one or both sides with plastic mesh netting to hold the mat in shape and help protect the soil from erosion. The mesh is usually designed to disintegrate after several years' exposure to sunlight. Mulch mat's high visibility acts as a deterrent to keep backcountry visitors from walking through restoration sites.

Seeding can be done by spreading seed over an area and then unrolling the mulch mat and anchoring it to the ground with rocks and woody debris. After the mat is laid out, install any transplants by cutting a cross through the matting 6 to 8 inches larger than each transplant. Peel back the mat, dig a hole, transfer the vegetation, then fold the mat in around the base of the plant.

CHAPTER 17

Rigging

The Guessing Game is no game for those in the Rigging Game.

W. G. Newberry
HANDBOOK FOR RIGGERS
(N.P., 1967), P. 69.

BACKCOUNTRY RIGGING—the use of ropes, pulleys, anchors, and other hardware to move materials for building and maintaining trails, rock structures, and wilderness bridges—draws heavily on techniques of mountain rescue, high lead logging, the outfitting of sailing ships, and rustic construction methods. Many trail crews will find that rigging is a welcome addition to their knowledge of traditional skills. Whether moving rocks, gravel, logs, or other materials, rigging can make work easier, more interesting, and much more lively.

This chapter is intended to familiarize readers with the basics of rigging systems, methods of judging safe working loads, and the designs of simple systems for moving materials at backcountry work sites. As with all traditional skills, the most important aspect of rigging is doing it safely.

Rigging Safety

Diligent observation of safety practices is vitally important when working with or around rigging. The mechanical advantage created by these systems allows workers to augment their physical strength many times over, but doing so places a great deal of strain on equipment. Correctly using gear that is rated within safe working parameters is an essential consideration when setting up rigging, as is understanding both what should happen and also what may occur while a system is in use.

All safety rules must be followed at all times regardless of the simplicity or complexity of the system. Proper working habits established while using basic setups should be second nature by the time a crew has developed the skill to put together more complicated rigging.

- Whenever working with rigging, do not operate beyond your limits of experience and knowledge. If you are not sure that the system you are planning to use is safe, STOP! Find a way to get the job done without the aid of rigging, or bring someone to the site who has the expertise to guide you.
- Allow no one near a rigging system in operation except those workers essential to the task at hand. Bystanders may be in danger, or may distract the attention of those running the system.

- Wear protective clothing. Long pants, a long-sleeved shirt, boots, a hard hat, and leather gloves are the standard uniform for working around rigging. Each item helps prevent abrasions caused by accidental contact with moving parts of a system. Gloves shield hands from friction burns when playing out line, and from jagger wounds inflicted by the sharp whiskers that sometimes protrude from strands of wire rope. Avoid loose shirt tails, baggy sleeves, or anything else that could be pulled into the rigging. Tuck long hair under your hard hat or into your shirt to keep it out of the way.
- Operate within the Safe Working Load limits of your equipment. Use only quality gear that is in good condition.
- Study every rigging system before putting it under tension, and imagine the consequences if any piece of equipment fails—anchors, blocks, shackles, main line, etc. Stay clear of areas that could be endangered by flying blocks, lines, or other gear from a failed system.
- Stay out of the bight. A *bight* is a bend in a rope or cable. A V-shaped bight is always formed by a line as it makes a turn through a pulley, and a rigging system may have several bights. Should the system fail, people standing inside a bight are likely to find themselves in the path of flying hardware and rope.
- Never step over or under a tensioned line. If the tension in a rigging setup suddenly changes, rope or cable may lift up, drop, or move sideways with tremendous force. That is most certainly not a moment when

Rigging systems can be set up in many ways. Here, a wire rope is anchored at two trees (1). The GripHoist at the left anchor augments the power of a trail worker to pull the slack out of the wire rope, lifting the load off the ground (2). A simple 2:1 system anchored to a third tree can then be used to move the load horizontally (3).

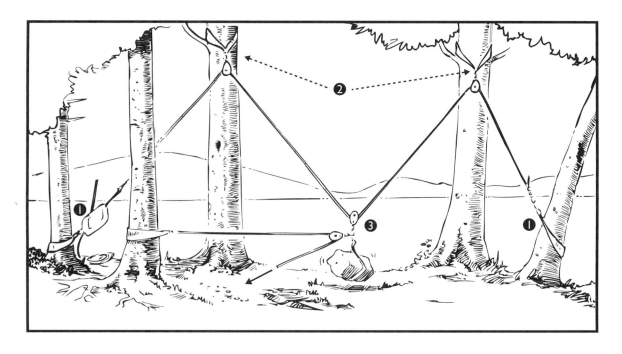

you want to be straddling the line. Always walk around tensioned lines rather than stepping over or under them.

- Beware of cable-swing arcs. A rock, log, or other load attached to a cable may roll sideways as it is being dragged or lifted, especially if it is on a slope. When it does, the cable will swing with it, endangering anyone standing in its path. Identify potential cable-swing arcs before putting tension on a system, and stay clear of them.

- Keep fingers and clothing away from pinch points where lines touch pulley parts or loads.

- Tension systems slowly. The first time a system is to be used, and every time you have made an adjustment in the rigging or the load, place tension on the system gradually. This is usually done by hauling the lead line on a block and tackle or by operating a winch or GripHoist. When the system begins to tighten, stop and inspect it to make sure there are no twisted ropes or hardware, that the anchors are secure, that there is sufficient clearance for the load to move, and that everyone is standing in a safe location.

Rigging Basics

Backcountry rigging may be as simple as a block and tackle used to drag a log up a hillside, or a zip line for sending buckets of sand from one bank of a stream to the other. It can be as complex as a tensioned high-lead cable outfitted with blocks and lines for lifting large stones and moving them horizontally for long distances. (For an example of a very practical rigging system, see *Bear Lines* in Chapter 3, "Camping with Work Crews.")

As with most aspects of backcountry work, using rigging is simply a matter of combining common sense, appropriate tools, and basic principles of physics. Reduced to its essential elements, every backcountry rigging system consists of three parts:

- A load to be moved
- A power source (usually human) sufficiently augmented by mechanical advantage (usually block and tackle or a winch) to move the load
- One or more anchors to secure the system in place while the load is being moved

(Additional components can be added to increase mechanical advantage or to change the direction of movement.)

It follows, then, that safe rigging can be set up by following four steps:

- Determine the approximate weight of the load to be moved.
- Determine the best path of movement for the load.
- Use proper hardware and rope to build a system that is sufficiently powerful to move the load.
- Secure the system to a suitable anchor.

Determining Load Weight

The following chart can be used to compute the weight of common backcountry construction and maintenance materials:

MATERIAL	APPROXIMATE WEIGHT IN POUNDS PER CUBIC FOOT
Earth:	
Dry, loose	75
Dry, packed	100
Mud, packed	115
Sand and gravel:	
Dry, loose	90 to 100
Dry, packed	100 to 120
Wet	120
Stone:	
Granite, basalt, gneiss	150 to 200
Sandstone	80 to 100
Shale	90

Timber:

Timber varies greatly in weight, depending upon the species and the amount of moisture in the wood. For rigging purposes, figure the weight of wood at a safe 60 pounds per cubic foot. Most dry wood will weigh less, while green wood may weigh a little more.

The weight of a load is only part of the consideration. The *resistance* of the load can add greatly to the strain placed upon rigging. Reduce the resistance whenever possible. A peeled log will skid more easily than one with bark. Using an axe to round off the leading end of the log will allow it to ride up over obstacles. Employing smaller logs as rollers under the load will greatly reduce resistance.

Safe Working Load

A chain is only as strong as its weakest link goes the old saying, and what is true for chains is every bit as important with rigging. Riggers must be certain that each piece of hardware and rope in a system is strong enough to withstand any demands placed upon it. To build a rigging system you can trust, find out every component's *Safe Working Load,* or *SWL* (also known as the *Working Load Limit,* or *WLL*).

The Safe Working Load indicates the maximum load that a piece of equipment, properly used, can be relied upon to handle safely. As a rule of thumb for rigging used in general backcountry construction and maintenance work, every component in a system should have a Safe Working Load rating of at least 4,000 pounds.

In most cases, the SWL of a component is one-fifth of the actual breaking strength. For *man hauling*—that is, people riding on a system—the Safe Working Load changes to one-eighth of the breaking strength. The large margin for error incorporated into SWL ratings allows the system to withstand expected and unexpected stresses placed upon it. For example, a 100-pound weight suspended from rigging may, if it is swinging or jerking up and down, place several hundred pounds of stress on rope, shackles, and anchors.

The Safe Working Load rating should be marked somewhere on each piece of sling and rigging hardware. The Safe Working Loads of various kinds and diameters of fiber and wire rope are listed on their original containers, or can be acquired from their manufacturers.

Sling

Standard anchoring slings made of 3-inch nylon webbing are ideal for rigging done in trail work and rustic bridge construction. The most useful lengths are 8 to 16 feet.

Dirty sling can be brushed clean or washed without soap. Keeping it clean will increase the useful life of a sling by preventing grit from abrading the fibers.

EYE-AND-EYE SLING

An *eye-and-eye sling* has a loop in each end. It is usually stitched in such a way that the webbing takes a half twist at the eye, keeping it open for a shackle, carabiner, or hook.

The manufacturer's label on an eye-and-eye sling should have three numbers that indicate its Safe Working Load (SWL) in pounds:

- Vertical (3600, for example)
- Basket (7200)
- Choke (2700)

Vertical refers to the Safe Working Load of the sling when it is hanging vertically and supporting a load at the lower end. *Basket* indicates the SWL of a sling that is cradling a load. Because the eyes of a basket setup are sharing the weight of a load evenly, *basket* SWL is always double that of *vertical* SWL.

Choke indicates the Safe Working Load of the sling when one end is passed through the eye at the other end so that the sling can be cinched around a load or anchor.

If you need more webbing length for setting an anchor or cinching a load, two eye-and-eye slings can be linked together by placing a shackle through one eye of each, or by interweaving all four eyes.

LOOP SLING

Webbing can be made into a loop by stitching the ends together or by tying them with a water knot. Because it creates no bends in the sling, stitching results in

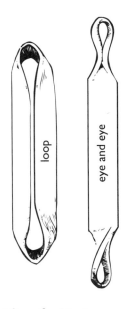

Slings for Rigging

loop

eye and eye

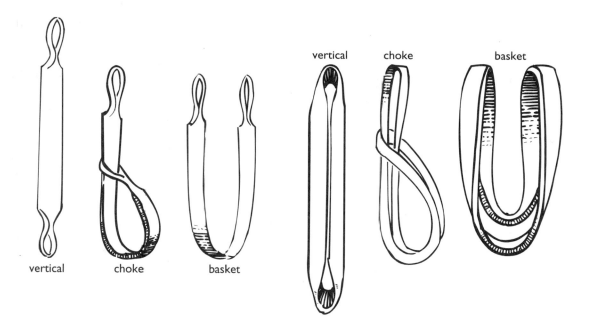

a stronger loop than does knotting. Loops of sling can be joined to one another with a shackle.

The label on a continuous loop gives the Safe Working Load for three sling orientations:

- Vertical (3200, for example)
- Basket (6400)
- Choke (5000)

As with an eye-and-eye sling, the *basket* orientation of a continuous loop sling has twice the SWL as *vertical*. The SWL of *choke* is much higher with a loop sling than an eye-and-eye sling because the load is cradled by two lengths of the looped webbing rather than by the eye-and-eye's single webbing.

The three ways a sling can bear the weight of a load—vertical, choke, or basket—have very different Safe Working Load limits. For general trail work, however, slings made of two-inch nylon webbing are usually suitable in any orientation.

CLIMBING SLING

Nylon sling designed for use by mountain climbers is very unlikely to have a Safe Working Load rating that nears the 4,000 pounds expected of rigging gear. Don't confuse the *Breaking Strength* rating given on some climbing gear with the *Safe Working Load* or *Working Load Limit* of rigging equipment.

Climbing sling is sometimes used in lightweight applications such as anchoring zip lines to carry gravel buckets. However, it is much better for crews to be equipped with the best gear right from the start, using only heavy-duty components rated with at least a 4,000-pound SWL that can be trusted in almost any backcountry rigging situation.

Shackles

Shackles are virtually essential for linking together the parts of a rigging system. The *standard rigging shackle* consists of a U-shaped steel body with an eye in each end, and a threaded pin that can be fitted through the eyes and screwed into place.

Each shackle should have a code printed on the side indicating the diameter of its pin and the safe working load in tons. For example:

¾"–T-2

This shackle's pin diameter is three-quarters of an inch, and the Safe Working Load equals two tons.

Some shackles have no SWL markings on them. They may be cheaper to purchase, but cannot be relied upon to be safe. Always insist on rigging hardware that has documented tolerance information.

Shackle pins can usually be hand-tightened to secure them in place. In rigging systems where repeated hauls may vibrate shackles, the pins should be hand-tightened and then wired in place. Loosen a jammed pin by using an adjustable wrench or by getting leverage from a spike fitted into the hole at the end of the pin.

A shackle can be attached to an eye fixed in a wire rope. Fiber rope may have an eye spliced into it; if not, use a clove hitch to tie the rope to a shackle. To free the rope even if tension has tightened the hitch, simply remove the pin from the shackle and allow the rope to fall loose. (For more on splices and clove hitches, see Chapter 18, "Knots.")

Shackle

Rope

Rope is one of humankind's oldest tools. Horse hair, vines, strips of leather, and plant fibers have been used through the centuries to make rope. Polyester, nylon, steel, and other materials form durable, modern-day ropes suitable for almost every need.

NATURAL FIBER ROPE

Stringy fibers of manila and sisal are spun into threads which are, in turn, twisted into strands that make natural fiber rope. Manila is stronger and more reliable than sisal. The best grade of manila rope—the only grade appropriate for rigging uses—is usually indicated by a colored yarn worked among the strands. Because they are made of natural fibers, manila and sisal ropes should be air-dried before storage to protect them from mildew and rot.

SYNTHETIC FIBER ROPE

Developed in the 1940s, ropes made of synthetic fibers are superior in a number of ways to natural fibers. Many short natural fibers must be twisted together to form manila and sisal rope, but each synthetic fiber extends the full length of the rope, resulting in a stronger line. Synthetics are easier to care for since they are less likely to rot.

Like natural fiber rope, synthetic rope should be kept as clean as possible to prevent grit from abrading the fibers. Long exposure to sunlight may also weaken synthetic rope. Keep every rope away from heat, and store it loosely coiled, hanging where air can circulate around it.

If either a natural or a synthetic rope becomes damaged, you may be able to cut out the flawed section and splice together the sound pieces. Splices can reduce overall rope strength by 10 to 15 percent, while knots may reduce strength 50 percent or more.

The Safe Working Load of new rope can be found on the box it comes in, or by contacting the manufacturer. Rope that has become loosely twisted, has dirt and grit inside the strands, or shows signs of abrasion or damaged fibers should be considered to have a significantly diminished Safe Working Load.

In determining the load that a rope can bear, remember to factor in any mechanical advantage present in the system. For example, the five lines sharing the load in a 5:1 block and tackle system are each bearing one fifth of the weight of the load. If the rope is rated at a Safe Working Load of 1,000 pounds, the 5:1 mechanical advantage gives the five lines working together in the block and tackle an effective Safe Working Load of 5,000 pounds. (The SWL of the blocks, anchors, and other parts of the system must be judged individually to be certain that all components exceed the 4,000-pound Safe Working Load required for backcountry rigging.)

CLIMBING ROPE

Rope intended for recreational climbing sometimes turns up in trail crew equipment caches. Most of this rope is *dynamic,* meaning that it is designed to stretch if someone falls and thus absorb weight gradually rather than jerking the climber to an abrupt halt. Its elasticity makes it unsuitable for use as a haul line or in systems that require the rope to be tightened.

WIRE ROPE

Wire rope, also known as cable, is made of high grade steel. Steel wires are twisted together to form a strand, and the rope is formed by wrapping the strands around a core of plastic, fiber, or metal. Cables used with chair lifts and gondolas usually have plastic cores that allow the cables a good deal of flexibility. A metal strand core, on the other hand, creates a stiffer cable and prevents the diameter of a wire rope from being distorted when the rope is wrapped around an anchor point, passes through a pulley, is pulled through a GripHoist, or is stored on a spool.

Wire rope is described in several ways:

- Diameter of rope
- Number of wires per strand
- Number of strands wrapped around the core

- Core material
  —FC = fiber core
  —WSC = wire strand core
  —IWRC = independent wire rope core

Thus, a spool of cable marked *½" 7 x 25 IWRC* would be a wire rope ½ inch in diameter composed of 25 wires per strand forming 7 strands wrapped around an independent wire rope core.

Rope that will be exposed for long periods of time to the elements may have a protective layer of zinc *galvanized* to its surface. Because the zinc stiffens wire strands, galvanized cable is appropriate for stationary applications such as the guy lines on transmission towers, but not for use in rigging systems where the rope must bend.

The Safe Working Load of a particular type and diameter of wire rope can be ascertained from the manufacturer. For general backcountry rigging, stick with 6 x 19 or 7 x 25 wire ropes. Fiber core rope is generally used for running rigging, while IWRC is better suited for static rigging such as tightlines. In diameters under ¾ inch, both fiber core and IWRC are flexible enough to work in running rigging.

CARING FOR WIRE ROPE

Wire rope requires care in handling, just as does any tool. Roll wire rope onto a spool for transport or storage. If no spool is available, roll the rope as if you did have one, then secure it with cord. Do not coil wire rope as a cowboy would a lariat—that puts twists into the rope and may lead to permanent kinks that can weaken the line and make it unreliable.

Storing Wire Rope

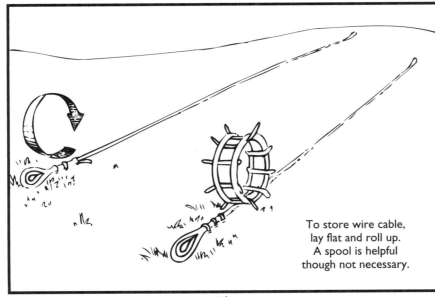

To store wire cable,
lay flat and roll up.
A spool is helpful
though not necessary.

right

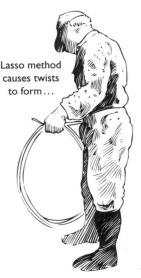

Do not use lasso method.

Lasso method
causes twists
to form...

wrong

CLIPS AND THIMBLES

Clips and thimbles are used to put eyes in the ends of wire ropes. Forming the eye by bending the rope around a thimble distributes the weight of a load throughout the eye and protects the strands from fraying. Each thimble is stamped with the diameter of rope with which it should be used.

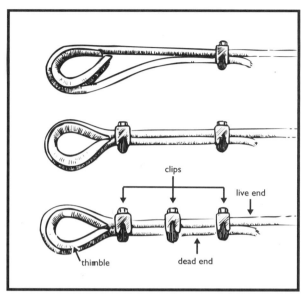

Once the eye has been formed around a thimble, use clips to secure the tail of the wire rope, known as the *dead end,* to the standing part of the rope, or *live end.* Each clip consists of a *saddle* and a *U-bolt,* and each is sized to fit a specific diameter of cable. The saddle must be placed on the live part of the rope, the U-bolt on the dead end.

The Safe Working Load of the wire rope and of the eye are dependent upon the number and placement of the clips as determined by the manufacturer. Even though it is properly made, forming an eye will reduce cable strength by 10 percent or more.

Form a loop of wire rope around a thimble by attaching the clips in the correct sequence.

Place the first clip a few inches from the end of the rope and alternately tighten the nuts. Place the second clip as close as possible to the loop and tighten the nuts. If more clips are required, space them evenly between the first two. Torque the nuts to manufacturer's specifications; for clips on a ½-inch-diameter wire rope, it's less than the force used to secure wheel lug nuts on an automobile. If it is deforming the rope, a clip is probably too tight.

Once the eye has been put under tension in the rigging system, check the security of the clips and, if necessary, retighten the nuts.

Never Saddle a Dead Horse

The riggers' warning, "Never saddle a dead horse," is a reminder that the *saddle* of a clip must always be placed on the *live* part of the rope.

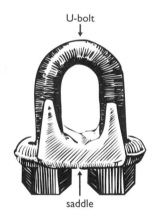

Cable Clip

Block and Tackle

A *block* is a wooden or metal shell in which are mounted one or more wheels called *sheaves.* Each block has an eye or hook that can be attached to a stationary anchor or to a movable load. Rope used with blocks is known as *tackle.* A rope threaded, or *reeved,* through one or more blocks redirects and often augments the force applied to the rope.

To determine the mechanical advantage of a block and tackle system, identify the *power block* (i.e., the block that moves while the system is being used). Grasp all the ropes coming off the power block and suspend the block from them. Notice that the weight of the block is distributed equally among all the ropes in your hand. If the block is hanging from five ropes, for example, each line is bearing a fifth of the weight.

When the system is in operation, workers haul on just one of those lines. In the instance of five lines coming off the power block, workers would be hauling only the weight borne by the lead line—a fifth of the total weight of the load. Thus, the mechanical advantage of that system is 5:1.

The amount of rope that must travel through the block will increase in direct proportion to the mechanical advantage. It will take five times as much rope to move a load with a 5:1 system than to move it the same distance without mechanical advantage. Friction will reduce the mechanical advantage somewhat as the ropes put pressure on the sheave axles in the blocks.

BLOCK AND TACKLE EXERCISE

A feature of many SCA Work Skills courses is an exercise that illustrates the basics of simple rigging systems and the methods of determining their mechanical advantage.

1:1   Mary and Bill, two people of equal strength, pull against one another in a tug-of-war. Neither can move the other. There is no mechanical advantage.

1:1   Pass the rope through a block anchored to a tree. Mary and Bill again pull against each other. Although the rope changes direction as it goes through the block, Neither Bill nor Mary can move the other person. There is still no mechanical advantage.

1:1

1:1

2:1   Anchor one end of the rope to the tree and pass the other end through a block that is free to move—the *power block*. Bill pulls on a sling shackled to the block while Mary hauls on the free end of the rope—the *lead line*. In doing so, she drags Bill off his feet. That's because the pulling force Bill is putting on the block is divided evenly between the rope that is anchored to the tree and the lead line in Mary's hands. There are two lines coming off the moving power block, and thus a mechanical advantage of 2:1. Another person must grab the sling and help Bill pull if he hopes to stop being dragged toward Mary.

2:1

5:1

5:1 Anchor one block of a block and tackle to the tree, then use a shackle to attach Bill's sling to the other block. Count the ropes coming off the power block; in this case, there are five. The system has a mechanical advantage of 5:1. When Mary hauls on the lead line, it will take five people pulling in the other direction to match her power.

10:1 Anchor the block and tackle to a tree for a 5:1 mechanical advantage. Now tie a rope to the power block, run that rope through a second block, and anchor the free end of the rope to the tree. Bill will pull on a sling shackled to the second block while Mary pulls the lead line of the block and tackle.

Notice that there are two moving blocks in this system, and thus two power blocks. To figure the mechanical advantage, count the number of lines coming off the first power block and multiply it by the number of lines coming off the second power block. In this example, the load on the first block is equally shared by five lines and the load on the second block is equally shared by two lines, creating a

10:1

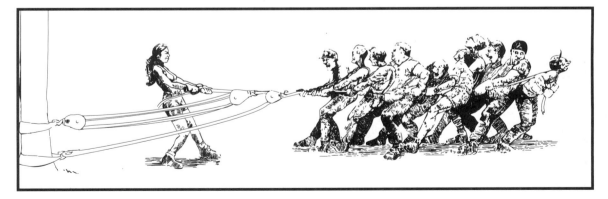

mechanical advantage of 10:1. Bill is going to need a lot of friends if he expects to hold his own against Mary.

SNATCH BLOCKS

Unscrewing a retaining bolt allows a side plate of a snatch block to swing open so that the block can be *snatched* onto any point of a line. That saves riggers the trouble of reeving lengths of rope through standard pulleys.

Klein and Havens Grips

Many rigging systems require that one line be attached to another with a hold that can be trusted not to slip. To do that, shackle the eye of a Klein or Havens grip to the end of a line such as that leading to block and tackle, then fit the body of the grip over a wire rope. (Each Klein or Havens grip is built to fit certain diameters of wire rope. The size should be etched in the body of the grip.) Tension placed on the line by the block and tackle will cause the grip to tighten on the wire rope. The greater the tension, the stronger the hold. Slacking off on the line will allow the grip to be moved to a new position on the cable, or removed altogether.

If dirt on a wire rope has made it slippery, you may need to clean that portion where the grip will be placed. A galvanized finish on a cable can also lessen the effectiveness of a grip.

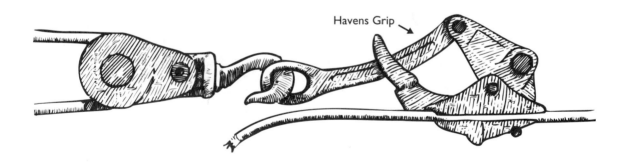

Havens Grip

Setting Anchors

From the simplest to the most complex, every rigging setup must have at least one anchoring point that will not move while the system is in operation. Use only good slings to establish anchors. Slings that have been abraded cannot be relied upon to live up to the Safe Working Loads cited on their labels.

Sturdy trees and large boulders are common anchoring points. If the tree is

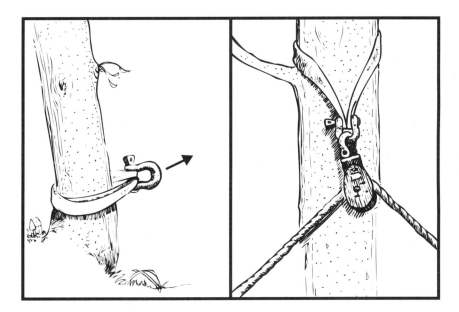

Left: *A sling shackled around the base of a sturdy tree makes a reliable anchoring point for a rigging system.*

Right: *A block anchored in a tree can lift a rope high above the ground.*

alive, orient the webbing so that it will not slip and rub through the bark. A sling made of wire rope can cut into a tree unless you wedge blocks of wood between the sling and the trunk before the system is tensioned.

The strongest anchor is a *basket* setup (the shackle passes through both eyes of an eye-and-eye sling or through both bends of a continuous loop sling). In a *choker* setup (the sling cinched around the tree), adjusting the sling so there is little or no bend in it puts the least strain on the webbing.

The closer to the ground the sling rests, the less the likelihood that the system under tension will uproot a tree. You may also be able to wrap one sling around two or three trees, or set separate slings around several trees so that the load of the system is distributed among them.

With a reliable anchor in place, you can devise rigging systems of all sorts, from a simple 2:1 pulley setup for dragging rocks into position in a retaining wall, to a tensioned high lead cable for hoisting materials across a river.

Packaging Loads with Slings, Baskets, Chains, or Chokers

The load that a system is expected to transport must be secured in such a way that it can be connected to the rigging, and that it will stay bound during the move.

SLINGS

Nylon 2-inch eye-and-eye sling is well suited for moving rock, especially if a large stone must be lifted off the ground. Cinch the sling around the center of a rock with a choke hold. Shackle the free eye of the sling to the rigging and align the sling so that it will tighten around the rock as tension is applied.

Upon reaching their final destinations, heavy rocks may lie on the webbing and make sling removal difficult. Try loosening the sling, then reattaching a free eye to the rigging and slowly applying tension. Jiggle the stone with a rock bar, and the sling should pull free.

Two-inch nylon webbing can also be used to move logs. If an eye-and-eye sling is long enough, cinch it around a log and then give the tail one more wrap before attaching it to the system. Tension on the sling will roll the log in the direction in which it is being pulled.

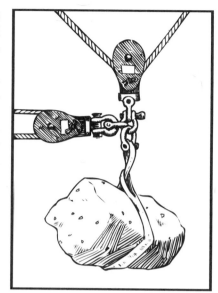

Cinch eye-and-eye sling around a rock or log and shackle it to a rigging system.

WARNING

Nylon webbing used to cinch loads will almost surely be abraded by being dragged across the ground. Though still reliable enough to wrap up loads, slings showing any signs of damage should *never* be used for anchors. Keep your anchor slings separate from those that have cinched loads.

TIRE CHAINS

The ladder-like configuration of tire chains makes them a practical choice for packaging rocks. Wrap the chain around a rock just as you would around a tire, then secure the links with shackles. The shackle that binds together the ends of the chain is usually the best point to hook into the rigging system; pulling on that shackle will cause the tire chain to cradle the rock.

The weight of tire chains can be a disadvantage, especially if you must carry them deep into the backcountry. Used chains are not always easy to come by, though if you keep your eyes peeled as you drive through mountainous regions in the spring, you can usually find enough chains discarded or lost on the shoulders of roads to keep you supplied for a summer of trail work.

ROCK NET

An alternative to tire chains is a rock sling of the same ladder-like design, professionally sewn from strips of 1-inch, heavy-duty nylon webbing. Have the

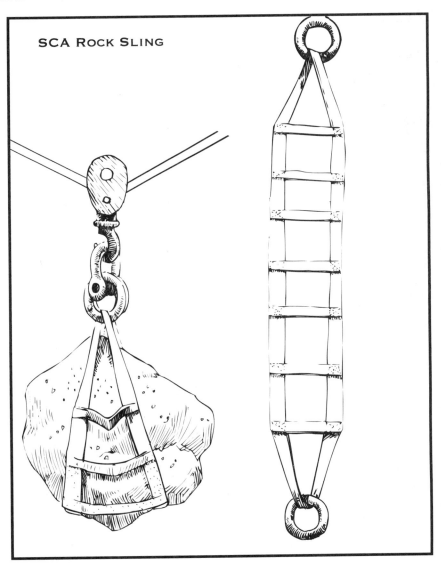

SCA ROCK SLING

A net sling sewn from nylon is ideal for hoisting large rocks.

sidepieces made about 8 feet long, with foot-long crosspieces spaced at 8-inch intervals. Eyes or metal rings stitched into the ends of the sidepieces will provide points for shackling the rock sling to the rigging system.

The net can also be made of 2-inch webbing. The added material will extend the working life of the sling, but the extra bulk makes it more difficult to pull the sling from under large rocks after they have been moved into place.

CLIMBING SLING AND CARABINERS

The use of climbing sling and carabiners is not recommended for wrapping up large loads to be moved with systems involving mechanical advantage. The mechanical advantage of the system and the weight of the load may break the sling. Carabiners securing a sling around loads are in danger of being bent and weakened when rocks or logs are dragged over them. Shackles and either tire chains or 2-inch anchor slings are far safer and, in the long run, more economical.

CHOKERS

Chokers made of cable are used throughout the logging industry to move timber. Wrap the cable around the log and insert the metal button on the free end into the sliding bell. As tension is introduced to the system, the choker will live up to its name by cinching tightly around the log.

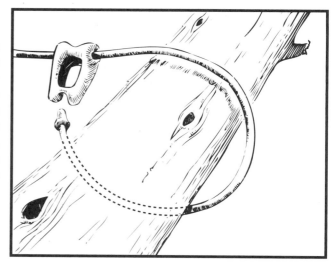

Choker

Tree Climbing

Rigging high-lead systems and zip lines may require installing anchors and blocks at points high in trees. The safest way to reach those points is with a ladder. Crews that will be doing a lot of rigging or are close to a trailhead should consider the convenience of having a ladder on-site.

If there is no ladder, free-climbing a tree may be an option, as is using lineman's spurs and a climbing belt. Climbing with spurs requires special training and, in some land-management areas, completion of a certification course. Whatever climbing method you choose, use extreme caution at all times.

CHAPTER 18

Knots

The field man who must be continually packing, saddling, tethering animals, raising and lowering articles by means of ropes, or using ropes in a number of other ways should be more or less familiar with those knots for which he may have the greatest use.

Jay L. B. Taylor
HANDBOOK FOR RANGERS &
WOODSMEN (NEW YORK:
JOHN WILEY & SONS, INC.,
1917), PP. 325-326.

ROPE AND THE LANGUAGE OF KNOTS and splices are indispensable tools for anyone traveling and working in the backcountry. The confines of this book allow only a brief review of the knots found to be effective for use by trail crews. More comprehensive knot books are available that explain in far greater detail the methods of tying these and many other knots.

As with many other traditional outdoor skills, knot tying and splicing are seldom common knowledge in our day and age. Even experienced crew leaders well-versed in other backcountry matters may feel at a loss when confronted with the need to tie a particular knot. Including several knot books and lengths of rope in a trail crew's tool cache can make the learning of knots a pleasant social activity. With the books as a guide, crew leaders and crew members can teach themselves and each other, practicing until basic knots and splices become second nature.

Knots

Knots work because of friction. The greater the friction created by the rope against itself or by contact of the rope with a surface such as a log, the more secure the knot. Knot strength is also affected by the diameter of the bends created as the rope forms a knot, and by the forces placed upon those bends. A rope subjected to a sharp bend will have many *compressed* fibers that will not help bear a load, and many other fibers that are *stretched,* and thus already stressed before a load is applied. Any knot in a rope involves these factors to some degree, and so any knot weakens a rope.

Three Tests of a Good Knot
- Is it appropriate for the task?
- Will it stay tied?
- Is it easy to untie?

Square or Reef Knot

SQUARE OR REEF KNOT

Without knowing they are doing it, most people tie their shoe laces with square knots, leaving loops in place to make untying the knots easier. Pull the loops on through, and the appearance of the square knot will become more recognizable.

The square knot is best known as a mariner's knot for securing, or *reefing,* furled sails by tying together the ends of a rope. Examine the architecture of the knot and you'll see that it is composed of two interlocking bends. The running ends of the rope are on the same side of the knot; the standing parts of the rope are also in line with one another, lending strength and stability to the knot.

Butterfly Knot

A square knot is a good utility knot where safety is not an important issue—securing loads to a pack frame, for example, or wrapping up a rolled tent. Unfortunately, a square knot under tension may slip out of synthetic rope or nylon cord, or it may become so tight that it is difficult to untie, especially in ropes and cords of smaller diameters.

BUTTERFLY KNOT

A butterfly knot puts a secure loop anywhere along the body of a rope. The construction of the knot allows the loop to be equally strong regardless of the direction in which tension is applied. The butterfly knot takes its name from the bends of rope that seem to resemble wings. To untie the knot, press the wings backward to break the tension in the knot and begin loosening it.

Butterfly knots are common in mountaineering where the middle climbers in teams of three use it to clip the carabiners on their harnesses to the centers of climbing ropes. Their partners tie in to the ends of the ropes with figure-eight knots.

Figure Eight Knot

FIGURE-EIGHT KNOT

Like the butterfly knot, the figure-eight knot takes its name from its appearance. A simple figure-eight knot can be used as a stopper to prevent a rope from running out through a pulley. Tying a figure-eight knot in the bight of a rope will create a dependable loop that will hold under great tension but can still be untied with relative ease.

BOWLINE

The bowline may be the knot most frequently used in the backcountry for rope work requiring a non-slip loop. A basic knot for mountaineers and sailors as well as trail crews, the bowline takes its name from its traditional use of securing the rope that tightens the weather edge of a square sail. It can be tied quickly and in a variety of ways, even one-handed. Loosen it by pulling forward on the collar-shaped bend.

Bowline

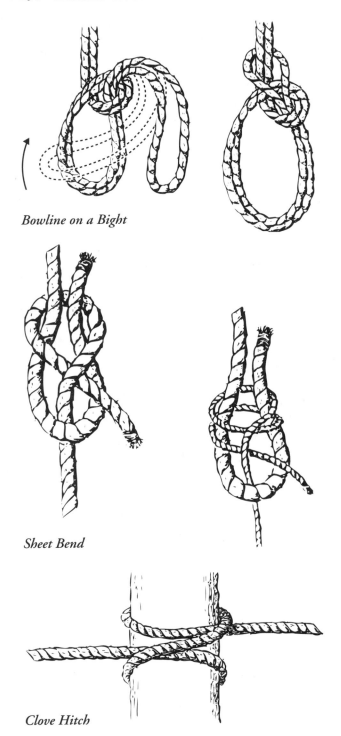

Bowline on a Bight

Sheet Bend

Clove Hitch

BOWLINE ON A BIGHT
Similar in appearance to the bowline but much different in the way it is tied, the bowline on a bight results in two loops rather than one. The knot is useful when a rope must be secured to a pair of anchoring points.

SHEET BEND
In nautical terms, a *sheet* is a line used with sails. A sheet bend, a knot traditionally used with sails, features a distinctive bend in one rope.

The architecture of a sheet bend is virtually identical to that of a bowline except it does not result in a loop. Instead, the sheet bend is used to join together the ends of two ropes. If the ropes are of unequal size, make the bend in the larger one and put an extra wrap around it with the smaller line to form a *double sheet bend*.

Hitches

Hitches are a family of knots used to secure a rope around something—a log, for example, or around the standing part of a rope. In short, hitches are meant to be hitched.

CLOVE HITCH
A clove hitch should be used only when a rope is pulling directly away from the object around which it is tied. Increasing the tension on the rope tightens the hitch. Since it is simply a series of wraps around an object, the clove hitch is easy to loosen.

Clove hitches are used to start lashings when binding together poles such as those used for a tripod, a camp table, or the chandelier of a bear hang. They are also the hitch of choice to secure a rope to a shackle in rigging operations; even though the knot may become very tight, pulling the shackle pin out of it will allow the clove hitch to fall from the rope.

TIMBER HITCH

Use a timber hitch when the direction of pull on a rope will be parallel to the load to which it is tied. The most common use of a timber hitch is to drag a log along the ground.

DOUBLE HALF HITCH

The double half hitch is better suited to take strain from a variety of directions than are the clove or timber hitches. It is a good utility knot for camp chores such as tying tent lines into grommets and lashing loads to pack frames. The disadvantage of the double half hitch is that it can become very tight and difficult to untie.

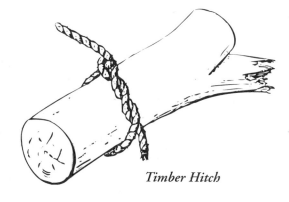

Timber Hitch

Double Half Hitch

TAUTLINE HITCH

The tautline is used on tent guy lines or in similar situations requiring a light, steady tension that can be easily adjusted. Pull some slack into the standing part of the rope, and you should be able to slide the hitch along it. When the rope is taut, the hitch will grip the standing part and stay in place.

Tautline Hitch

PRUSIK KNOT

In a manner similar to the tautline hitch, the Prusik knot slides along a rope, or relies on friction to hold a loop of cord or sling in place on the rope. The Prusik is a mountaineering knot used for ascending a fixed line. For trail work, the Prusik can be tied on a haul line and used as a safety brake by securing the loop on the Prusik to an anchor.

Prusik Knot

Splicing

The splices most commonly used by trail crews are the *eye splice, short splice,* and *back splice.* The eye splice makes a fixed loop in the end of a rope. It is the usual way that the end of a rope in a block and tackle system is fastened to one of the blocks. The short splice permanently joins the ends of two ropes of equal size. The back splice secures the strands at the end of a line so that they will not unravel. Since each of these splices increases the diameter of the rope, they should not be used on sections of rope that must pass through a block.

Tying a Mantie Load

In the Western states, a mantie load is a bundle of gear or provisions wrapped and cinched so that it can be carried on a pack animal. It requires a *mantie cover*—a 6-foot square of waterproof canvas or heavy plastic—and a 25-foot length of ⅜-inch manila rope with an eye spliced in one end. A feature of the mantie load is that it is secured with a series of loops; untying it is simply a matter of loosening the final knot and letting the rope fall free.

1. Lay a mantie cover so it faces you as a diamond. Organize a load of gear on it just below the centerfold of the cover, and square up the pile to make it as compact as possible. (Group your gear into manageable and compatible piles. Do not pack stove gas with food and clothing, for example. Keep the points of tools away from water jugs and other easily damaged goods.)
2. Fold the bottom of the mantie cover over the load.
3. Crease the sides of the cover and fold them over the load.
4. Keep all the folds tight.
5. Fold the top of the mantie cover down over the load.
6. Holding onto the eye, toss the rope so it uncoils away from the mantie load.
7. Slide the rope under the pack and bring the eye around to the center of the pack.
8. Form a bight in the rope and feed it through the eye. Pull on the bight to tighten the rope around the pack.
9. Make a loop in the bight big enough to go around the pack end-wise. Tilt the pack and slide the loop around and underneath the pack end for end, swinging the loop away from the running end of the rope rather than over it.
10. Again cinch down on the first loop, then take up the slack in the second loop and cinch it with the running end.
11. Tie off the running end with several half-hitches on a bight.
12. Lift the mantie load onto the decker saddle or sawbuck of the pack animal.

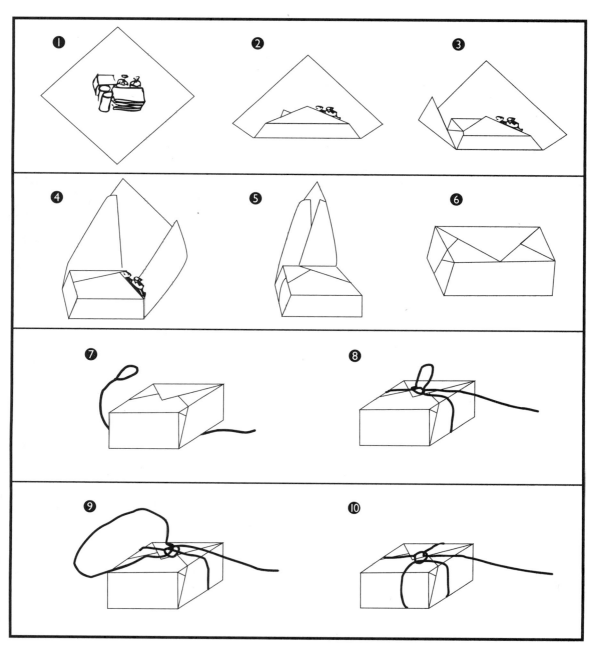

Tying a Mantie Load

CHAPTER 19

History of the SCA Work Skills Program

THE WORK SKILLS PROGRAM of the Student Conservation Association traces its heritage to trail crews working in the backcountry since the 1800s, though the true model for Work Skills and for the Association as a whole was the Civilian Conservation Corps. Established in 1933 during the Great Depression, the CCC was a federally funded relief program designed to provide work on public lands for unemployed young men. Over the nine years the CCC existed, three million men took part at more than two thousand sites.

Much of the CCC's work involved construction of trails, campgrounds, and recreation facilities in parks and forests across the United States. Crew leaders often possessed a high level of competence in a given trade, bringing to the projects an understanding of carpentry, masonry, surveying, and road work. Stone cutters accustomed to laying the walls of office buildings and cathedrals redirected their efforts to raising retaining walls for hiking trails. Unemployed loggers used their skill with woods tools and rigging systems to construct bridges of native timber.

The manpower needs of World War II absorbed the CCC's applicant pool, and the program was disbanded. However, it had involved such a large number of people and had lasted so long that the backcountry skills of the CCC era were widely disseminated among its participants. That was especially important to parks and forests as those people returned from the military and took positions in land management agencies.

In the decade following World War II, no comparable rustic construction programs were attempted by either the government or private enterprise. As the years went by, state and federal land-management agencies could point to fewer and fewer employees who had mastered their craft in the CCC days. There were younger trail workers who learned many skills from the CCC veterans and continued the traditions of the Corps in the woods, but never in the numbers active during the Depression years.

Mechanization also played a role in the mid-century fading of many rustic backcountry skills. The advent of gasoline-powered chain saws, rock drills, and trail-building machines made it less likely that agency personnel would know much about crosscut saws, hand drilling, or even, in some cases, how to use a shovel very well. Increased use of prefabricated bridges and other structures, coupled with the growing reliance on milled lumber rather than native timber, gave trail crews fewer incentives to practice timber notching and complicated rock construction.

Although the number of people skilled in backcountry work was declining throughout the 1950s and 1960s, interest in conservation service continually resurfaced among nonprofit organizations. Among them was the Student Conservation Association.

The idea for the SCA originated in 1955 when Elizabeth Cushman Titus, then a student at Vassar College, completed a senior thesis entitled, "A Proposal for a Student Conservation Corps." Concerned that the nation's parks were suffering from neglected maintenance and the demands of growing numbers of tourists, Titus believed that student volunteers could complete important park projects that would otherwise not be done. She also felt that students would benefit in many ways from their experiences in the field, and would increase their understanding of the environment and their place in it.

Encouraged by National Park Service Director Horace Albright and by others, Titus spent two years exploring the possibilities of a conservation corps for students. She found sponsorship from the National Parks and Conservation Association, and funding from other organizations and individuals.

In the summer of 1957, the Student Conservation Association fielded pilot programs in Olympic and Grand Teton National Parks with a total of fifty-four participants. Since then, the SCA High School Program has continued to provide opportunities for young adults ages sixteen to eighteen to spend a month or more in the backcountry completing meaningful conservation work. SCA's Resource Assistant Program, open to persons older than eighteen, offers twelve-week internships with federal and state land-management agencies.

The Student Conservation Association was incorporated as a nonprofit organization in 1964. The success of SCA's programs, though at the time small in scale, came to the attention of Senator Henry M. Jackson of Washington State, who visited SCA crews working in Olympic National Park. Jackson and other legislators became convinced that a federal program combining the best aspects of the Student Conservation Association with the strengths of the old Civilian Conservation Corps could be of enormous value to young people and to the nation.

In 1969, Jackson introduced legislation in Congress establishing the Youth Conservation Corps (YCC). Among those who gave Congressional testimony were officers of SCA. Almost three decades after the disbanding of the CCC, the federal government was again exploring the possibilities of a conservation corps, this time for a younger generation.

The Youth Conservation Corps was administered by the Departments of

Agriculture and Interior. Between 1971 and 1980, the Corps provided work opportunities to 213,000 teenagers. A companion program, the Young Adult Conservation Corps (YACC), offered similar opportunities to older participants.

The combination of YCC veterans and experienced backcountry leaders who had learned their craft from members of the CCC gave SCA a talented pool from which to draw leaders for the crews making up its own High School Work Group Program. In 1980, however, funding for the Youth Conservation Corps disappeared, the Youth Adult Conservation Corps was severely reduced, and SCA lost an important source of experienced leaders. Whereas the Association had once been able to attract candidates who came equipped with strong backcountry living and working skills, applicants in the early 1980s often possessed impressive leadership abilities, but not the hands-on labor experience necessary to oversee the completion of rustic construction projects.

Weekend workshops intended to provide new supervisors with basic work skills proved too short to be effective, so in 1985, veteran SCA crew leaders conducted four week-long training workshops on the Tower Falls Trail in Yellowstone National Park. Participants learned by doing, completing timber cribbing, rock retaining walls, tread work, and the revegetation of eroded hillsides. Enrollment was intended primarily for SCA's crew leaders, but spaces were also made available to agency personnel and others who wanted to learn trail construction and maintenance. A surprising number of people enrolled, coming from the National Park Service, U.S. Forest Service, and several conservation corps. SCA returned to Yellowstone the following year for two more weeks of workshops and the complete reconstruction of the Tower Falls Trail.

Buoyed by the success of the two summers in Yellowstone, SCA sent the Work Skills Program on the road. Through the winter and spring of 1987, Work Skills instructors and volunteers converted a delivery truck into a field kitchen and resurrected an old van that had for many years been SCA's primary vehicle in the Northwest, a fact attested to by the thick mantle of moss growing on its roof. Contributions of equipment and tools from manufacturers gave the Work Skills Program the gear required for teaching rustic skills, and visits to secondhand tool stores around Puget Sound turned up a wealth of crosscut saws, axes, winches, and other vintage tools.

The first Work Skills road trip was a grueling siege of hard highway miles and intense teaching and learning. The courses began in April in the High Sierra, then migrated to projects in Arizona, New Mexico, Colorado, Wyoming, Washington, and New York, finally ending in late September in Virginia. In the years since, Work Skills instructors have taken the course to parks and forests up and down the east and west coasts, areas in Arkansas, Oklahoma, Minnesota, Michigan, and throughout the Rocky Mountain region. Participants have come from all over the country, too, representing every federal land-management agency and many from the state level, as well as crew leaders and members of conservation corps, youth organizations, volunteer groups, and outing clubs.

SCA Work Skills courses have allowed people from across the country to share their skills and philosophies with each other. The accumulated backcountry work wisdom is a storehouse of knowledge of great value to conservation and resource management. It forms the backbone of the skills that SCA crew leaders take with them into the field, and it has served as the basis of this book.

Glossary

Abney level—A hand-held surveying tool used to measure grades of slopes and trails.

Abutment—The foundation at either end of a bridge that supports the sill, stringers, and deck.

Backslope—The excavated bank on the uphill side of trail tread.

Barrier-free trail—A pathway with no structures or other limitations that would impede easy passage of a wheelchair.

Bed—The excavated surface on which a trail tread lies.

Bench—A relatively flat, stable surface on a slope occurring naturally or by excavation.

Berm—The raised outside edge of a trail. Berm is usually undesirable because it can prevent water from escaping the tread.

Blaze—A mark used to signify the route of a trail.

Blowdown—Trees that have been toppled by wind. Also known as *windfall*.

Borrow—Fill material taken from a site other than the trailway excavation.

Bull rail—A beam affixed to the outside edge of bridge decking to prevent the hooves of animals from slipping off the walkway.

Canting—Hewing a flat face on a surface of a log.

Climbing turn—A wide, ascending curve that gradually reverses the grade of a trail as it ascends a hillside. Climbing turns work only on gentle slopes of 15 percent or less.

Clearing limits—The edges of a trail corridor beyond which brushing is not required.

Clinometer—The direct descendent of the Abney level, used in trail work for measuring grades of slopes and heights of trees.

Cribbing—Retaining walls, usually constructed in the backcountry with rock or notched logs.

Daylighting—Clearing a ditch or drain so that water can run *all the way to daylight.*

Decking—Planks spiked onto stringers to form the travel surface of a bridge.

Drain dip—A carefully shaped depression built into an existing trail to divert water from the tread.

Drip line—The outer growth perimeter of the plant. The term is derived from the circle formed on the ground by water dripping off a plant's outermost foliage.

Duff—Ground cover consisting of leaves, needles, and other forest material.

Fall line—The steepest route of descent down a slope. Water flowing down a hillside will travel along the fall line.

Fill—Gravel or soil used, as the name implies, to fill voids in trails and to pack behind retaining walls and other structures.

Full bench cut—A tread lying completely on a bench of undisturbed earth. Most trails excavated into the side of a slope are *full bench cut.*

Gabion baskets—Rectangular containers made of heavy galvanized wire. Gabions can be wired together, then filled with stones to form quick and dirty retaining walls.

Grade dip—A reversal of grade surveyed into a new trail. The slight rise in the tread diverts water from the trail surface.

Heartwood—The older, nonliving wood in the center of a timber. It is more durable and harder than the sapwood surrounding it. Heartwood is often darker than sapwood.

High lead—A rigging system featuring a tensioned cable. Loads slung beneath the cable can be moved horizontally.

Mineral soil—Earth containing little or no organic material.

Outrigger—A bridge plank extending beyond the sides of the decking to serve as an anchor for bracing handrails.

Outslope—A slight tilt in the surface of trail tread to promote drainage.

Puncheon—A simple wooden walkway constructed through boggy terrain. Terminology varies regionally. In New England, puncheon may refer to two flattened logs nailed to sills, also known as a *topped log bridge.* In Western states, puncheon usually includes stringers, sills, and decking.

Sapwood—The younger, living layer of wood just beneath the bark of a timber. Sapwood is usually lighter in color than the more durable heartwood beneath it.

Sill—The timber upon which the end of a bridge or length of puncheon rests.

Slough—Silt and organic debris collecting on the inside edge of a trail tread.

Spline—In advanced bridge construction, a tapered member driven into a dovetail notch cut across two or more stringers. The spline reduces the flexing of individual stringers.

Stringer—A deck-supporting beam, usually resting on sills.

Switchback—A sharp reversal of direction in a trail, allowing the tread to maintain a reasonable grade while ascending a steep slope. The switchback includes a turning platform.

Tread—The travel surface of a trail.

Trail corridor—The full dimensions of a route, including the tread and a zone on either side and above the tread from which brush will be removed.

Turnpike—A structure used to carry a trail across saturated ground. Logs or rocks embedded along the sides of the tread hold fill material in place to form an elevated travel surface.

Water bar—A drainage structure composed of an outsloped segment of tread leading to a rock or log barrier embedded at an angle across the trail. Water flowing down the trail will be diverted by the outslope or, as a last resort, by the barrier.

Index

THE STUDENT CONSERVATION ASSOCIATION fosters lifelong stewardship of the environment by offering opportunities for education, leadership, and personal development while providing the highest quality public service in natural resource management, environmental protection, and conservation.

SCA is the largest and oldest organization in the conservation arena providing volunteers to national parks, forests, and other natural resource areas in the United States. In the last forty years, over thirty thousand "SCA's" have served in more than three hundred sites, including leading the recovery efforts in Yellowstone National Park after the great wildfires of 1988 and recovery efforts in the Everglades after Hurricane Andrew. SCA trains more than a thousand volunteers annually in traditional conservation work skills and is considered a national leader in the archiving and instruction of this valued heritage.

Student Conservation Association, Inc.
P.O. Box 550
Charlestown, NH 03603
(603) 543-1700

ROBERT BIRKBY has been leading SCA backcountry work crews since 1983. For more than a decade he has been an instructor of SCA Wilderness Work Skills Programs, teaching and learning rustic skills in dozens of locations across the United States. His understanding of backcountry work began during six summers as a trail crew foreman and then Director of Conservation in northern New Mexico at Philmont, a national camp of the Boy Scouts of America. He has hiked the length of the Appalachian Trail, much of the Pacific Crest Trail, and a fair number of the pathways in between. A writer by profession, he is also the author of the current edition of *The Boy Scout Handbook* and numerous other manuals on conservation and outdoor skills.

Notes

Notes

Other titles you may enjoy from The Mountaineers:

WILDERNESS BASICS, 2d Ed.: The Complete Handbook for Hikers & Backpackers, *Jerry Schad & David S. Moser, editors*
Comprehensive resource covers all aspects of backcountry use: planning, equipment, navigation, weather; coastal, mountain, and desert travel; first aid, and winter mountaineering.

STAYING FOUND, 2d. Ed.: The Complete Map and Compass Handbook, *June Fleming*
Updated and revised handbook presents easy-to-use, unified map-and-compass system. Includes instruction on route planning, winter navigation, teaching kids to "stay found," coping when you're lost, and more.

MOUNTAINEERING FIRST AID, 4th Ed.: A Guide to Accident Response and First Aid Care, *Jan D. Carline, Steven C. MacDonald, Martha J. Lentz*
A team of medical experts provides expert, straightforward first aid instruction for outdoor enthusiasts. Conforms to the latest MOFA classes.

THE AVALANCHE HANDBOOK, 2d. Ed., *David McClung & Peter Schaefer*
Classic and comprehensive reference on avalanches, their formation, and their effects.

THE ABC OF AVALANCHE SAFETY, 2d. Ed., *F.R. LaChapelle*
Comprehensive handbook on how to determine avalanche potential, traveling safety in avalanche terrain, what to do if caught in an avalanche, and search & rescue.

MEDICINE FOR MOUNTAINEERING & OTHER WILDERNESS ACTIVITIES, 4th Ed., *James A. Wilkerson, M.D., editor*
Thoroughly revised and updated "bible" written by climber/physicians for travelers more than 24 hours away from medical aid, and for climbing expeditions.

THE MOUNTAINEERS, founded in 1906, is a nonprofit outdoor activity and conservation club, whose mission is "to explore, study, preserve, and enjoy the natural beauty of the outdoors. . . ." Based in Seattle, Washington, the club is now the third-largest such organization in the United States, with 15,000 members and five branches throughout Washington State.

The Mountaineers sponsors both classes and year-round outdoor activities in the Pacific Northwest, which include hiking, mountain climbing, ski-touring, snowshoeing, bicycling, camping, kayaking and canoeing, nature study, sailing, and adventure travel. The club's conservation division supports environmental causes through educational activities, sponsoring legislation, and presenting informational programs. All club activities are led by skilled, experienced volunteers, who are dedicated to promoting safe and responsible enjoyment and preservation of the outdoors.

If you would like to participate in these organized outdoor activities or the club's programs, consider a membership in The Mountaineers. For information and an application, write or call The Mountaineers, Club Headquarters, 300 Third Avenue West, Seattle, WA 98119; (206) 284-6310.

The Mountaineers Books, an active, nonprofit publishing program of the club, produces guidebooks, instructional texts, historical works, natural history guides, and works on environmental conservation. All books produced by The Mountaineers are aimed at fulfilling the club's mission.

Send or call for our catalog of more than 300 outdoor titles:

 The Mountaineers Books
1001 SW Klickitat Way, Suite 201
Seattle, WA 98134
1-800-553-4453